SCHOLARS, TRAVELLERS AND TRADE

Today, the National Museum of Antiquities in Leiden is internationally known for its outstanding archaeological collections. Yet its origins lie in an insignificant assortment of artefacts used for study by Leiden University. How did this transformation come about?

Ruurd Halbertsma has delved into the archives to show that the appointment of Caspar Reuvens as Professor of Archaeology in 1818 was the crucial turning point. He tells the dramatic story of Reuvens' struggle to establish the museum, with battles against rival scholars, red tape and the Dutch attitude of neglect towards archaeological monuments. It was Reuvens who trained archaeological agents to investigate and excavate ancient sites, and bring back the antiquities on which the museum's importance rests. Though he was operating long before the current debate on whether collecting antiquities is legal trade or cultural looting, Reuvens recognized the potential ethical problems inherent in achieving a world-class collection. In this, he was ahead of his time.

Scholars, Travellers and Trade throws new light on the process of creating a national museum and the difficulties of convincing society of the value of the past – issues with which museums are still wrestling. It also highlights the difficulties that an archaeological pioneer had in establishing his discipline as a fully accepted branch of academia.

Ruurd B. Halbertsma is Curator of the Classical Department at the National Museum of Antiquities, Leiden, The Netherlands.

SCHOLARS, TRAVELLERS AND TRADE

The pioneer years of the National Museum of Antiquities in Leiden, 1818–40

R.B. Halbertsma

Routledge
Taylor & Francis Group
LONDON AND NEW YORK

First published 2003 by Routledge

Published 2017 by Routledge
2 Park Square, Milton Park, Abingdon, Oxon OX14 4RN
711 Third Avenue, New York, NY 10017, USA

Routledge is an imprint of the Taylor & Francis Group, an informa business

First issued in paperback 2012

Typeset in 11/12pt Garamond 3 by
Graphicraft Limited, Hong Kong

British Library Cataloguing in Publication Data
A catalogue record for this book is available
from the British Library

Library of Congress Cataloging in Publication Data
Halbertsma, Ruurd B.
Scholars, travellers and trade: the pioneer years of the National
Museum of Antiquities in Leiden, 1818–1840 / R.B. Halbertsma.
p. cm.
Includes bibliographical references and index.
1. Rijksmuseum van Oudheden te Leiden. 2. Reuvens, Caspar
Jacob Christiaan, 1793–1835. 3. Archaeologists–Netherlands–
Biography. 4. Netherlands–History–1815–1830.
5. Netherlands–History–1830–1849. I. Title.
AM101.L536H35 2003
069'-09492–dc21   2003043147

ISBN 978-0-415-51855-0 (pbk)

TO THE MEMORY OF HERRE
HALBERTSMA (1920–98)

CONTENTS

CONTENTS

FIGURES

FOREWORD

Only in recent years has the history of museums become established as a field of academic enquiry in its own right. It is nevertheless surprising that the fascinating, sometimes painful story of the birth of the National Museum of Antiquities in Leiden has not been told before. The challenge is now happily taken up by Ruurd Halbertsma, who has ransacked the museum's own archives to reveal its origins in the eighteenth century and to trace its rise from the modest collections of Leiden's ancient university. The result is an important and compelling new chapter in Dutch and indeed European cultural history.

The central hero of the narrative is Caspar Jacob Christiaan Reuvens. He was professor at the university and an early pioneer of the new nineteenth-century discipline of archaeology. He conducted systematic excavations in Holland itself and laid the foundations of modern understanding of the Roman province there. In Leiden he had care of the *marmora Papenburgica*, that is to say, the classical marbles bequeathed to the university by Gerard van Papenbroek (1673–1743), who is described by Halbertsma as a 'representative of the Dutch "sedentary" school of collecting'. Reuvens was not himself of that persuasion, but travelled less in his short life than he should have liked and set about augmenting the founding collection of the museum by employing agents operating abroad on his behalf. He did, however, twice visit England, first in summer 1819, to take inspiration from the public museums there. In the then maturing British Museum he found a model for his own vision of a museum as universal index of ancient civilizations. His untimely death in 1835 at the age of 42 robbed the Netherlands of a figure of extraordinary energy and vision. It fell to his successors to realize his dream in the fine museum we see today in Leiden.

Ian Jenkins
Keeper of Greek and Roman Antiquities, British Museum

PREFACE

The Greek vase which adorns the cover of this book may well be a symbol of both the period and the subject treated in the next chapters. The vase, painted by the Ixion Painter around 325 BC in South Italy, shows the final battle between Achilles and Memnon before the walls of Troy. The warriors are supported by their mothers, Thetis on the left, Eos on the right. The scene shows the dramatic moment when their souls are weighed in heaven by the god Hermes, with the result that Memnon is killed, his throat being cut by Achilles' javelin. The vase was bought in Rome around 1738 by Frederic Count de Thoms, an adventurous German gentleman of fortune, who took the amphora with him to the Netherlands when he married Johanna Maria, the daughter of the famous physician Herman Boerhaave, who had been professor at the University of Leiden. After De Thoms' death the vase came into the possession of the Stadtholder, Willem IV of Orange. His son Willem V lost many of his belongings when he had to flee the country to England, after the invasion of the French troops and the proclamation of the Batavian Republic in 1795. The amphora did not remain in the Netherlands, but was taken by the French troops to Paris, where it could be admired in the halls of the Musée Napoléon alongside other treasures from the European capitals. In 1815 the vase returned to Holland, now to Amsterdam, where it was placed in the Rijksmuseum, the first national museum of the Netherlands. After the founding of the National Museum of Antiquities in 1818, the director of the Rijksmuseum refused to part from his trophy: battles as fierce as depicted on the vase were fought between the directors and the ministry to decide the issue. Finally in 1844 the decision was taken to place the vase in Leiden, where it has been kept ever since.

The eventful pedigree of just one object may illustrate the restless era in which collectors, scholars, nationalists and politicians were so active that they created collections and institutions that are still in existence today and whose history explains the reasons why objects are where they are. Each object has its own history: its meaning and function in different epochs. When whole collections, huge amounts of money and national politics are concerned, the history of collecting becomes part of general cultural history.

It has been my intention to add a chapter to this history and to describe the events which led to the creation of a national Museum of Antiquities in Leiden with collections from Greece, Rome, Egypt, the Netherlands, the Far East and the Americas. It is, in short, a story about archaeology, about why and how and by whom.

ACKNOWLEDGEMENTS

This book is the result of the research I did for a series of lectures at the University of Leiden on the history of archaeology in the Netherlands. I thank my students for their enthusiasm and for their critical remarks, which led to further investigations. My predecessor at the National Museum of Antiquities, Dr F.L. Bastet, first introduced me to the history of archaeology and brought me into contact with Professor H.D. Schneider, who supervised my doctoral thesis, which was dedicated to the archaeological travels of Jean Emile Humbert (1771–1839). I thank them both for the way they have influenced my scholarly life. Dr J.A. Brongers was so kind to let me read his manuscript on the life of C.J.C. Reuvens, which contains much unpublished archive material. I have endeavoured to write this book in English, but publication would not have been possible without the correction of the text by Mrs Anne Reichart. I thank Anne for her work and her critical reading of the manuscript, which forced me more than once to express myself more clearly. The correction of the text was made possible by a generous gift of the Gratama-Stichting, for which I am very grateful. Fortunately I am not the only museum curator with an affection for the history of the pieces under his or her care. I am obliged to Dr Ian Jenkins, Keeper of Greek and Roman Antiquities in the British Museum, for his willingness to write a foreword to this book. My colleagues at the National Museum of Antiquities helped me in many ways to realize the publication of this book. The museum also provided most of the illustrations. Permission to reproduce photographs has been given by the authorities of archives and by owners of other collections. Their names may be found in the captions of the illustrations. Finally I express my gratitude to my editors, Richard Stoneman and Catherine Bousfield. Richard was immediately intrigued by the subject of this book and his enthusiasm gave me the impetus to go ahead with the endeavour. The support and the professionalism of the staff at Routledge did the rest.

1

INTRODUCTION

POLITICAL DEVELOPMENTS, 1795–1840

The development of the National Museum of Antiquities and the biographies of the main characters involved in the growth of the archaeological collections in Leiden cannot be understood without paying attention to the history and the cultural climate in the Netherlands in the period before and after the years of Napoleon's occupation of the Low Countries. The Dutch Republic under the rule of Stadtholders from the House of Orange ceased to exist in 1795, when French revolutionary ideas spread to the Netherlands, resulting in a French invasion, the flight of Stadtholder Willem V to England and the proclamation of the Batavian Republic. The most important cultural treasures were taken to Paris to be placed in the confiscated royal palace of the Louvre alongside other European works of art. With the rise of Napoleon and the growing French influence in Europe, the short-lived Batavian Republic was converted in 1806 into the Kingdom of Holland, with Napoleon's brother Louis Bonaparte as its first monarch. Louis Bonaparte did his best to introduce the example of French institutions in his new kingdom. In the capital Amsterdam the first National Museum (Rijksmuseum) was created. In 1808 he founded the Royal Academy of Arts and Sciences in Amsterdam, which organized exhibitions of contemporary art and awarded prizes for literary and artistic achievements. The popularity of Bonaparte in the Netherlands rose remarkably due to his independent politics (which often collided with his brother's imperial ideas), the care for his people and his interest in Dutch culture: he even tried to learn Dutch, and the results of his efforts produced benevolent sympathy among his subjects. More sinister years followed his forced abdication in 1810 and the subsequent annexation of the Netherlands by Emperor Napoleon. The imperial war machine needed young men, who were conscripted and forced to join the Napoleonic armies. Nearly 15,000 Dutch soldiers died during the campaign against Russia. Culture suffered too: many works of art were selected by the French art committees, confiscated and transported to the Musée Napoléon in Paris. In 1815, after the defeat of Napoleon, the royal houses in Europe were restored. The son of Stadtholder

1

Willem V (who had died in exile) was proclaimed king of the Netherlands. King Willem I ruled over a kingdom which comprised the Netherlands, Belgium and Luxemburg (a union that was to prove difficult to rule because of differences in religion, language and wealth). The government alternately resided in The Hague and Brussels. The economy began to prosper as new roads and canals were built, trade possibilities increased and the colonies in the East Indies, which had been under English rule during the Napoleonic era, were restored to Dutch rule. In this climate of growing economic wealth, the need to create unity in a new kingdom and a sense of nationalism, it is understandable that proposals to create new national institutions met with approval in governmental circles.

The political union of the Kingdom of the Netherlands came to an end in 1830, when riots broke out in Brussels against the king. These riots led to an insurrection and the proclamation of an independent Belgian state. The Ten-Days' War of 1831 between the Netherlands and Belgium resulted in European intervention and the official recognition of the Belgian Kingdom under the rule of King Leopold I. Worries about the future and an economic depression led to sharp retrenchments, which affected the whole country. In 1840 King Willem I abdicated and left the Netherlands. He died in Berlin in 1843.

MUSEUMS, MINISTRIES AND DEPARTMENTS

By royal decree of 13 June 1818 Caspar Reuvens was appointed Professor of Archaeology at the University of Leiden. Together with this function he also became director of the 'Archaeological Cabinet' of the university, a collection of about 150 Greek and Roman statues, busts, altars and inscriptions. These antiquities had been bequeathed to the university seventy-four years earlier and led a dormant existence in the orangery of the botanical gardens. As a *professor extraordinarius*, Reuvens was the responsibility of the *Curatoren* (trustees) of the university: they were responsible for his teaching, publications, caretaking and housing of the collection of antiquities.

The University of Leiden fell under the jurisdiction of the Ministry of Education, National Industry and the Colonies, headed by the influential minister Anton Reinhard Falck (1777–1843), who had arranged the nomination of Reuvens as professor of archaeology. The relationship between Reuvens and Falck was very strong and had a remarkable influence on the development of the archaeological museum. When Falck left the ministry in 1824 to become ambassador of the Netherlands in London, Reuvens felt this as a personal loss, to be compared with losing a 'dear member of the family'.[1] In 1824 the ministries were reorganized: the Department of Education, Arts and Sciences came into existence, which became part of the Ministry of the Interior. Head of this department was D.J. Baron van Ewijck van Oostbroek en de Bildt (1786–1858), who took a personal interest in the development of the national collections of art. The first ten years of the archaeological museum's existence can be described as the 'golden decade', which brought large collections of ancient art to Leiden and saw the start of the first excavations in the Netherlands. During this period an interesting division can be observed in the function of the professor of archaeology. At the university Reuvens fell under the jurisdiction of the trustees, but as director of the Rijksmuseum van Oudheden (National Museum of Antiquities, as Reuvens preferred to call the archaeological cabinet), he stood in direct contact with the ministry, where ideas about fostering the cultural policy in the Netherlands by acquiring collections of art began to develop. More than once Reuvens addressed the king directly, without consulting his direct superiors, the board of trustees. The result of this dichotomy in Reuvens' function was an enormous growth of the archaeological collection in a university town, where no decent museum building existed and where the trustees were faced with a growing and money-consuming institution, which they had never envisaged.

After Reuvens' death in 1835 the trustees decided to change this state of affairs and to reorganize the administration of the museum. No new director was appointed, but a 'first curator', Reuvens' former student and assistant Conrad Leemans. All dealings with the ministry now went through the office of the trustees, who bought a new building for the collection and ordered Leemans to organize the instalment of the antiquities. In 1838 the museum opened its doors to the public and in 1839 Leemans was rewarded with the directorship. Although formally the rules were thus set, the museum's archive with its 'unofficial letters' shows that Leemans, too, had his informal contacts with the ministry: for example, the Canino collection of Greek vases was bought through these channels, with private funding by the king of the Netherlands.

THE PRICE FOR ANTIQUITIES

Every decision to buy larger collections had to be authorized by a royal decree. The king was advised by the minister of the interior and the finance minister, who in their turn had been informed by Reuvens' letters and reports. The finances for larger acquisitions were found according to the exigencies of the case. A collection of Punic monuments from Carthage was bought in 1821 for 17,000 guilders and paid out of the budget surplus of the Ministry of Education.[2] An acquisition of Etruscan antiquities was made in 1826 for the sum of 33,000 guilders. As there was no budget available, the king decided to use the country's contingency fund for 1826, although these finances were generally reserved for catastrophes such as damage by hurricane, flood and dam-bursts.[3] The same fund was used for the largest acquisition of the 'golden decade': the purchase of the Egyptian collection of D'Anastasy, which was sold in Livorno to the Dutch government for 113,000 guilders.[4] The lack of a regular fund for the acquisition of works of art shows that a real cultural policy with an adequate budget was non-existent: the government, inspired by feelings of nationalism and European competition, reacted benevolently to the possibilities offered by the activities of zealous museum directors and their agents. During the prosperous years this policy produced impressive results, but in times of economic decline the buying, housing, restoring and conserving of works of art were neglected to such an extent that opportunities of buying famous collections were lost and the condition of the antiquities in Leiden deteriorated rapidly.

The question of the value of the sums spent on archæological collections in the early years of the National Museum of Antiquities is difficult to answer. The amount of money is easier to establish. For the most important purchases during the 'golden decade' of 1820–30, the Greek antiquities of Colonel Rottiers, the Punic collection of Lieutenant-Colonel Humbert, the statues from Utica, the Punic collection of Alexander Tulin, the Egyptian antiquities of Signora Cimba and Jean D'Anastasy, the Etruscan bronzes of Count Corazzi and the manuscripts of Count Borgia, a total of *c*.210,000 guilders was paid. The costs of the expeditions to the Mediterranean of the officers Rottiers and Humbert amounted to a total of 35,000 guilders. The excavations during the years 1827–33 directed by Reuvens at Arentsburg (Forum Hadriani) cost the government around 12,000 guilders. When we place these amounts of money against the yearly income of Reuvens himself as a full professor of archæology (2,600 guilders) or the yearly pension of a retired major (1,500 guilders) we must conclude that the zeal of the government to found an important archæological museum in the Netherlands did really exist, although the implications of all the purchases and activities were not always foreseen.

SOURCES

For the reconstruction of the way in which the National Museum of Antiquities in Leiden was created, the motives behind the actions of the main characters, the organization of travel and trade and the political background, archives are of paramount importance. All the incoming and outgoing letters of the museum are kept in the archives of the National Museum of Antiquities. In the footnotes this archive is referred to as 'Museum Archive', followed by a specification of the reference where a certain document can be found. Outgoing letters and documents which had to be returned to the sender were copied by Reuvens and kept in his archives. Apart from the official correspondence there are also private archives in the museum, including Reuvens' notes on various subjects and the private correspondence of the traveller Jean Emile Humbert. The letters between Reuvens father and son, prior to Reuvens' appointment in Leiden, are at the moment in a private collection. In the footnotes they are referred to as 'Archive Reuvens'.

The deliberations on a ministerial level and the correspondence between the ministries and the king are kept in the National Archives in The Hague. Here also are the archives of the Dutch embassies and consulates in the Mediterranean area, which were often involved in the acquisition and transportation of antiquities. The logbooks of the ships used for archaeological voyages and the transportation of antiquities to the Netherlands are also kept in the National Archives. They are useful for reconstructing travel routes and checking the information given in the letters of the travellers.

2

EARLY COLLECTIONS OF CLASSICAL ART IN THE NETHERLANDS

The seventeenth and eighteenth centuries

'WORKS OF ART AND BEAUTIES FROM VENICE': THE REIJNST COLLECTION

The history of collecting ancient art and artefacts in the Netherlands dates back to the seventeenth century, the 'Golden Age', which brought international contacts and prosperity after eighty years of war with Spain. Before that period some archaeological objects were present in art cabinets or ecclesiastical treasuries, but the Golden Age saw the beginning of purposeful collecting of archaeological artefacts.

In seventeenth-century Amsterdam the jewel in the crown was without doubt the impressive art collection of the brothers Gerard and Jan Reijnst, both wealthy merchants.[1] In 'De Hoop' (The Hope), their house on the Keizersgracht, a large art collection was displayed, which comprised around 200 Italian paintings and more than 300 classical sculptures. Apart from this collection of *artificalia*, many *naturalia* were also exhibited, as was usual in seventeenth-century art cabinets. The initiative of creating such a collection had come from Jan Reijnst, who in 1625 became the representative of the family firm in Venice. *Giovanni Reynst*, as he is called in the Venetian archives, became impressed by the Venetian way of life of his Italian colleagues in impressive *palazzi*, filled with crystal chandeliers, colourful paintings and sculptures from classical antiquity. Venice, which until this period had prospered economically through monopolies on eastern trade, counted numerous art collections along its canals. But in the first half of the seventeenth century the tide had turned for *La Serenissima* due to the economic recession following the discovery of the trade route around the Cape of Good Hope. The monopoly on the spice trade was lost and many merchants had to sell their collections, mostly to west European buyers.

Jan Reijnst, inspired by the world of art around him, began to foster the ideal of creating a Venetian *palazzo* with an art collection on the Keizersgracht in Amsterdam. The realization of this dream was one of the great successes of the renaissance ideal in seventeenth-century Holland. But, unlike the Italian collectors, the brothers Reijnst were no *cognoscenti* with knowledge, taste and patience to let their collection grow organically. Both practical and purposeful, they bought parts of the inventory of one of Venice's palaces: the Palazzo Vendramin along the Grand Canal in the neighbourhood of the Abbey of San Gregorio, between the Campo San Vio and the Punta della Dogana.[2] The first mention of a large collection of paintings and antiques belonging to a certain Andrea Vendramin was made in 1615 by V. Scamozzi in his book about architecture:

> Il clarissimo Signor Andrea Vendrameno à San Gregorio nella sua casa sopra Canal Grande ha disposto due stanze, dove con triplicato ordine si ritrovano non poche statue, e 140 petti di varie grandezze, e torsi, e bassirilievi, e vasi, e pietre nobili e altre petrificate, e buon numero di medaglie antiche, e sette statue del Vittoria in un suo scrittoio d'olivo e ebano e forsi 140 quadri grandi e piccioli di buone pitture.[3]

Andrea Vendramin was born in 1556, a close relative of the famous collector Gabriele Vendramin. He was married to Elena Contarini and had one daughter, Chiaretta. Two years before his death in 1629 he decided to describe his whole collection, which he did in seventeen handwritten catalogues with illustrations in brown ink and watercolour. His antiquities were subdivided in six catalogues: *De Sculpturis*; *De Deis Oraculis Idolis et Antiquorum Sacerdotibus*; *De Sacrificiorum et Triumphorum Vasculis, Lucernisque Antiquorum, Urnis a Liquoribus, Lacrimis atque Vasculis Vitreis*; *De Antiquis Romanorum Numismatibus; De Antiquorum Tumulis*; and *De Annulis et Sigillis Aegyptiorum*. Other catalogues described his paintings, Venetian coins, books, manuscripts and the collections of natural history. Only six volumes of this catalogue still exist today in libraries in London, Oxford and Berlin with the lists of the paintings, ancient ceramics, Egyptian rings and scarabs, animals, minerals, and sepulchral monuments. Shortly after the death of Vendramin his widow sold part of the collection to Jan Reijnst. He acquired most of the sculptures, antiquities and parts of the collection of paintings. The fate of the other Vendramin items is unknown: probably they were sold by the widow to other collectors in Venice and hence dispersed.

The Vendramin collection was shipped to Amsterdam, where it was placed in 'De Hoop' on the Keizersgracht. The Reijnst brothers had entered the circle of learned collectors overnight, as Anne-Marie Logan put it concisely: 'Thanks to this collection he [Gerard Reijnst] obtained the image of a collector, before he really started seriously collecting himself.'[4] Later purchases in Venice (mainly pictures) by Jan Reijnst added considerably to the collection.

Due to the cosmopolitan character of Amsterdam, the Reijnst collection soon became famous in Europe. The earliest mention of it was made in 1639 by a certain Aernout van Buchell, who described royal interest for a certain piece in the collection:

> Be aware that Reijnst, an inquisitive man in Amsterdam, has received many antiquities, works of art and beauties from Venice, collected in Turkey, Greece and Italy: statues, tombs, paintings, medals, prints, etcetera; which were desired to be seen by the Princess Amelia (who did not know this collection), who was accompanying Her Highness the Queen of France. She was very pleased with a female statue representing Cleopatra. It was donated to her.[5]

In another passage by the same author we read that the smaller antiquities were arranged in two rooms; in the courtyard he noticed '*cassen* [chests] with antique marble statues, more than life-size'.[6] Logan suggests an arrangement of the statues in the courtyard in wooden chests,[7] but this seems an unlikely display for objects which were bought to impress the visitor. Maybe the *cassen* refer to (wooden) niches, in which antique sculptures were often displayed, as can be seen in contemporary drawings of, for example, the sculptures in the courtyard of the Villa Sassi in Rome by Maarten van Heemskerck.[8] The list of visitors includes illustrious names such as Cosimo de'Medici, Carlo Ridolfi, Joost van den Vondel, Knorr von Rosenroth and Constantijn Huygens.[9]

The seal on the collector's work was the publication of an illustrated catalogue and in this respect Gerard Reijnst followed the lead of contemporary art collectors. He ordered Jeremias Falck to make engravings of thirty-three of his best Italian paintings, among them works by Titian, Tintoretto and Veronese. They were published by Clement de Jonghe under the title *Caelaturae* around 1665–70. A selection of the classical sculptures was published by Nicolaes Visscher around 1670 under the title *Signorum Veterum Icones*. Unfortunately Reijnst did not live to see the publication of either volume: he died in the winter of 1658 after falling into the water of the Keizersgracht.

The title page of *Icones* (Figure 2.1) was made by the artist Gerard de Lairesse. It shows an allegorical and somewhat violent representation of Old Father Time, who takes a powerful swing with his scythe at a tremulous-looking statue of a Muse. A mutilated torso of a male statue is lying at his feet. Broken columns testify to earlier acts of violence by this aggressive senior. The destructive work of Time is stopped by Prudentia, the personification of reason and judgement. This allegory praises Reijnst as a wise man, who safeguards works of art from the destructive power of Time.

In *Icones* many sculptures bear historical and mythological names, most of which are distributed haphazardly (e.g. Cleopatra, Germanicus). Furthermore,

Figure 2.1 Title-page of Reijnst's *Signorum Veterum Icones*, by Gerard de Lairesse, Amsterdam (1670).

it is striking that all the sculptures look suspiciously complete and undamaged. A comparison with still existing pieces in, for example, Dresden and Leiden makes it clear that the *Icones* show an idealized version of the statuary. Also restoration marks are not indicated in the engravings.[10]

After the death of Gerard Reijnst in 1658 the collection was dispersed. The first sale occurred in 1660. On the occasion of the visit of the English King Charles II to the Dutch Republic it was decided to offer him a prestigious gift. The sovereign's predilection for Italian paintings and ancient sculptures was the reason for asking the widow Reijnst to sell part of her collection to representatives of the Dutch Republic: twenty-four of the best paintings and twelve sculptures were bought for the considerable sum of 80,000 guilders. The 'Dutch Gift', intended to secure diplomatic relations between England and the Republic, aroused interest in British newspapers: 'an excellent collection of pictures of the most famous, auncient and moderne masters, with a great number of statues of white marble of excellent sculpture [. . .]'[11] Nevertheless, the two nations were at war again four years later. The ancient sculptures were to suffer a similar fate: most of them were lost during the Great Fire of Whitehall in 1698. At the moment only one piece in England can be identified as having been part of the Dutch Gift of 1660.[12]

In 1670 the remainder of the Reijnst collection was sold and divided between collectors such as Nicolaes Witsen, Jan Six and Gerrit Uylenburgh. In Germany the Elector of Brandenburg was interested, with the result that apart from the objects in Dutch and English collections, pieces of the Reijnst collection can also be found in Germany.

THE SMETIUS COLLECTION: IN SEARCH OF THE *OPPIDUM BATAVORUM*

A collection of a very different nature was formed in Nijmegen by Smetius father and son.[13] Johannes Smetius (Johann Smith, 1591–1651) was summoned to Nijmegen as a minister in 1618. He had received his education at the academy of Harderwijk, where he had been a devoted pupil of the historian Pontanus, a well-known authority on Roman antiquities. During Smetius' stay in Nijmegen, he became fascinated with the Roman finds made frequently in Nijmegen and the surrounding countryside. His collections comprised coins, inscriptions, sculptures, glass, jewellery, statuettes, pottery and utensils. Being a minister, his favourite object became a Roman cornelian gem, in which the Christian symbols of an anchor and a fish were carved. On his official portrait he holds this object, the *gemma Smetiana*, in his hand.

Smetius took an active part in the scholarly debate about the interpretation of Tacitus' geographical description of the Netherlands. The location of the *Oppidum Batavorum*, the main centre of the famous *gens Batavorum*, was the subject of especially heated controversy. In the western provinces of the

Netherlands scholars maintained that the oppidum had to be located in the southern part of Holland, with its manifold Roman finds. The Batavian Revolt of AD 69 had started in a sacred grove, the *sacrum nemus*, as it was called by Tacitus.[14] Philologists connected the name *sacrum nemus* with the country estate Schakerbos near The Hague: all possible and impossible arguments were used to connect the Batavi with the western part of the Netherlands. The eastern provinces naturally reacted to these pretentions. Scholars from these regions stated that the *Insula Batavorum*, the island of the Batavi, the homeland of the tribe according to Tacitus, had to be located between the rivers Rhine and Waal, just west of the city of Nijmegen, which had to be identified with the *Oppidum Batavorum*. Archaeology came to the aid of philology by producing numerous Roman finds, which were gathered by Smetius and presented in his *Oppidum Batavorum seu Noviomagum* (1644), published by Blaeu in Amsterdam with financial support from the city council of Nijmegen. This publication made Smetius' collection well known and so began a correspondence with international scholars and politicians, whose names we also encounter in the visitors' book of the collection.

Smetius handed on the torch of Roman archaeology to his son Johannes Smetius junior (1636–1704), who also became a minister in Nijmegen and curator of the famous collection. He wrote the illustrated catalogue *Antiquitates Neomagenses* (1678), which gives us an idea of the size of the collection: no less than 4,500 Roman antiquities are listed, and more than 10,000 coins. In his visitors' book we encounter more than 3,000 *spectatores antiquitatum*. Shortly before his death Smetius junior tried to sell his precious collection to the town of Nijmegen, but times had changed: the city council had lost interest in scholarly debates and antiquities, and the collection was eventually sold to Johann Wilhelm, elector of the Paltz. So, for 20,000 guilders, the Roman antiquities were moved to Düsseldorf, and from there they moved in the course of time to untraceable other locations. A few fragments are in Mannheim and Munich. Four inscriptions (a gift from Smetius to the city of Nijmegen) were built into the wall of the town hall, and are now kept in the municipal museum of Nijmegen: the sole tangible remains of the collecting activities of the two erudite clergymen.

ADVENTURES AND ANTIQUITIES: FREDERIC COUNT DE THOMS

A collection of quite a different nature, which was formed in Italy but went to the Netherlands, was formed by the adventurous German collector Frederic Count de Thoms. Frederic (then called 'Friedrich') was born in the city of Giessen in 1669. His father was owner of the local pub 'Zum wilden Mann'. The young Friedrich lost his mother when he was three years old. His grandfather, a Professor F. Nitzsch, took care of his studies and secured a place at the university for his promising grandson. As a real social climber the young Friedrich invented an impressive French ancestry of his own (the family De Thomas) and started reading history, politics and law at the University of Giessen. In 1712 he wrote his doctoral thesis *De rebus sub lege commissaria delatis*, which was followed in 1715 by a biography of the French king Louis XIV, who had died in that same year.

The bright young man's connections in diplomatic circles led to travels to Vienna, Budapest, Regensburg and London, where he met King George I and became his secretary in 1719. In England he acquired a considerable capital by speculating and gambling. Lending parts of his capital resulted in more favours and influence. In the thirties he travelled extensively in Italy, where he set up his residence in Naples, entered the service of King Charles VII, became member of the Accademia Etrusca and was awarded the title of count in 1737. A life of leisure in Italy could never be complete without a collection of at least some antiquities, and De Thoms followed the example of his peer group: he started collecting ancient coins, carved stones and other antiquities. The most interesting pieces of his collection were a Campanian grave amphora, a marble statue of an owl with a Greek inscription and a marble relief with a representation of Asclepius and Hygieia. He acquired the large amphora in Rome: the earlier history of the piece is unknown. The vase (see cover) has a rare representation of a psychostasia (weighing of souls) on the front: Hermes is weighing the souls of Achilles and Memnon in the presence of their mothers Thetis and Eos. The artist chose the dramatic moment when Memnon's soul went down, his fate killing him instantly on earth through Achilles' lance. Eos leaves the scene in tears, Thetis is watching contentedly. On the reverse two *papposilenoi* are depicted, each one carrying a winged Eros. The soft boots of the sileni suggest a scene from the theatre, perhaps a satyr play following the grim tragedy of Memnon. It is known that both Aeschylos and Sophocles wrote a tragedy *Memnon*, in which his tragic fate was treated.

The marble owl had been owned by the Roman prelate Francesco Bianchini, who gave the piece to Violante Beatrix, princess of Baviera, the widow of Ferdinand de'Medici. After her death the antiquarian A.F. Gori bought the owl in 1731 and gave the piece to his friend Frederic de Thoms. The owl is standing in an 'Egyptian' pose, with one foot advanced and the wings tight against the body (Figure 2.2). Beneath his claw a small mouse is held captive. The head seems to be covered with a hood. On both sides of the pedestal are representations of a Victory holding a crown. The awkward Greek inscription on the front has been a puzzle for every owner of the piece. Most probably the text should read: 'Archates Petrios the soothsayer predicts the future for four *asses*', the whole statue thus being a kind of shop-sign. Possibly an owl played some role in the prophecies of Archates Petrios.

De Thoms bought the interesting relief with Asclepius and Hygieia around 1737 in Rome from the art dealer Borioni. The relief shows Asclepius

Figure 2.2 Marble owl with inscription, second century AD. National Museum of
Antiquities.

sitting on an Attic *klismos* with his hand in a protective gesture above a
snake's head. The *klismos* is standing on two pedestals, a curious mounting
probably invented by the artist to create some space for the curling body of
the snake. Opposite the god his daughter Hygieia is depicted, standing erect
and making a libation with a jug and a bowl in front of her father. Although
the relief was considered by some to be a fifth-century BC Greek original,
and by others a clever fake, it is now clear that it is a neo-Attic work of art,
dating from the Roman imperial period.[15]

After his prolonged stay in Italy Frederic de Thoms settled down in Leiden, where in 1741 he married the 30-year-old Johanna Maria Boerhaave, daughter of the world-famous physician, who had died three years earlier, leaving his daughter a considerable bequest. The antiquities were divided between the town house on the Rapenburg canal and the family castle Poelgeest in the neighbouring village of Oegstgeest. The owl found a place in the bedroom of the couple, where he was a silent witness of the birth of two daughters, Sybilla Maria (1742) and Hermina Jacoba (1744). De Thoms planned to crown his collecting activities with a publication of his collection, for which a series of engravings was prepared. A special drawing was made of the Asclepius relief: De Thoms ordered the engraver to replace the divine heads by those of his late father-in-law and of his wife, thus honouring the memory of Leiden's most famous doctor.

De Thoms' marital happiness did not last long. In 1746 he died suddenly after a fatal stroke. His antiquities were sold for 30,000 guilders to the stadtholder Prince Willem IV and remained in the family of Orange till 1795, when they were seized by French troops and, with the exception of the owl, transported to Paris. They remained in the Musée Napoléon till 1815, when the war spoils were returned to the original countries. The amphora and the Asclepius relief went to the Rijksmuseum in Amsterdam, where they became the favourite pieces of the director Cornelis Apostool and for this reason did not go to Leiden till 1844, as shall be described later. The coins and gemstones, among which was a superb portrait of the Empress Livia, went to the Royal Coin Cabinet in The Hague. The owl entered the archaeological museum in 1823 and was published by the first director of the museum, Caspar Reuvens, in 1830.[16]

GERARD VAN PAPENBROEK: *VANITAS VANITATUM*

Gerard van Papenbroek (1673–1743) was the owner of one of the largest Dutch art collections in the eighteenth century. His collection of manuscripts, portraits and antique sculptures was bequeathed to the universities of Amsterdam and Leiden and thus did not share the fate of Reijnst's and Smetius' antiquities but remained intact in these two cities.

Van Papenbroek belonged to the municipal elite in Amsterdam. He served terms as an alderman on several occasions, held different public offices and became one of the burgomasters in 1723. He owned two houses: in Amsterdam a mansion on the Herengracht and a country estate near Velsen, named 'Huys te Papenburg': an allusion to his family name. His collection of paintings and manuscripts was kept in Amsterdam. The ancient sculptures were in the estate near Velsen. A description of this idyllic castle is to be found in a contemporary eulogy of the beauties of Velsen and surroundings:

Neatly trimmed hedges, high trees along manifold paths, ponds, sweetly purling rivulets of lively dune water, amusing avenues, starry groves, fruitful orchards, kitchen gardens and an illustrious country house, adorned with a treasure of books and old marble remains of Greeks and Romans.[17]

As a collector Van Papenbroek was a typical representative of the Dutch 'sedentary' school. He did not travel to the Mediterranean to see the ancient remains and buy antiquities (as many British, French, German and some Dutch travellers did on their Grand Tour), but enlarged his collections mainly by buying antiquities from other collectors or by bidding at auction. In this manner he bought some pieces from the collection of Gosuin van Uylenbroek in 1729. They in their turn had been part of the Reijnst collection. In this manner other *Reynstiana* also turned up in the estate of Van Papenbroek from smaller collections, such as those of Six, Witsen, Heydanus, De Witt, Graevius and Van der Wolff. Parts of these collections also had interesting origins, for example, like two Roman funerary urns and an early Christian sarcophagus from the collection Van der Wolff, which previously belonged to the Flemish painter Peter Paul Rubens.[18] Other pieces in the Van Papenbroek collection came from less famous collectors such as De Bosch, Chevalier, De Flines, Fremeaux, Grill, De Hochepied, De Neufville, Scholten and De Wilde. The collection of inscriptions, altars, grave reliefs, busts and statues comprised around 150 pieces. Greek or Roman pottery was lacking, as appreciation of *vasi Etruschi* only came with the publications of Sir William Hamilton in the second half of the eighteenth century.

The earliest mention of Van Papenbroek's antiquities dates from 1725. In the 'Great Universal, Historical, Geographical, Genealogical and Judicious Lexicon' mention is made of:

Greek and Latin inscriptions, altars, gravestones, funeral urns, sublime sculpture, statues and busts, which were found and excavated in various parts of Asia, in Greece, in Rome, and in the surrounding neighbourhoods, also in the Dutch Republic, and which were brought hither.[19]

In this description of the country house 'De Papenburg' mention is made of an inscription, which can shed some light on the reasons why Van Papenbroek accumulated such a number of Greek and Roman antiquities. The inscription was seen by the visitors 'when entering the porch' on the left-hand side. It contained a clear admonition, or lesson, for those who were about to look at the ancient treasures. After the words 'All ye, who enter, pay attention' (*Omnes, qui huc introitis, attendite*) a long list followed of all the antique treasures which were on display: portraits of emperors, famous men and women from antiquity, Greek and Roman inscriptions, representations of ancient deities, etc. Whoever studied these remains of classical antiquity had to bear in mind this important lesson: 'Be mindful of human frailty, vanity and instability, remember that all worldly things die, perish, collapse and change, and that nothing is permanent and stable; that only the word and the name of Jehova the Lord remains to all eternity.' (*Memor esto humanae fragilitatis, vanitatis ac inconstantiae, et omnia mundana mori, perire, labi, transferri, nihilque stabile ac diuturnum esse; solum vero verbum et nomen Jehovae Domini manere in aeternum.*) It was of great importance for Van Papenbroek to convey this Calvinist lesson to his visitors: a *vanitas* admonition combined with a collection of classical art.

Following the examples of Reijnst and Smetius, Van Papenbroek also thought of publishing his collection. A first attempt was made by Daniel Bedber in 1726, but his early death put an end to this endeavour. Sigibert Havercamp, professor of Greek at the University of Leiden, discussed the possibilities of finishing Bedber's manuscript with Van Papenbroek. However the catalogue of the *marmora Papenburgica* was never published, because of the professor's other pressing occupations.

PAPENBROEKIANA MARMORA, NUNC LEYDENSIA MARMORA

When Van Papenbroek felt the presages of death, he began to search for a proper destination for his possessions. On 1 April 1739 he composed his will, 'a bit diseased, but in perfect possession of his senses, mind and judgement'.[20] In the first version of his will all antiquities, manuscripts and paintings were bequeathed to the University of Leiden, probably because of his close friendship with two of the university's trustees, Jan van de Poll and Arent van der Dussen. In 1742 he changed his will to the effect that the paintings which were already hanging in the Athenaeum and the Nieuwe Kerk in Amsterdam should remain there after his death. The other portraits, nineteen in total, his collection of manuscripts (except those of P.C. Hooft) and the antiquities were intended for Leiden. On Saturday 12 October 1743 Gerard van Papenbroek died. He was buried in the Westerkerk in Amsterdam: *memor esto omnia mundana mori.*

The first task of the university's trustees was to find a suitable place to house the *marmora Papenburgica.* In his will Van Papenbroek had stipulated that his collection should be exhibited so that all interested would have free access. A public space belonging to the university was needed. It was decided that the new orangery, which was planned in the botanical garden, could house the antiquities, as the building had not yet been finished and could be adapted to become a kind of art cabinet. The original design was changed by the highly regarded architect Daniel Marot, who designed a building 'with pilasters that will be made of Scottish stone'.[21] Stylish material for an elegant building.

Van Papenbroek's executor and brother-in-law, Simon Emtinck, sent parts of the antiquities, inventories and engravings to Leiden in the winter of 1743–4. On 26 June 1744 Professor Esgers informed the trustees that all antiquities from Velsen and Amsterdam had arrived and been placed temporarily in the right wing of the orangery, awaiting the completion of the central hall. In the Leiden City Archive are preserved five drawings of the ground plan and four views of this central hall, adorned with the Papenbroek marbles.[22] The peculiar arrangement of the antiquities deserves closer inspection. The size and shape of the objects were decisive for the arrangement along the four walls. The gallery of honour consisted of sixty-three sculptures arranged along the wall opposite the entrance, divided in three by two niches and a central *aedicula* with tympanum (Figure 2.3). The reddish-marbled wooden panels in the niches and the pedestals contrasted favourably with the white marble sculptures. The predilection for symmetry is conspicious in every detail. Above the antiquities an honorary Latin inscription was placed by 'Trustees and Burgomasters of Leiden to commemorate and honour Gerard van Papenbroek Esquire, once Burgomaster of the City of Amsterdam, because of his donation of Greek and Roman antiquities to the University of Leiden'.[23]

The side walls of this *salon*, as it was called, had doors and two niches, in which five sculptures were placed, the largest one in the middle. The larger objects were placed on pedestals and on the floor. The fourth wall consisted mainly of windows and doors, with a few statues in between them. Around 120 sculptures were in the *salon*; the rest were placed in other academic buildings, even in the open air in the botanical garden.

After the sculptures had been satisfactorily arranged, an academic session took place to thank all those involved in the project and to stress the importance of Van Papenbroek's bequest. This was held on 27 September 1745. Franciscus Oudendorp, professor of history and eloquence, delivered a Latin speech with a high content of rhetoric, in which he sang the praises of Van Papenbroek's generosity, the mediation of Simon Emtinck (*Emtinckius*) and the cares of Professor Esgers (*Esgerius*) in arranging the statues. After a short review of earlier collections of classical art in the Netherlands, Oudendorp thanked Van Papenbroek in a grateful albeit sinister way for his bequest:

> The collection has been transferred to Leiden and arranged in such a fashion, that, if you were to rise from the dead and you approach to give a judgement, you would not regret your benefaction.[24]

The University of Leiden had been rich in academic collections, but until now one jewel in the crown had been missing:

> She could not show inscriptions on marble, no religious or artful remains of antiquity. Papenbroek has – bravo! – supplied this want,

Figure 2.3 The *marmora Papenburgica* in the orangery of the botanical garden. Drawing by J. van Werven, *c.*1745, Leiden City Archive.

added this jewel, dedicated these firstlings to the *alma mater* of the Academy, and obliged us all to the veneration of his name.[25]

Oudendorp tried to stress the importance of ancient artefacts and inscriptions for the study of antiquity. The works of the highly revered classical authors have come to us only fragmentarily. A necessary and incorrupt addition to our knowledge of antiquity is provided by antique coins, inscriptions, statues and portraits: direct sources, which present the past to us in a tangible way. Oudendorp finished his lecture with an appeal to use this collection for study and pleasure. In one of the jauntier parts of his lecture he addressed the academic youth as follows:

> In the meantime, youngsters, enjoy your good luck, dear pupils of the Academy, chained by love for the free arts, and be happy with merry excitement. You have received a basket with all kinds of antiquities, which might contain the sweetest nourishment for your studies. If it is pleasant for you to stand eye to eye with Roman generals, laurelled emperors and young caesars as commanders of the youth, then it will now be possible to see a number of them with your own eyes. If you find pleasure in seeing queens and empresses, then the female portraits and representations, carved with utmost skill, will leave you astonished. If you prefer men of learning, you will not find them absent. Or do you prefer to look at the hollow gods and demigods of the pagans, and treat them with a smile? Then look! Jupiter, Sarapis, Apollo and Bacchus in different attire and ornamented with their own attributes, naked Venuses, beautiful Cupids, Silenus, Pan, Fauns, remarkable in their attitudes, Hercules struggling with Antaeus, or proud with the golden apples of the Hesperides, and finally the goddesses Domina Urbs, Fortuna, Salus, Abundantia and Nehalennia, and the frightful head of Oceanus with his fishermen: the *Papenbroekiana Marmora*, now the *Leydensia Marmora*, present them all to your judgement.[26]

A year after this public lecture Oudendorp published a catalogue of the inscriptions and sculptures with the engravings made earlier for the intended publication of Daniel Bedber.[27] The catalogue describes the Greek and Roman inscriptions first, then the statues, busts and reliefs. The sequence in the catalogue is determined by the arrangement in the botanical *salon*, for example: 'the following nine heads stand below Papenbroek's honorary inscription.' The origin of each object is given from documents and notes which Van Papenbroek himself had assembled.[28]

As a reward for his efforts and his swift publications, Oudendorp's salary was raised by 200 guilders yearly, but his eloquence and efforts were to no academic avail. Apart from Oudendorp, no other professor showed any interest in using the marbles for their lectures or research. They considered Oudendorp's publication enough attention paid to this new academic collection. After the busy years of 1744–5 the collection started to lead a dormant existence. Trustees of the university were not interested in enlarging the collection, in spite of the good example of some individuals who donated pieces to the university, which were later described in the *Auctorium Legati Papenbroekiani*.[29] Due to the high humidity in the orangery and changes in temperature, the condition of the pieces deteriorated rapidly: the iron pins, used for restorations and connecting loosened pieces of marble, began to rust and caused damage to the sculptures. The first official curator of the collection commented in 1820:

> Exposed to the insults of air and people, and without custody, many pieces have suffered: the rusting of the iron, with which they were restored, has deformed and broken the attached pieces. Subsequently the marbles have also been damaged deliberately. I will do my utmost best to cure these deficiencies, as much as my feeble abilities and the finances of the Academy will allow.[30]

The circumstances surrounding the ancient marbles were far from ideal, but the presence in Leiden of these *marmora* were to be the decisive factor for the creation of the first academic chair of archaeology in the Netherlands.

3

C.J.C. REUVENS AND THE ARCHAEOLOGICAL CABINET IN LEIDEN, 1818

LAW, CLASSICS AND ARCHAEOLOGY

On 13 June 1818 Caspar Jacob Christiaan Reuvens, 25 years old, was appointed Professor of Archaeology at the University of Leiden, after a brilliant and swift career in the study of law and classics. Reuvens was born in The Hague on 22 January 1793, to Maria Susanna Garcin and Jan Everard Reuvens.[1] Caspar remained the only son and lost his mother at the early age of five. His father was a jurist with a high position in society: he became councillor at the Court of Justice of Holland and Zeeland, and for a short time minister of justice. During the French administration he became president of the National Court of Justice: in this function he was ordered by Napoleon to work at the Imperial Court of Cassation in Paris.

The young Caspar Reuvens was an industrious and highly gifted student. After the Latin School in The Hague he went to Amsterdam in October 1808 to study at the Athenaeum Illustre, where he became imbued with the classics through the teaching of Professor David Jacob van Lennep. His father, who wrote letters weekly with all kinds of advice, wanted him to become a lawyer, in those times still a *nobile officium*, which could provide Caspar with esteem and a steady income. After Amsterdam the young Reuvens started reading law in Leiden, but he continued his classical studies with the aid of the inspiring professor Daniel Wijttenbach. Reuvens' stay in Leiden did not last long. In 1811 his father was transferred to Paris to work at the imperial Court of Cassation. He took his son with him and arranged the continuation of his juridical studies with professors Boutage, Cotelle and Delvincourt, the founders of the *Code Napoléon*. In 1813 the young Reuvens was awarded his licentiate by the University of Paris.[2] But for a young man with more than average interest in classical studies, there was more to be enjoyed in Paris: he started reading classics with Professor Jean François Boissonade and had ample opportunity to visit the Musée Napoléon, the French national collection, which in those days enjoyed enormous success, after the rather tumultuous years of its creation.

The French revolution had been the source of drastic changes in the way art collections were looked at. The former happy few, the royal household, the church and the aristocracy, had lost their possessions. Their art collections had been confiscated and redistributed between newly created public museums. In this process many works of art were deliberately or accidentally destroyed or damaged before they reached safety in one of the new institutions. Warehouses were set up in ancient convents to house paintings and sculptures for which no new place was available. A central role was assigned to the king's Palais du Louvre, which was appropriated in May 1791 for objects of art and science. In 1793 this 'Museum of the Republic' opened its gates to the public, although ordinary visitors were welcome only three days a week. The other seven days of the new revolutionary week were reserved for cleaning and for artists to study, copy and admire the masterpieces inside: the improvement of the contemporary arts was one of the main functions of the new museum. The whole cultural atmosphere around the Louvre is best evoked by an extract from a letter, written by Minister Roland to the painter David:

> As I conceive it, it should attract and impress foreigners. It should nourish a taste for the fine arts, please art lovers and serve as a school to artists. It should be open to everyone. This will be a national monument. There will not be a single individual who does not have the right to enjoy it. It will have such an influence on the mind, it will so elevate the soul, it will so excite the heart that it will be one of the most powerful ways of proclaiming the illustriousness of the French Republic.[3]

Between 1792 and 1795 several other museums were created, including the Musée des Arts et Métiers, the Muséum d'Histoire Naturelle and the Musée des Monuments Français. The French artists and the general public, after having had the opportunity to admire the confiscated treasures of the king, the church and the nobility, were treated in the years following the French conquests in Europe to the best objects that other European collections had to offer. From 1794 special commissions followed the conquering troops, selecting classical sculptures, Greek vases, medieval and Renaissance paintings, books, furniture, instruments and stuffed animals for the collections in the Louvre. In triumphal processions the war booty entered the city of Paris, the new capital of Europe. The masterpieces of classical art – including the Apollo Belvedere, the Laocoon, the Medici Venus and the Ariadne-Cleopatra – found a place in the Louvre, next to so many other objects from the conquered countries.

In November 1802 several museums and services were placed under the guidance of a new director, the colourful Dominique-Vivant Denon, 'the eye of Napoleon',[4] who had been a member of the Egyptian campaign with

Bonaparte and became the first real director of the Musée Central des Arts, which was rebaptized as the Musée Napoléon a year later. Léon Dufourny was appointed curator of the paintings. The antiquities were placed under the care of the curator Ennio Quirino Visconti, an Italian scholar who had worked in the Capitoline and Vatican museums in Rome.

Denon was a man with an intangible, lively character: scholar, traveller, collector and artist, but at the same time a political chameleon, poseur, ladykiller and pornographer. Without scruples he had selected works in various European museums which were worthy to be taken to Paris, referring to the law of war and with the visionary idea of creating a 'European Museum' in the capital of the empire. The central idea in Denon's mind was the conviction that classical art had to play a paramount role in improving contemporary taste. Sculptors such as Canova and Thorvaldsen were esteemed: they were able to adopt and to revive the classical spirit. Denon offered his own collection of Greek pottery from Southern Italy to the porcelain factory at Sèvres, to be used as a source of inspiration.[5]

The 17-year-old Reuvens must have been impressed. There are no direct sources from this period, but his later pleas for a national archaeological museum, for archaeological expeditions to the Mediterranean and for archaeology as the inspirational source for contemporary architecture and applied arts must have been rooted in the intellectual climate he encountered during his formative years in Paris.

After Napoleon's fall from power, father and son returned to the Netherlands in the spring of 1814. Both were temporarily out of work, but the young Kingdom of the Netherlands under King Willem I needed competent lawyers, regardless of whether they came from Napoleon's apparatus. Caspar became a lawyer in The Hague, and his father was appointed as one of the four presidents of the High Court. Caspar continued his classical studies: he started working on commentaries on Latin authors, especially playwrights, and on a treatise about the correct pronunciation of ancient Greek. These *Collectanea litteraria* were published in 1815 and were well received by scholars in the literary faculties.[6]

After finishing the manuscript of the *Collectanea* Reuvens allowed himself a trip to the spa of Pyrmont (Germany) to find relief for his continuous complaint of constipation. The many letters to his father written in this period characterize him as a silent, withdrawn young man, 'little in touch with his surroundings'. His doctor in Pyrmont tried to encourage him by writing in the *album amicorum*: '*Les grands parleurs sont souvant* [sic] *de tonneaux vides, qui rendent plus de son que de tonneaux pleins*' ('Great talkers are often like empty barrels, which make more noise than full ones'). After the medicinal water in Pyrmont had done its salubrious work, Reuvens returned to the Netherlands through Göttingen and Kassel, where he visited the brothers Grimm. In the meantime his father had taken care of the galley proofs of the *Collectanea*, prepared their publication and set wheels in motion that were to be germane in his son's future as a professor of classics.

FROM HARDERWIJK TO LEIDEN:
PER ASPERA AD ASTRA

On 2 August 1815 King Willem I assented to the foundation of an Athenaeum in Harderwijk, a small town on the eastern shore of the Zuiderzee. It was thanks to the timely publication of the *Collectanea* that Caspar Reuvens was appointed professor of Greek and Latin. He had six fellow professors of theology, law, anatomy, botany, mathematics and eastern languages. On 25 January 1816 he gave his inaugural lecture about the benefits of the classics for scholarly studies.[7] Reuvens started his academic career with zeal, but he had only a few students, and the cultural climate in the small town was hardly tolerable. Reuvens received letters from his father encouraging him to make his name known by publications: the only way to earn an appointment at a better university.

In the meantime Jan Everard Reuvens left for Brussels in May 1816 to prepare a revision of the Civil Code. For this man, a *homo novus* always concerned about his social position, the trip ended in disaster. A few days after his arrival 'having too much time and feeling bored' he took a long evening walk, which took him to a public garden. Here he encountered a group of youngsters, who managed to bring him into a precarious situation of blackmail, probably by performing compromising acts in the presence of some 'witnesses'. They threatened to make these deeds public, if Reuvens was not willing to pay a considerable sum of money. Being a law-abiding civil servant he did not yield to blackmail, but went to the authorities instead, not quite foreseeing the dramatic consequences of this deed. In the hope of arresting the gang, Reuvens was followed discreetly the following evenings by some police officers, but nothing happened. In the meantime the affair, which implicated Reuvens as a high-ranking Dutch official, became known in Brussels, and beyond. Reuvens wrote his version of the events to the minister of justice, who informed King Willem I, who was 'hurt and indignant' by the affair. In Brussels a trial of the (still missing) suspects was prepared, in which Reuvens had to testify: the catastrophe was entering its last phase. On 10 July Reuvens was seen for the last time. His body was found four days later in the water of a city canal. Two young men were arrested and convicted for 'assault' and sentenced to the improbably light punishment of six months in prison. The body was buried hastily, the 'murder case' was closed. The truth never surfaced.[8]

Caspar Reuvens had followed all these events through his father's letters. He had offered to come to Brussels to assist his father, but this was rejected as 'out of proportion for such a case'. The news of his father's death must have been devastating, after so many years of a close relationship and joint travels; and now Caspar had not a single relative left. After his father's accident he went to Brussels to take the body with him to The Hague, where Jan Everard Reuvens was reburied. The tragic and sudden death of his father left Reuvens orphaned in a small town on the Zuiderzee, where the prospects of continuing his teaching deteriorated rapidly.

In 1818 the Ministry of Education decided to put an end to the languishing existence of Harderwijk's Athenaeum.[9] Of the six remaining professors, three were given emeritus status. The three others, all, according to Minister of Education Falck, 'young people, and worthy to be placed in more suitable surroundings', were offered new positions at other universities. The future for Caspar Reuvens was more difficult, as vacancies for classical languages were not available. Minister Falck contacted Reuvens' former teacher Van Lennep in Amsterdam, and a new project came into being. Falck wrote to King Willem I:

> The profession of ancient languages, that of Mr Reuvens, is well taken care of at all universities, and there is no special vacancy at the moment. But Mr Reuvens has acquired a special taste for Archaeology, the knowledge of antiquity, elucidated by remaining monuments, about which until now at our universities no teaching has taken place. This profession could be offered to him, and he could be placed in Leiden, where the means for this profession are available.[10]

On Saturday 13 June 1818 the king signed a royal decree, in which the appointment of C.J.C. Reuvens as extraordinary professor of archaeology was made official.[11] He was also appointed director of the 'archaeological cabinet', consisting of the *marmora Papenburgica*, the 'means for this profession', which still languished in the damp orangery of the botanical gardens.

PROFESSOR IN LEIDEN: THE PRAISE OF ARCHAEOLOGY

On 24 October 1818 Reuvens gave his inaugural lecture in the auditorium of the university in the presence of the rector, trustees, professors, city council and students. His lecture *De laudibus archaeologiae* ('the praise of archaeology') was composed according to the laws of the genre, but without the usual grandiloquence and extreme flattery. The result was a clear location of the new discipline of archaeology in regard to the well-established chairs of history and philology. Reuvens pleaded for a worthy place for archaeology beside these disciplines in the large 'building of the humanities', the *humanarum scientiarum aedificium*. He did not fear that other professors would scorn this novice-discipline as an inferior part of the humanities, a *pars levior litterarum*. The newcomer was able to contribute to the cross-fertilization of

Figure 3.1 Portrait of Professor C.J.C. Reuvens. Lithograph by L. Springer (1835) after a painting by Louis Moritz. Archive, National Museum of Antiquities, Leiden.

disciplines, a process well known to all scholars: *notum est enim quantum lucis altera pars litterarum ab altera accipiat* ('for it is known how much light one part of the humanities can receive from another').

Generally speaking, according to Reuvens, a division could be made in the study of ancient cultures: on the one hand the written sources (*opus ingenii*, 'work of the mind'), on the other the artefacts, the tangible remains of antiquity (*opus manuum*, 'work of the hands'). Ancient written sources had quite a few problems: most of the literature had been lost, many texts were incomplete and the remainder had suffered from inaccurate transcriptions by medieval monks. The antiquities, less eloquent than Greek or Latin texts, had the advantage that they had not been corrupted by mice or monks, so they could give additional information to the ancient texts. As an example, Reuvens gave a short review of Roman history, as illustrated by the different coinages. Political and economic changes, rival emperors and usurpers, devaluation and prosperity could all be distilled from the study of Roman coinage but were scarcely or not at all to be found in the ancient written sources: *haec { . . . } non narrata audimus, aut vix intellecta legimus, sed in ipsis monumentis quotidie vidimus, cernimus, animadvertimus* ('these stories we do not hear told, nor do we read them in an understandable way, but we see, discern and notice them daily in the monuments themselves'). In short, no other discipline than archaeology could show the magnitude of our ignorance regarding antiquity: *nulla est, quae tam evidenter nos doceat, quantum sit illud quod nesciamus, quam haec Archaeologia.*

And the lack of knowledge was overwhelming: scholars hardly knew anything about remote and overgrown cities in India, rock graves in Egypt, cyclopean walls in Italy or Greece, or ancient inscriptions in the Punic, Etruscan, Iberian or Palmyrene languages. And, closer at home, which classical author could be consulted to gain some knowledge about the megalithic monuments, the goddess Nehalennia, Hercules Magusanus or the Matres Aufoniae? This is where the realm of philology ended and the reign of archaeology began: the discovery and the elucidation of the unknown. Reuvens continued his oration with a sketch of the archaeological tradition in the Netherlands. The activities of learned predecessors such as Scaliger, Smetius and Oudendorp had only been flickers in the dark and after their deaths nobody had been there to take over the torch of archaeology. Tradition had been lacking. At the end of the eighteenth century archaeology in the Netherlands was as good as dead, whereas in Germany the discipline flourished through the activities of Winckelmann and Heynius (Christian Gottlob Heyne). Today at the University of Leiden archaeology had risen as a phoenix from the ashes, and hope for the future was renewed: *quod tunc { . . . } negatum fuit, id nunc adfert Fortuna Redux, mutataeque temporum rationes* ('what at that time was denied, is now brought to us by *Fortuna Redux* and the altered state of affairs'). The fatherland should do its best to foster the study of archaeology by assembling the various smaller collections of *archaeologica* in Leiden, the centre of all future archaeological activities.

Reuvens ended his lecture with the traditional call for support from his fellow professors, many of whom had tutored him as a young student, reading law and classics. He asked sympathy for his youth and inexperience, as it was better to acknowledge one's weaknesses than to conceal them: *habet aliquam veniam veritas* ('the truth gives some forgiveness'). With an exhortation addressed to the academic youth to show interest in the new discipline of archaeology and a promise to help his future pupils to the best of his abilities, Reuvens ended this declaration of principles.

The praise of archaeology had been sung. After a successful start to his academic career, his personal life, too, experienced happiness: in 1822 he married Louise Sophie Blussé, the daughter of a well-known publisher in Leiden. The marriage brought the serious and rather reticent Reuvens into contact with lively in-laws and was blessed with three children: Maria (1823), Louis (1824) and Margaretha (1827). Reuvens and his wife spent their honeymoon in Germany, where they visited Düsseldorf (in the hope of seeing some Smetius antiquities), Cologne, Bonn (where Reuvens met Professor F.J. Welcker, but failed to see the Dorow collection), Trier, Mainz, Frankfurt, Dresden and Berlin. In this last city Reuvens had a meeting with the eminent scholar F.A. Wolf. Business and pleasure were combined in a happy way and important contacts with foreign scholars were made.

EXAMPLES FROM ABROAD: CAMBRIDGE, OXFORD AND LONDON

For all parties concerned it was obvious that the Papenbroek marbles could no longer stay in the damp surroundings of the orangery in the botanical gardens. In the summer of 1819 Reuvens travelled to England to seek inspiration about what a new museum could look like. Oxford and Cambridge were interesting places for Reuvens, because of the similarities with Leiden: in all three old university towns collections were kept, which were originally assembled and donated to the university by private collectors. In Cambridge Richard Viscount Fitzwilliam (1745–1816) had been active. His collections were built on those of Clarke and Colton; in Oxford the collection of Sir Elias Ashmole (1617–1692) was considered the oldest public museum. In his diary Reuvens made sketches and interesting notes about the arrangement of the antiquities in these museums, the colours used in the galleries and the different efforts to get the best lighting for the sculptures.[12] Reuvens proved enthusiastic about the display of antiquities in the Perse School in Cambridge, because of the 'contextualization' of the objects:

> Most of the antiques in Cambridge Clarke's marbles are in round niches, of wood, placed in the walls, and then painted white. Has a very good effect. A single big inscription is in a rectangular niche. The bas-reliefs are simply built in. The niches take up lots of space.[13]

The display in the Old Schools in Oxford was judged less favourably: 'in Oxford everything built in, or placed at random, wherever space is available. The wall has been left unfinished, not even plastered; it makes a miserable impression.'[14] On a drawing by William Westall, *The Sculpture Gallery 1813*, it is indeed obvious that the sculptures were placed without any thought for their arrangement on a rough wooden floor. Roman capitals and altars served as pedestals. Black lettering on the wall was a silent remainder of an earlier function of this gallery.[15]

Reuvens was more enthusiastic about the galleries in the British Museum in London. As during his stay in Paris, he was visiting an archaeological collection during a very dynamic period.[16] The older Hope and Hamilton collections were already an established part of the museum, but the Towneley marbles had only been on display since 1808, in the so-called Towneley Gallery, adjacent to Montague House. In a further extension, the spectacular Elgin marbles were housed in a temporary setting, finished in 1817, just a few years before Reuvens' visit. The Phigalian marbles from the temple of Apollo at Bassae had also been put on display only recently. Reuvens was impressed with his first encounter with original classical Greek sculpture: he immediately ordered plaster casts of both the Elgin marbles and the Phigalian sculptures for later use in his lectures about the history of ancient sculpture.

Concerning the way in which the antiquities were exposed, Reuvens was pleased with the high windows with the resulting light skimming on the object from above and sides. He described at length the colours used in the different galleries. The floor of the Towneley Gallery was 'pale-green, with black and white'. The shelves, on which the busts were displayed, would make a better impression if painted 'white as marble'. The blue of the temporary Elgin Hall and the yellow of the Hope Gallery were 'both bad, but Hope the worst'. The nicest part of the museum was in his view the room with the Hamilton collection. These antiquities were placed in a hall with 'light rose-red colours, with many white marble pedestals'. The impression was very good: 'Most charming, merry and at the same time the best for the display of statues.' In his diary he did not comment on the quality of the sculptures, but only on the arrangement of the objects and the use of colour and lighting, forming his own ideas for the collection in Leiden.

Financing the 'archaeological cabinet' became a difficult task during the first years of its existence. A few months before his inaugural speech Reuvens was asked by the trustees of the university what he needed to start working as a professor of archaeology and keeper of the cabinet. He replied with a report of eleven pages consisting of 'a list of the things I deem necessary for the creation of the material resources for the teaching of archaeology'.[17] He put special emphasis on a new building for the collection, on new purchases and on the creation of an archaeological library, which was non-existent in Leiden. Evidently the Kingdom of the Netherlands wished to compete with countries like England, France, Germany and Italy 'for the price of scholarship' but it was 'probably the poorest country in Europe' as far as archaeological facilities were concerned. This had to be changed in due time. For the moment Reuvens asked for a wooden cabinet with fifty drawers to house his collection of ancient coins, which he wanted to use for his first lectures: the study of numismatics was the starting point for every course in archaeology. Trustees reserved a modest sum of 500 guilders for the year 1818 and another 500 guilders for 1819. They did not comment on any of Reuvens' further wishes.[18] In April 1819 Reuvens was again asked to give a list of his wishes for the year 1820. He answered dryly that this was 'hardly possible', because he had not received any answer to his earlier demands about housing, a library and his other wishes, nor any commitment for the future.[19]

Two months later he had quite another experience concerning financial matters. In June 1819, during his stay in London, he asked the minister of education if the department was interested in 'placing some orders on behalf of the archaeological cabinet'. He suggested buying the casts of the Elgin marbles and the Phigalian reliefs, which would be useful for his next term of lectures about the history of ancient sculpture. Falck submitted the question to the king, who without hesitation signed a royal decree, which allotted 1,200 guilders to the archaeological cabinet for the casts and their transportation to Leiden.[20] Officially this extraordinary subsidy should have been arranged through the treasury of the trustees, a task which Reuvens later performed in a diplomatic way.[21]

These financial matters during the first year of his professorate made one thing clear: support for his ideas about the future of archaeology was to come from the Ministry of Education and the benevolence of the king. Subsequently problems were to arise with the trustees of the university, who were frequently being bypassed by one of their professors. But Reuvens, determined to realize his ideas, could live with this state of affairs.

4

COLLECTIONS AND CONFLICTS

Be wiser than other people if you can, but do not tell them so.
Philip Dormer Stanhope, 4th Earl of Chesterfield
(1694–1773)

A NATIONAL MUSEUM AND THE STUDY OF ARCHAEOLOGY: ORGANIZATION

In Paris, Reuvens had encountered the organization of the French museums in the post-revolutionary years. The central role of the Musée Napoléon was undisputed, but in the provinces and conquered countries, especially in the university towns, adjunct museums for the schools of art had been created, with curators and lecturers as staff. In 1800 Jean Chaptal, minister of the interior, had advocated distributing works of art to cities with a large population to enlighten the general public and to give opportunities to students to get acquainted with a complete range of paintings by masters of different schools. In total fifteen cities in France and conquered Europe benefited from this initiative and received works of art from the central depots of the Louvre. During the second year of his professorate and even before the first museum building came into being, Reuvens theorized about the possibility of creating more than one archaeological museum and more chairs of archaeology in the Netherlands. Apart from the situation in France, the examples from other neighbouring countries showed that a healthy competition between museums and universities helped to promote archaeology. But the Netherlands were a small country and establishing one museum was already a difficult task. Reuvens wrote to the department:

> I would dare say that our country is too small and not rich enough
> to maintain more than one archaeological museum. If it is possible
> to have various good ones, for example like London and Oxford,
> then I consider this preferable (however tempting the thought may
> be to unite everything); because this fosters scholarship in more

than one place, and thus the scholarly competition. It keeps monopoly and aristocracy, if I may express myself in this way, outside of the realm of the humanities. Also Germany maintains various museums of first and second rank: Vienna, Munich, Dresden, Berlin, Kassel etc. These belong to different sovereigns, and this fosters competition in buying and extending, and none of them is disused or neglected. And nobody should wish that the study of antiquity, which now thrives in the whole of Germany, would be confined to one single spot in that country.[1]

Following the French example, however, he saw the possibility of creating museums related to the central archaeological museum with numismatic and plaster-cast collections, which could serve to promote the taste for archaeology and train young archaeologists. These 'introductory' museums in university towns could also provide job opportunities for curators and lecturers of archaeology. The academic teaching of 'full archaeology' could be limited to two universities (Leiden in the north, Ghent in the southern part of the country), while the other universities could teach numismatics – 'basic archaeology' – as an introduction for full archaeological education at the two vintage universities.

In Reuvens' view Leiden was to become the central assembly point of all archaeological collections, which until then had been owned by different public institutions and private collectors. In Leiden he could start with the antiquities from the Papenbroek collection and other university collections. Of particular interest were the Egyptian and Roman antiquities from the Theatrum Anatomicum, the first 'museum' of the Netherlands, dating back to 1591. This Theatrum was situated in the Beguinage Chapel (*Faliede Bagijnen Kerk*) given to the university in 1577. An amphitheatre had been built in this church, which was used for public dissections during the winter months from 1590 onwards.

Round the theatre skeletons of men and animals had been set up and a varied collection of curiosities was exhibited either in the open space or in cabinets. A printed catalogue of the collection saw sixty-four editions between 1669 and 1761 in Dutch, Latin, French and English.[2] That most of the antiquities were of Egyptian origin was due to the fact that the first professor of anatomy and keeper of the Theatrum, Otto van Heurn (Heurnius), ingeniously availed himself of his valuable contacts with an alumnus of the university, who was at that time employed in the Levant. This David le Leu de Wilhem made a journey from Aleppo to Egypt in 1619. He may have been the first citizen of the Netherlands to visit the cemetery of the ancient capital of Memphis. On the site near the present Saqqara he found, or bought from the native population, antiquities, which were put on display in the Theatrum labelled with the donor's name and surname: mummy coffins, mummies, mummified skulls and limbs, funerary images, a canope.

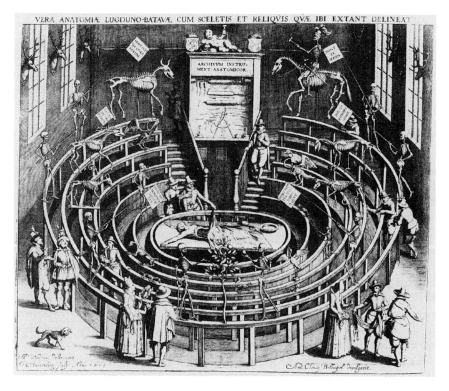

Figure 4.1 The Theatrum Anatomicum in Leiden. Engraving by W. Swanenburg after a drawing by J.C. Woudanus (1610). Archive, National Museum of Antiquities, Leiden.

For two centuries the Theatrum Anatomicum was one of the main attractions of the town of Leiden. When the arts and sciences were more differentiated and became more specialized, antiquities and other strictly anatomical materials were regarded as discordant with the collection. A number of them were discarded in 1771 and soon afterwards the whole cabinet was closed, although anatomical dissections continued to take place here till 1860. Luckily the most important antiquities survived and were transferred to the National Museum of Antiquities in the summer of 1821.

Outside Leiden, too, there were collections that aroused Reuvens' interest, such as the antiquities which had belonged to the stadtholder Willem V and been taken to Paris by French troops. After Napoleon's fall most of these pieces were recovered by the director of the Rijksmuseum in Amsterdam and kept in that institute. In The Hague was the Royal Cabinet of Curiosities (*Koninklijk Kabinet van Zeldzaamheden*) with a very rich ethnological collection, interspersed with archaeological finds from the Netherlands. The Hague was also the seat of the Royal Coin Cabinet (*Koninklijk Penningkabinet*) with ancient and modern coins, medals and precious gemstones. Smaller collections of antiquities were owned by private collectors, art academies or local authorities and church councils. With support from the ministry, Reuvens tried to move all these dispersed antiquities to Leiden, as with the objects which Reuvens acquired at the auctions of the collections Johannes in de Betouw (1822–3), D. Versteegh (1823) and J. Delescluze (1826). From time to time private persons donated antiquities to the museum, like Minister Falck: in 1823 he presented the museum with a fourth-century Attic grave inscription of Philon from Aixone (the father of the Syracusan tyrant Kallippos) and a superb Hellenistic torso, which was found in the ruins of Eleusis. Falck had acquired these precious pieces from Jean-Baptiste Delescluze, a Bruges shipowner, about whom more will be said in the next chapter.

Most of the institutions did not object to parting with the *corpora aliena* in their possession. For example, in 1825 the Royal Art Academy in Amsterdam sent to Leiden a colossal marble head of Dionysos, one of the most important antiquities in the Netherlands (Figure 4.2). The head was shipped from Smyrna to Amsterdam in 1732 by the Dutch consul D.A. de Hochepied and after some time in the Chamber of Commerce was transferred to the Art Academy. Probably the head belonged to the Roman cult statue of Dionysos in the temple of Teos, which replaced a Hellenistic statue, which together with the temple was destroyed in the first century AD.[3]

Other museums opposed Reuvens' views vigorously, sometimes out of sheer unwillingness to part with their objects, but more often because a fundamental discussion was possible about the legality of Reuvens' claims. For example about the question which objects belonged in an archaeological museum and which in an ethnological collection.

ART FROM THE EAST INDIES: 'CONTEMPORARY OR ANCIENT CIVILIZATIONS?'

With the emergence of differentiated museums, of coins, of carved stones, natural history, archaeology, ethnography and 'national' art, the question of boundaries between these institutions began to play an important role. Reuvens' claim that ancient Hindu and Buddhist art belonged to the realm of archaeology, especially, led to a collision with the director of the Royal Cabinet of Curiosities in The Hague. This museum housed mainly ethnological objects, but in the view of the director ethnology comprised 'the history of foreign countries and peoples, including our fatherland and the Dutch people': many archaeological finds from the Netherlands were to be found in this cabinet, alongside church treasures, reliquaries, furniture, doll's houses and a mass of Asian artefacts from all periods and countries.

Figure 4.2 Marble head of Dionysos, early second century AD after a Hellenistic original. National Museum of Antiquities.

With his legal background, Reuvens had a clear view of which objects should be collected and presented in an archaeological museum. As a rule these were the material objects of the ancient civilizations of Greece and Rome, and of the ancient peoples who had been conquered or influenced by the Greeks and Romans. From this perspective it followed, too, that the ancient Buddhist art of Afghanistan (Gandara) and India should be placed in an archaeological museum, as it was influenced by Hellenistic and Roman art. Consequently Hindu and Buddhist antiquities from the Dutch Indies, which had derived many motives from the Indian examples, also had to be shown in an archaeological museum, and not in an ethnological collection. An ethnological museum had to confine itself, according to Reuvens, to still existing peoples. The artefacts of the ancient Indonesian civilizations were too far removed from the modern, Islamic community to be placed in an ethnological collection. Reuvens applied this rule very strictly: archaeological objects from cultures unknown by the old world were less suitable for an archaeological museum. When in 1828 a collection of Mexican artefacts was offered to Reuvens, he answered:

> I would not cut off the possibility of enlarging our Dutch museum collections with the so unknown objects from Mexico, but these objects should not be placed in a Museum of Antiquities, which should confine itself to classical antiquity and to those regions, which were known by the Greeks and Romans and which were influenced by their civilization, e.g. India.[4]

But of course discussion was possible about the question of boundaries. Where to place ancient objects from a still existing people? Where is the borderline between an ancient and a contemporary civilization?

> There is no doubt about categorizing as antiquities the artefacts of peoples which either no longer exist, or have changed completely due to foreign occupation or a change in religion. And thus in a Museum of Antiquities, Egyptian, Babylonian, Greek, Roman and northern artefacts should be placed. But if a people of antiquity, known to us either by its own writings or by those of Greeks and Romans, still exists today, and exists in nearly the same form as in the past, should it then be counted among the contemporary or the ancient civilizations? Such peoples are the Indians, the Hindus, and part of the Javanese, and the other inhabitants of the Indonesian archipelago, who partly have preserved the Indian religion in spite of the Muslim majority, like some mountain tribes on Java and the whole population of the island of Bali.[5]

These considerations were put to the test in 1820 when Reuvens asked the Department of Education, Arts and Sciences to remove twelve ancient Javanese statues from the Royal Cabinet of Curiosities in The Hague. The director of the Cabinet of Curiosities, R.P. van de Kasteele, strongly opposed Reuvens' view in a letter to the Ministry of Education, in which he pointed out that the statues in question belonged to a still existing people and that they, therefore, belonged in his cabinet, and not among the antiquities in Leiden. When confronted with this opposition to his ideas, Reuvens explained his point of view more clearly. Antiquities as old as Roman artefacts, from a culture influenced by the Greco-Roman world, belonged in an archaeological museum. Otherwise Roman art, too, could leave the museum and find its place in a collection of Italian culture:

> The diligent and deserving director of this cabinet has understood from a decision unknown to me, that Indian antiquities should also be part of that cabinet *as belonging to a still living people*. To deny

the old age of the Indian religion and its statues and temples, only with a view to placing them in an ethnological cabinet, would be preposterous. I do not think that this can be the case, and I will not bother to prove their antiquity. These Indian antiquities are from a dim and distant past and it cannot be the intention of this decision to place objects, which are of equal or higher antiquity than Egyptian, Persian or Greek artefacts, in a *modern* cabinet, only because the people still exists. I reply that essentially the borderline between a Museum of Antiquities and a Museum of Curiosities of Living People cannot be found in the respective antiquity of the objects, which is impossible to establish with certainty, but that the borderline should be drawn quite differently. It is important for scholarship that the Indian antiquities are not separated from the Egyptian and other artefacts. Otherwise, in the near future, there will be no longer a Museum of Antiquities, because also *Roman* and *Greek* objects will be placed in a Museum of Living People, the former labelled as *Italian*, and the latter among the objects from the *Hellenic Commonwealth*. The borderline, as I may repeat, is this: the disappearance of a people, or its later civilization, by its complete transition to the *Christian* or the *Muslim* faith.[6]

The department took a decision in accordance with Reuvens' views and ordered the removal of the ancient Indonesian statues from The Hague to Leiden. Also Indonesian ancient art from the Royal Academy of Arts and Sciences in Amsterdam went to Leiden, where Reuvens started working on the publication of these monuments. He published a monograph on the iconography of the Javanese statues from Amsterdam[7] and he began to take an interest in measures to safeguard Indonesian monuments and antiquities still in situ against vandalism, looting and neglect by his fellow countrymen: 'There seems to be a feeling on Java that those monuments are common property and that everyone, especially the higher civil servants, can take away what they like.'[8]

Reuvens was thinking about measures to stop the destruction of these works of art and to safeguard this part of the archaeological heritage of Java. A law forbidding the removal of antiquities would not suffice:

To stop this misconduct completely by declaring the monuments property of the government, from which nothing can be taken, is probably impossible and could have bad side effects. Supervision in these remote places is impossible and the monuments could be demolished, and their reliefs exported, without the government knowing anything about it. Consequently, they would be even less known in Europe, and the public would be even less interested in them. Also, concerning smaller antiquities, our experience in Europe teaches us that it is dangerous to declare them government property. These antiquities may be melted down (if they are made of metal) or otherwise obscured without any benefit for academic studies. I would consider it best, if all future owners of large pieces of antiquity, especially those of stone, were obliged to hand over to the government a drawing of them, with notes about the place where the object was found and the circumstances of the find. The owners of smaller antiquities of gold, silver, bronze or another material should be obliged to hand over these objects to the government for a little more than the intrinsic value of the metal, or for another reasonable price. Both drawings and antiquities should be handed over to the future *Society for the Publication of the Javanese Monuments* or should be sent to the fatherland.[9]

Reuvens saw two possibilities for moveable objects: either sending them to Leiden or creating an archaeological museum in Batavia (in West Java): in theory he favoured the latter idea, but he rejected this plan on practical grounds. Batavia lacked the presence of a university, there were no culturally educated classes and the general neglect would make the erection of such an institution a non-starter. A better project would be the creation of a society to describe and publish the ancient monuments and safeguard them against pillaging:

I take the liberty to ask if it is possible to create a domestic institution on Java, entrusted permanently with these tasks, in order to let the work continue on a solid foundation, independent of external conditions. First, could this institution be financed totally by the Government? Second, should the first question meet with difficulties, is it possible with support from the Government to create a private scholarly society, which fosters these activities with voluntary contributions from its members? This society could bear the name of *Society for the Publication of the Javanese Monuments* or *Monuments of the Dutch East-Indian Colonies.*[10]

As examples for such an institution Reuvens mentioned the British Society of Dilettanti and the Society of Antiquaries: 'Why would Dutch money and Dutch patriotism not be able to create a similar thing?' Reuvens thought about giving a start to this society by a large private donation and continuing to act as an advisor for the archaeological activities involved. Three tasks were of paramount importance: the publication of illustrated descriptions of the monuments and antiquities, the study of Javanese language and literature, and the creation of a good library in Batavia. Special interest lay in the publication of the Indonesian temple reliefs:

Very important for academic research is the shape of the temples, with complete details of all the decoration on, inside and around these monuments. This is the only way to get a thorough knowledge of the Indian religion and its Javanese adaptations. Very often the reliefs on the temples show a complete mythology and sometimes historical representations. How much remains to be done can be deduced from the innumerable reliefs with which the temple of Boro Bodor is covered on all sides: only twenty or so are illustrated in the drawings of Professor Reinwardt, and six of them in Crawford. And their exact location on the monument is not even known.[11]

Reuvens ended his memorandum with a list of clauses for the creation of such a society, in which the organization was described in detail, including the financial obligations of the members and the necessary support from the government. Apparently other items were higher on the agenda of the governor-general of the Dutch East Indies, with the result that this memorandum of Reuvens' remained in the archives of the colonial palace in Batavia. Indonesian antiquities did go to Leiden occasionally, but the opportunity to make a start with safeguarding cultural heritage and the creation of a society was not taken.

THE ROYAL COIN CABINET: 'A DIFFERENCE IN SCHOLARLY VIEWS'

Another confrontation concerning the indistinct boundary between archaeological objects and other ancient artefacts took place in 1824, when a conflict arose with the director of the Royal Coin Cabinet in The Hague. This cabinet was responsible for the collection of coins, medals and carved stones, which originally came from the Royal Collections. As pointed out before, Reuvens did not have any objections against collections of ancient coins in other cities, because they could serve as an introduction to the study of archaeology. Problems did arise when a definition was needed for the category 'carved stones': in 1824 a collection from North Africa arrived in Leiden which contained coins and Egyptian scarabs, among various other objects. Dutifully Reuvens sent the coins to The Hague, but the director of the cabinet, J.C. de Jonge, also claimed the scarabs, which were 'carved stones' in his view. Reuvens reacted irritably:

> The coins are of course at your disposal. But I have left the decision about the scarabs to the Ministry, because these pieces do not seem to belong in your collection and if I am to be robbed of even the smallest and cheapest items, I will lose all possibilities for my teaching.[12]

De Jonge was sure that the matter could be settled amicably and asked to view the scarabs in order to form an opinion about them: 'Without having seen them I cannot hand them over, because *stricto jure*, as a manner of speaking, they belong to me.'[13] Reuvens sent him the scarabs, but the words *stricto jure* ('according to the law') aroused his legal interest, because the lack of any legislation was precisely the reason for the present state of affairs, in which unwritten, customary laws ruled. A few days later de Jonge sent the scarabs back to Leiden, having judged them unworthy for his cabinet and stressing the fact that it was his decision to do so, because 'carved stones' did belong to his realm. Reuvens refused to accept the scarabs on these conditions, if *stricto jure* they did not belong to him. In a long and important letter to de Jonge he expressed his feelings about this case, in which he wanted a fundamental decision and not a compromise:

> I have received the four scarabs and your letter of the 19th. I thank you very much for the offer to leave them at the Museum of Antiquities and regard this as a proof of your friendship. Notwithstanding our friendship, please allow me to refuse this offer, because you wrote to me that also the Government differs from my view about the legality. And because you mean to have reasons to disapprove of my conduct, I ask you to excuse me for explaining myself in a more extensive way.
>
> I do not know of any 'yielding' or 'handing over' of Government's property. I understood that the Government alone is master and in case of doubt has to make a decision after having received scholarly considerations from both sides. I further understood that negotiations between cabinets were not needed, but only a simple notification to the Government if there were objects in a collection whose destination might be doubtful. To me these scarabs were not beyond any doubt, and, without giving any opinions pro or contra, I have asked a simple decision, awaiting should further considerations be asked or not. Instead of finding fault with this behaviour I hope that, on second thoughts, you will concede that I have chosen the only straightforward 'royal way', so to speak: the only way which could not lead to dispute and dissension.
>
> Indeed you cannot blame me for having doubts from time to time: I have never received any information about the right boundaries between museums, for reasons that I do not know. If a *strictum jus* can be alleged against me, then this rule must come forward from a clear governmental decision. If this decision is not shown to me, then it is natural that I bring back the question to its prior state. If I were summoned to give my opinion on neutral ground, for example in a foreign country, about the dividing lines between museums, then in a cabinet of coins and carved stones I would place only objects which belonged there according to the most rigid rules, for fear 1) that nowhere else could a natural borderline be found, and 2) that too many objects would be lost for serious study.

First, as far as the so-called carved stones are concerned, I would consider only the precious stones engraved with images, from Greek and Roman craftmanship, and the ancient glass pastes to be part of such a cabinet. Persian, Egyptian and Gnostic stones do not belong to the fine arts, but simply to scholarship and I would not consider placing them in that cabinet. The Egyptian ones are not even made of precious stones, but of hard, rocky materials like granite, syenite, basalt and the like. When in doubt I would always decide in favour of scholarship and to the detriment of a collection, which has beauty as its principal aim.

I repeat that I absolutely do not know the government's definition of engraved stones, let alone – if it exists – the quality of this definition. Therefore I have expressed my doubts whether two stones, one merely basalt the other sandstone and both unengraved, could be counted as carved stones; and whether two other stones, engraved but made of limestone, could be considered as precious? If all seal stones are to be categorized as 'carved stones' – and this goes for all signet rings as well – then I understand the protests when a golden ring from Java was placed in the Coin Cabinet. But should all rings go there, even the most ordinary ones of rusted copper and iron?

Egyptian scarabs are neither precious stones, nor seal stones: has someone made a separate classification for these objects? And is the definition extended to all carving in hard stone? But then all Egyptian objects with reliefs, sarcophagi, cippi, statues etc. would be included: they are all made of hard stone, the same stone as the scarabs, and all covered with the same representations and carvings. If the cabinet claims all scarabs, then items of earthenware also have to go there, which the ministry has always placed in the Museum of Antiquities. And finally, if one desires all small objects with hieroglyphs, which were used as amulets, to be in the Coin Cabinet, then no Egyptian statuette of earthenware will be left in the collection of antiquities. And if we were to acquire a scarab with a diameter of five feet, like the one of Lord Elgin, or of one foot, like the one of Denon, would you also consider those 'carved stones'? Or a gemstone?

If you think it necessary to inform the Ministry that I will not make use of your kind offer to keep the scarabs, because they are not considered mine, it is all right with me. Otherwise I will find an opportunity to do so in the near future. In the meantime do not be angry with me or my words: these are not disputes between you and me, but a difference in scholarly views between the Director of the Coin Cabinet and his counterpart at the Museum of Antiquities.[14]

It is clear that Reuvens was not interested in the four scarabs as such: by sending them back he wanted to provoke a discussion about the boundaries between his museum and the Coin Cabinet. Other correspondence about this question is lacking, but all future shipments of scarabs found their way into the collections of the archaeological museum.

THE RIJKSMUSEUM: 'ONE OF THE LARGEST AND FINEST EXAMPLES OF THE SO-CALLED ETRUSCAN VASES'

A year later a conflict arose between Reuvens and the influential director of the Rijksmuseum in Amsterdam, Cornelis Apostool. The Rijksmuseum, the national treasury founded in 1807 as the Royal Museum by King Louis Bonaparte, housed collections of paintings, furniture and applied art of a very varied origin: private collections, donations to the state, permanent loans, and the war booty recovered from Paris after Napoleon's fall. Among the art objects, antiquities and objects related to antiquity could also be found: sculptures, vases, gemstones, fragments of Pompeian frescoes, pre-historic axes and models of ancient architecture. Apostool was asked by the department to hand over these archaeological objects to the new museum in Leiden. Apostool made no objections to sending the rougher artefacts to Leiden, but he kept the most precious and beautiful objects in Amsterdam, especially the gems and the cork models of ancient architecture. Reuvens, who *de jure* could not claim the gemstones from The Hague, had placed his hope on this collection:

> I have made clear that all possibility is taken away from me to get some practice in the knowledge of engraved precious stones. I was able to train myself in antique sculpture by travelling, which I had to do on my own expenses. But in a foreign country it is of course impossible to take the precious stones in your hands to inspect them properly and compare them. And because it cannot be asked of me to pay personally for a small or large collection of these stones, my knowledge and my teaching will be confined to book learning.
> About the models of ancient temples I would like to say that these are the only way of rendering ancient architecture perceptible to the senses, as we lack the buildings themselves: they are most useful for my lessons in history of ancient architecture, which I have postponed deliberately till next year. Because I need them urgently, I take the liberty of asking you to allocate them to the Leiden Museum of Antiquities.[15]

When the shipment from Amsterdam arrived it became clear that other items were missing: 'a piece of fresco or wall-painting from Pompei, a seal stone for eye unguent (*sigillum medici ocularii*).' And the most important

42

object: the large Campanian grave amphora which came from the collections of Frederic Count de Thoms and the stadtholder, as has been described earlier (see front cover), which Apostool refused to hand over before his retirement as a director:

> Finally I have to draw Your Hon. attention to the fact that the Amsterdam Museum possesses one of the largest and finest examples of the so-called Etruscan vases, originating from the cabinet of the Stadtholder and shining brilliantly in Millin's *Peintures des Vases Grecs*. The Director of the Amsterdam Museum has made his intention clear to me that he will not hand over this vase, because he arranged its return from Paris in 1815 with much difficulty. But he has also promised me, that once his association with the Museum is ended, he will not try to obstruct the delivery.[16]

The department did not want to hurt Apostool's feelings: the Campanian amphora of the Ixion Painter remained in Amsterdam together with the relief of Asclepius and Hygieia and was not handed over to Leiden until 1844, after the death of both Reuvens and Apostool.

A smaller collection of prehistoric stone axes came to the museum in 1826 from the Museum of Natural History. The director of this institution, C.G.C. Reinwardt, was not unwilling to yield the axes to Reuvens, but he claimed to have every right to keep other artefacts because of the variety and type of stone. Again Reuvens had to complain about the arbitrariness of the arrangements with his fellow directors and the lack of cultural legislation. He wrote to the ministry responsible:

> Who would say that the big carved onyx, bought recently by the King for the Coin Cabinet, should belong in the Museum of Natural History because of the type of stone? Yet an onyx of that enormous size is quite remarkable. The type of stone used for the weapons of the nordic peoples, like axes, is very useful for historical conclusions. In other countries these objects belong without argument in an archaeological museum: an arrangement like the present one is likely to provoke strife and jealousy, which between two national museums is not appropriate.[17]

ARCHAEOLOGY VERSUS PHILOLOGY: 'BENEATH THE DIGNITY OF STUDY AND RANK'

The growing collections of the Museum of Antiquities attracted the attention of philologists in the Netherlands and abroad. In his inaugural address *De laudibus archaeologiae* Reuvens had treated the relation between archaeology and long established professions like history and philology: archaeology could shed light on aspects of antiquity about which the ancient authors remained silent. The study of coins, inscriptions and newly excavated finds could complement or even alter the established views of the past. Reuvens' colleagues had listened to his words benevolently, but their state of mind altered when their young colleague acquired objects for the archaeological museum, whose publication could lead to a place in the hall of academic fame.

The litmus test of the relation between archaeology and philology presented itself in 1822, when Reuvens planned to publish a collection of Punic stelae from Carthage, three of which bore inscriptions. For the philological interpretation of the inscriptions (written in the Punic language) Reuvens asked the help of his colleague H.A. Hamaker, professor of oriental languages. Their co-operation soon came to an end: when discussing the Punic stelae an argument arose between the two scholars about the function of the stones. Reuvens interpreted them as gravestones, considering the form and decorative elements. Hamaker compared the inscriptions with Hebrew and came to an interpretation of them as votive offerings. The argument was such that they could not agree on a joint publication of the important stones with the result that in 1822 two separate works were published: Hamaker's *Diatribe philologico-critica monumentorum aliquot Punicorum nuper in Africa repertorum interpretationem exhibens* and Reuvens' *Periculum animadversionum archaeologicarum ad cippos Punicos Humbertianos Musei Antiquarii Lugduno-Batavi* with archaeological arguments for his hypothesis that the objects were gravestones and not votive reliefs.[18]

After this incident Reuvens' idea of academic co-operation was severely frustrated, but worse was to come. When the museum acquired collections of Egyptian antiquities, which due to the publications of Champollion le Jeune, Young and Letronne had become the subject of intense academic interest, Hamaker decided that it was time to act. It was insupportable for him that a mere archaeologist like Reuvens should have the prerogative to publish these philological treasures of Leiden's university. In April 1826 he wrote to the ministry a request that he alone should be responsible for the publication of all archaeological objects bearing Punic, Egyptian or other 'Eastern' inscriptions. Before taking a decision, the ministry asked Reuvens' advice about this unprecedented request. Reuvens saw himself confronted with an attempt at scholarly theft of his collection, and the threat of a blemish on his academic reputation. He answered the ministry as follows:

> The circumstances are very sad indeed if an academic is confronted with the necessity of praising one's own capabilities, or of comparing them with those of others: it is beneath the dignity of study and of the rank which Mr Hamaker and I occupy in society. I will therefore have nothing to do with such a practice. The difference in

years, the altered direction of one's studies, the delay by circumstances and a different amount of knowledge of subjects during different periods in time can cause an ebb and flow of wisdom and capability, which makes the weighing of merits a very hazardous task, even for an impartial judge, living now or in the future.

It is especially sad in this particular case to have to defend my more or less adequate personal capabilities or my profession, which I alone am called upon to found (if I may say so), against the repeated and unfounded refusal of Mr Hamaker to publish the Eastern Monuments of Leiden's Museum together.

Why should this lack of compliance give Mr Hamaker the right to discredit and to stigmatize my person and my profession before our compatriots? Did I try to rob Mr Hamaker of any honour which was due to his extraordinary Eastern Studies? On the contrary, have I not tried to secure him that honour and even to improve the value of his studies by informing him in advance, before publishing, about my professional thoughts concerning those Punic objects? Perhaps I should clarify a particular point, which might have escaped one's memory: most of the archaeological collections are published by their directors alone, who are on the whole unfamiliar with the Eastern languages or have studied them to an extent that they might be called not totally ignorant. For the Eastern inscriptions in those collections scholars of Eastern languages are consulted and their philological comments are inserted in the publication and further archaeological research. I on the other hand, respecting the common bond of all studies, have placed the work of Mr Hamaker on the same level as mine and I have taken care that both studies before the publication were able to benefit from each other. This co-operation was refused by Mr Hamaker and now he asks – and this is the gratitude I earn – to be able to publish all Eastern monuments with writing by himself.[19]

The department suggested that a possible solution for the future might be found in separate publications, but according to Reuvens this idea was a chimera: no publisher would be willing to produce two expensive illustrated volumes about the same subject. Reuvens feared the outcome if the department had to take a decision. The long-established profession of Eastern languages had more chances of winning this conflict than the newly created academic branch of archaeology:

As Mr Hamaker continues to refuse a combined publication, a choice has to be made whose publication will be first (and thus most important). And then the inscriptions seem to be the most important part of the monuments and will take precedence.

Just as it is beneath my dignity to start arguing about capabilities, it is similarly improper to challenge my opponent (as I might do) by proving that the reasoning should be inverted. Surely it is something quite different to consider an inscription a necessary element in explaining the whole monument and to consider it the most important part. No, I will leave that question be completely and I confine myself to asking the Government not to take a disastrous decision. If precedence in the publication is given to philology on these grounds, then the good name of archaeology will be strangled in its infancy, and with all my other troubles this would be a very bitter reward for all my lengthy troubles. Can a Government by power or authority decide whether the legend or the image is the most important element on a coin?

I know, and I do not deny it either: for a very long period I will be opposed not only by Mr Hamaker, but by all philologists in this country. To consider inscriptions the most important element is the prejudice of all those people among our compatriots, who in this respect are at the same level as the rest of Europe before the time of Winckelmann and Visconti. Gradually this prejudice will be overcome by deeds, by scholarly results. But how shall this be done, if the Government starts obstructing archaeology and consolidating the prejudice by an act of authority? I repeat once more: I for myself do not ask for priority of archaeology over philology, but I ask for equality. And while, at present, respect for archaeology has not been sufficiently established, I believe to have gained enough credit by my scholarly endeavours to be able to ask the Government to hold the scales in balance between Mr Hamaker and myself.[20]

Reuvens did not want to sacrifice his ideas about academic collaboration to the unpleasant turn this case was taking. In his view a solution could be found in starting a new series with the title *MONUMENTA ANTIQUA MUSEI LUGD.BAT. ET ALIA INEDITA*. The Punic objects could be published in volumes titled *Monumenta Punica et Punico-Romana Musei Lugd.Bat. et alia inedita*; the Egyptian antiquities could find a place in the *Monumenta Aegyptiaca et Aegyptico-Romana Musei Lugd.Bat.* To give room to the philological and archaeological aspects each volume would contain two *sectiones*: a philological commentary with the *interpretatio Hamakeri* and a second archaeological part with the illustrations and the *annotationes C.J.C. Reuvensii*.

The ministry decided otherwise. On 8 November 1826 a ministerial decree was passed, which permitted both professors to publish the 'Eastern' antiquities of the museum with the only restriction that they were obliged to arrange the plates in such a fashion, that they could be used in both their publications. This Solomonian judgement displeased both parties. Hamaker had not succeeded in his attempts to obtain exclusive rights on publication of the inscriptions: he refused to accept these terms and ended his relations with Reuvens officially. He continued to work on his own on the Punic inscriptions and in 1828 published his *Miscellanea Phoenicia*.[21]

Reuvens, confronted with the impossibility of co-operating with the leading orientalist of his country, decided to publish the increasing Egyptian collection on his own. He spent months in the Egyptian collections of the Louvre and the British Museum and corresponded with the leading scholars in Europe. He developed as a specialist in papyrology and put the crown on his efforts by publishing, in 1830, the *Lettres à Mr Letronne*, which earned him the membership of numerous European learned societies.[22]

ANTIQUITEITEN: AN ARCHAEOLOGICAL JOURNAL

Co-operation with specialists on Dutch archaeology proved to be more fruitful. Soon after his nomination as a professor in Leyden, Reuvens made a journey to the northern provinces of Drenthe and Groningen and came into contact with Nicolaas Westendorp, a clergyman living near the city of Groningen. Westendorp was a typical nineteenth-century zealous amateur of antiquities, spending all of his free time on the study of the history of his native country. A publication about the megalithic monuments in the province of Drenthe was awarded a first prize by the Royal Academy of Arts and Sciences in Amsterdam. He kept in touch with a great number of correspondents and wrote extensively about subjects such as the runic script, German mythology, church history and the archaeological monuments of the north. In 1820 he founded the journal *Antiquiteiten* ('Antiquities'), which he planned to publish yearly. In the period after the French occupation strong nationalistic tendencies could be detected in the study of the past. In Westendorp's eyes patriotism could stop the neglect of monuments and the ignorance of local and national history. In the justification of the first volume of *Antiquiteiten*, he wrote:

> If one considers how amazingly little has been done concerning the ancient history of our country, how few monuments there are of the past ages, how disgracefully many monuments, indispensable for the knowledge of our history, laws and customs, are neglected; and if one considers how bright and lovely light is spread by the knowledge of these things, of so many important questions and institutions; and finally if one considers what power there is in securing the attachment and love for one's country, and the rest of the civilians; if one considers these things, then patriotic men will without any doubt foster our unselfish project with their influence.[23]

The preface was concluded with the following device:

Qui manet in patria et patriam cognoscere temnit
Is mihi non civis, sed peregrinus erit[24]

The articles in the first volumes of *Antiquiteiten* were typical of Westendorp's fields of interest: reflections on newly discovered burial mounds, the excavation of prehistoric urns, antiquities from the island of Borkum, peat corpses from the province of Drenthe, ecclesiastical jurisdiction in the city of Groningen, and the provenance of northern dialects.

From the start Reuvens had a subscription to *Antiquiteiten*. He was interested in this regularly published forum of Dutch archaeology, and he had perspectives of changing this rather regional periodical into a more scholarly journal. The possibility of bringing new finds and archaeological news quickly before a varied and interested audience led him to contact Westendorp with the offer of editing the journal together. From 1822 onwards Reuvens' name is listed as the co-editor. Reuvens' influence is immediately visible in the higher quality and diversity of the articles published, which now covered the whole archaeological field. In the first volume articles appeared about the Elgin marbles (with an analysis by Reuvens about their meaning, the legality of the export, the supposed damage done to the Parthenon and the reliability of the eye witnesses concerned).[25] The public had the opportunity to learn about the latest developments in the study of hieroglyphs through Reuvens' reviews of publications by Letronne, Young and Champollion. Colleagues of Reuvens also contributed to *Antiquiteiten*, with articles, for example, about recent discoveries in Germany, and the archaeology of the New World. After six years the curtain fell on this first archaeological journal of the Netherlands. The reason for ending the publication was given in the preface to the last issue of 1826:

> The reasons are mostly connected with the great distance between the cities of both editors and the ever-increasing professional activities of the second editor. These reasons are so important, that they have decided to end their co-operation with this issue.[26]

The ever-increasing professional activities took their toll in other fields as well, but Reuvens continued to write about the results of his activities. He published his later articles about the excavations at Arentsburg (Forum Hadriani) in the Dutch Official Gazette, trying to reach an even wider public for the benefit of archaeology. He did not preach only to the converted.

5

THE GREEK COLLECTIONS
OF B.E.A. ROTTIERS

Nothing great was ever achieved without enthusiasm.
Ralph Waldo Emerson (1803–82)

It is unfortunate, considering that enthusiasm moves the world,
that so few enthusiasts can be trusted to speak the truth.
Arthur James Balfour (1848–1930)

GREEK ANTIQUITIES FROM ATHENS

In early November 1820 Reuvens received a letter from the Department of Education, Arts and Sciences with the news that a collection of Greek antiquities had been offered to the Dutch government.[1] Minister Falck suggested that Reuvens inspect the collection, which belonged to the retired Flemish Colonel B.E.A. Rottiers, and draw up a report 'about the artistic value, and as far as possible, about its pecuniary value'. The letter contained a list of objects with a brief indication of the provenance of the pieces. The collection comprised five Greek grave reliefs, two marble grave lekythoi, fragments of statuary, pottery, terracotta statuettes, bronze objects and some Egyptian antiquities. Reuvens travelled to Antwerp, where he inspected the collection for six days and talked with the owner.

Reuvens' host, Bernard Eugène Antoine Rottiers, turned out to be an adventurous, enterprising and entertaining man.[2] He was born in Antwerp in 1771. Although predestined to become a priest, he had changed the soutane for the tunic to make a military career in the Austrian and Dutch armies. After the expulsion of the Stadtholder in 1795 he had fled to England and took part in the Anglo-Russian campaigns in Holland in 1799. After arrest and internment in the Temple in Paris for three years, he was released to enter the army of Louis Napoléon, king of Holland, who in 1810 gave him permission to offer his services to the czar of Russia; Rottiers was sent to the southern part of the Russian empire. He moved with his family to Tiflis (Tiblisi) and joined military campaigns against the Persians and the

Figure 5.1 Portrait of B.E.A. Rottiers. Engraving by J. van Genk after a painting by Sir Thomas Lawrence. From the book *Les Monumens de Rhodes* (1830).

Turks. In 1818 the czar accepted the resignation of Rottiers, who went back to the Netherlands via Turkey, Greece, Italy, France and England.

In Russia Rottiers had started to collect antiquities. In Turkey he created a collection of more than 600 coins, medals and gemstones, which he sold later to the Duke of Blacas, the French ambassador in Rome. In the publication of Blacas' collection the name of Rottiers is duly mentioned.[3] The events of his trip from Tiflis to Constantinople were published by Rottiers in a book in which fact and fiction are often difficult to discern.[4] In 1819 he arrived in Athens with his family.

In Athens Rottiers started collecting seriously. Influence and money were the two most important assets for acquiring and exporting antiquities in this city, which was subject to whimsical Turkish legislation.[5] After his Russian adventures money was no problem for the retired colonel and influence was easily bought. The two central figures in Rottiers' quest for antiquities were the Austrian vice-consul Georg Gropius[6] and his French counterpart, Louis Fauvel.[7] Both diplomats had quite some experience collecting antiquities: Gropius with his activities in the service of von Humboldt and the Count of Aberdeen, Fauvel as the agent of Count de Choiseul Gouffier. They both knew the diplomatic circuit in Athens inside out. The other players in Rottiers' game were the Corsican C. Origone, who held the

Dutch consulate in Athens (allegedly arranged for him in Constantinople by Rottiers), and his chancellor Paul Giuracich, who also held that office in the consulate of Gropius.

In this colourful company Rottiers felt like a fish in water. In March 1819 the three diplomats and Rottiers started excavations in the surroundings of Athens. The data about where and by whom excavations were carried out are very confused. Rottiers later stated that he 'occupied himself with excavations in the neighbourhood of Athens, which were rather lucky'.[8] This assertion is in direct contradiction with remarks by his fellow treasure-diggers, who wrote that Rottiers found nothing, but bought pieces from them. Giuracich, for example, stated that 'Rottiers did some digging, but did not succeed in finding anything, because he started too late and had too few workers.'[9] It has been suggested that Rottiers financed most of the venture and by doing so could consider all results 'his' property. During the final transactions the finds were divided, exchanged and resold according to now untraceable arrangements. The inscriptions on some of the finds point to a location of the excavations in the ancient deme of Aixone: Fauvel probably dug at Helliniko, near the ancient road. Rottiers worked a mile further along the road, between Glyphada and Voula. Giuracich and Gropius excavated north-east of Rottiers, near Hagios Nikolaos (Pirnari).[10]

'THE LITERARY GLORY OF A NATION'

Reuvens had to ascertain the importance of the collection for the museum in Leiden. Of course the unique chance to buy original Greek statuary from the classical period could not be missed, but not at any price. In his report to the department, Reuvens estimated the value of the collection in comparison with pieces in the museums of Paris and London, which he had studied in recent years.[11] For an institution like the British Museum the collection of Greek pottery would be 'of little or no value'. For Leiden, which had nothing in the field of Greek ceramics, the collection was 'highly important'. Some sculptures would have value for the collection of the British Museum or the Louvre, others were less interesting for London or Paris: for Leiden, which lacked original Greek sculpture completely, all pieces were extremely valuable: 'Some pieces in this collection are so important, that any museum of the first rank would like to acquire them.'

Reuvens started his letter to Minister Falck with the assertion that the Van Papenbroek bequest in Leiden could develop into a 'reasonable museum' if new collections were acquired with an eye for the gaps in the existing collection. The antiquities of Rottiers fitted very well in this project. The Attic grave reliefs from the 'best period of Greek art' (especially a monumental relief) were 'unique for the Low Countries' and would be an acquisition of the highest importance. Less spectacular pieces like the ceramics and the

Egyptian objects still had value for Leiden, because the museum was lacking those classes almost completely. Although Reuvens was enthusiastic about the collection, he warned not to buy it at any cost:

> In praising the collection of Colonel Rottiers, whether in general terms or in view of its merits for Leiden, I am cautious not to suggest acquiring it at every price. Also in the antiques' trade there is a fixed value, which only because of considerations of higher importance should be exceeded.[12]

In his report Reuvens summed up the most recent auctions of antiquities, of the collections of Count de Choiseul Gouffier (Paris, 1818), of Léon Dufourny (Paris, 1819) and of Sir J. Coghill (London, 1819). Furthermore he mentioned the prices paid for the collections of Towneley, Hamilton, Elgin and Borghese.

The most important piece, the grave relief of Archestrate found by Gropius (Figure 5.2), could be compared in size and depth of the carving with the metopes of the Parthenon. But the price should be lower, because the Parthenon metopes were 'much more interesting and offered more nude'. The relief could also be compared with the price of two statues 'of reasonable quality' or with half the price for 'one single outstanding statue'. In that case the price should be around 3,000 guilders. A grave relief of a nude standing young man with a dove (found by Giuracich) could be compared in size and relief with the slabs of the Parthenon frieze. But on those fragments generally four to six figures were depicted. On these grounds Reuvens suggested basing the estimate for the grave relief on one-third of the price paid for the single slabs of the Parthenon frieze, i.e. 500 guilders. The long inscription (a lease contract) with names of Athenian archons (found by Giuracich) was classified according to three classes of inscriptions: the most important ones were of historical or cultural value, such as political treaties and poetry. The second class contained inventory lists or contracts between private persons. The third and least valued class consisted of grave inscriptions. Rottiers' lease contract belonged to the second category and, after comparing its length with inscriptions in London and Paris, its worth was estimated at 750 guilders.

In this manner all sculptures, vases, statuettes, enamels and bronzes were compared with similar or comparable pieces in recent auctions. It is clear that Reuvens took no chances with this first report to the ministry about a collection he was eager to buy. On 4 February 1821 Falck answered that the Rottiers collection had been bought according to Reuvens' taxation for 12,000 guilders. The colonel had hoped to receive 3,000 guilders more, but agreed to this price due to personal reasons connected with the purchase of a new house.

Every curator knows the elation which comes with the successful end of negotiations over an important acquisition and Reuvens was no exception.

Figure 5.2 Attic grave relief of Archestrate, *c.*325 BC. National Museum of Antiquities.

Moreover it was the first collection he had acquired for the museum. He answered Falck that he was 'fully prepared' to receive the collection, 'I would say, the sooner, the better'.[13] The first step towards the realization of his dreams had been made. The lucky chance of an expatriate colonel moving back to the Low Countries, his own swift and adequate actions and the support of the ministry and the king had made the first important enlargement of the museum possible. Reuvens wrote to Minister Falck:

> Extremely honoured I haste to convey you my gratitude for Your Excellency's benevolent attitude towards the Academy and for the trust you were willing to put in me. A trust that I will try to earn more and more. I dare to ask Your Excellency also to convey my sincere and most respectful thanks to His Majesty the King for the

generous support of a profession, which forms part of the literary glory of a nation.[14]

ROTTIERS' SECOND COLLECTION: 'AN IMPORTANT ENLARGEMENT'

A year after the successful purchase of Rottiers' first collection, a second collection was offered on sale. These antiquities had been acquired by his son Jean Népomucène on a journey to Greece in the spring of 1821 with the shipowner Jean-Baptiste Delescluze from Bruges. Two ships belonging to Delescluze, the *Triton* and the *Thérèse*, were bound for the Black Sea via Piraeus. On 25 June both ships anchored in the harbour of Piraeus, where the crew encountered chaos due to the outbreak a month earlier of the *epanastasis*, the Greek War of Independence from Turkish domination. The Turkish forces were intent on recapturing the city of Athens and everybody with ways and means prepared to flee the city and the threat of violence. The French vice-consul Fauvel and Giuracich, chancellor of the Dutch consulate, had left Athens and sheltered on the island of Zea. Origone, the Dutch consul, presented himself and his family on board the *Triton*. The ship's owner, Delescluze, was not scared by the imminent danger but showed himself a true philhellene by organizing a rescue operation with his two ships. He transported more than 1,100 refugees to the island of Salamis. In August the Greek authorities, in view of the great danger, forced Delescluze to leave Piraeus and to set sail for Zea, where Jean Rottiers now met his father's acquaintances, Fauvel and Giuracich. On the island Giuracich sold a collection of about 200 antiquities to Jean Rottiers, according to one version of the story.[15] Giuracich thereupon left for Trieste. Delescluze and Jean Rottiers continued their journey aboard the *Thérèse* and returned to Flanders in November 1821.

In March 1822 Rottiers informed Reuvens that he had sent a list of 200 objects to the ministry: 'Greek objects, which my son by miracle has found during the four months that he was aboard the *Triton*, when he was part of an expedition to the Black Sea.'[16] In May Reuvens had the opportunity to travel to Antwerp and see the collection, which was less important than the first one, but still contained some valuable pieces. In his report Reuvens was particularly enthusiastic about an exceptional bronze bust from Egina:

A female bust, life-size, made of bronze. Very rare, because nearly all large bronzes were melted down during the destruction of the arts in the early Middle Ages. Only the museums in Naples can boast to have some, which they fortunately found in Herculaneum and Pompei. The present piece is well preserved, although without the fine patina (veneer or rust), which covers the Herculanean antiquities.

Also the sharpness of the hair and the contour of the nose have suffered, the latter probably due to a fall. Fine style and work. The hair is very elegant, but the whole piece is not to be placed among works of the first rank.[17]

Of importance were three black-figure plates (*pinakes*), 'very rare objects of antiquity', and an Attic red-figure pelike with a representation of a boy flute-player in the presence of a judge and a flying Nike, 'of a very good style'. The other pieces 'without much art value' were bronze utensils, terracotta statuettes, some Egyptian shabtis, oil lamps and pottery, mostly black-figure lekythoi. For the whole collection Reuvens named a price of 3,000 guilders. The bronze bust alone was estimated at 700 guilders, the three black-figure pinake together at 600 guilders and the red-figure pelike at 250 guilders. It is clear that these pieces made the collection. The ministry offered 2,500 guilders to Rottiers, which he accepted without any difficulties.

'JUDGING THE AUTHENTICITY':
DOUBTS AND FORGERIES

Reuvens tried to ascertain the provenance of the second collection on various occasions. At first he was made to believe that Jean Rottiers himself had dug up the antiquities during his stay in Greece (his father had mentioned 'Greek objects, which my son by miracle has found'), but in Antwerp Rottiers let slip a remark about Giuracich being involved in the acquisition of the pieces. When Reuvens later returned to this subject, Rottiers was very out-spoken: 'Mr Giuracich played no role whatsoever as a dealer.'[18] At first Reuvens took these contradictions for granted, busy as he was with other dealings, but when years later he received a visit from Jean-Baptiste Delescluze in Leiden, the conversation inevitably touched upon the events of the summer of 1821. Delescluze told Reuvens that he himself had bought some 'small vases' in Athens, a collection which out of sheer fancy he later enlarged by buying antiquities from Giuracich on the island of Zea.[19] It was this collection that *father* Rottiers had bought, when Delescluze returned to Belgium in November 1821. But more important was the fact that neither in Delescluze's nor in Giuracich's collection had a bronze female bust from Egina figured among the antiquities. The item had never been on board the ship. Serious doubts arose concerning the origin of this 'masterpiece'. Reuvens suddenly realized that Rottiers had added the bronze bust in Antwerp and not in Greece, to a collection of average importance, which by this action had acquired additional pecuniary value. For Reuvens, a man with a compulsive sense of honesty, this must have been a terrible moment.

In the draft catalogue of his first collection in 1819, Rottiers had mentioned a 'bronze bust found in Pompei'. This piece does not appear on the final list of antiquities, but was replaced by another object. Apparently Rottiers had bought the bust in Italy on his way home and saved it for later use. Looking back Reuvens realized that he had felt doubts about this rare piece, but the lack of comparable antiquities had implicitly made him trust the allegations of the colonel:

> Already when inspecting the antiquities in 1822 I realized that I had to be careful with this piece. But because in general Roman bronzes are widely known, and Greek ones are not, I lacked all means to judge the authenticity of this piece. I had to be content with telling Mr Falck 'that the character of Mr Rottiers was respons-ible for the authenticity of his antiquities' and that I left the decision to that.[20]

Reuvens continued his letter to the department with other specimens of Rottiers' actions, which were worthy of a place in the memoirs of Giacomo Casanova:

> At the same time that I was warned in Antwerp about this head, I was told that Mr Rottiers had bought a fine painting and had asked for a document of authenticity from the Academy of Fine Arts. When subsequently he acquired a copy of the same painting, he sold the good picture in England, and the fake in Russia, using the certificate of the Academy. I remember remarks made by Mr Rottiers that in his youth he had liked to mislead a clergyman in Ghent with faked antiquities. At the time I saw this as a youthful folly, as indeed it was presented to me. After he had sold his second collection Mr Rottiers told me in Leiden that he had sold a collection of fake oil lamps from Rome to Mr Hary in Antwerp. And to the same person, or to someone else, a fake gold Mithridates. He added that he did these things to enjoy himself at the cost of this would-be connoisseur, but would never do this to me. It takes only a small amount of judgement of human nature to mistrust such a declaration. Later I was told that it was common knowledge that he had deceived the Duke of Blacas in Rome with an engraved gemstone.[21]

It is clear that with age Rottiers had not bidden farewell to all his youthful follies. The affair came to light in a period when Reuvens had other serious difficulties with the colonel, as will be described later. The fact that the bust is not antique at all had escaped both Rottiers and Reuvens. The piece cannot have come from Pompei, but is a modern cast in bronze of a marble head in Florence from the Niobid group (head of the Trophos). The fact that this is a cast may also be the explanation for the deficiencies in 'the sharpness of the hair and the contour of the nose', which Reuvens had observed earlier.

AN EXPEDITION TO THE AEGEAN, 1824–6

Rottiers was not an average pensioner. His profitable transactions with the developing archaeological museum in Leiden led to a project which, with support of the ministry, he realized between the years 1824 and 1826, before his fall from grace: an archaeological expedition to the Greek archipelago to collect antiquities and to undertake excavations. The history of this expedition is one of the strangest in the annals of the Dutch archaeological museum: a mixture of private enterprise, good intentions and hidden agendas.

The idea for this journey came solely from Rottiers: on 7 May 1824 he mentioned a project to Minister Falck, who (without consulting Reuvens) presented the ideas to the king as follows:

> Colonel Rottiers has proposed on basis of his former travels in Greece and on his knowledge of archaeology to be enabled to collect Greek antiquities known to him with the aid of the squadron of Your Majesty's Navy, which is cruising in the Mediterranean. This could be done at no extra or very low costs.[22]

First of all the finances were settled. It was calculated that Rottiers needed 1,600 guilders for travelling to Toulouse and Minorca, an increase of 3,300 guilders in his pension, and a sum of 2,000 guilders for minor purchases 'with the restriction of accounting for everything'. For larger acquisitions he had to ask permission first. Travelling in the Mediterranean could be done on board of one of the Dutch warships, which were anchored at Port Mahon, on the island of Minorca. Once the king had approved of this proposal, plans gained momentum. On 18 July a contract was signed for the financial arrangements and the involvement of the Dutch Navy. It was only at this moment when all the preparations were settled that Reuvens was informed about the project. On 16 July he received an invitation to come to The Hague 'to discuss a matter, which could be of interest for archaeology. It concerns a journey, which might be made by Colonel Rottiers to the Greek Archipelago.'[23] Reuvens was asked to draw up a list with instructions for the colonel.

Reuvens did not show himself very enthusiastic about the whole project. He had serious doubts about 'Rottiers' knowledge about archaeology', so he composed a list of books for the colonel, to be read before the start of the expedition. The rest of the instructions show the way Reuvens looked at organizing an archaeological journey:

A It is important to receive: plans, sections, elevations, perspectives, details and orientation of buildings. No so-called restauration on paper, or only with exact indications of which part is antique, and which part is guessed. Samples of the stone of which the building is made. The drawings do not gain value by their number, but by their use for archaeology, completeness and accurate design. If in a funerary monument vases or other antiquities are found and taken away, I desire a precise indication where each piece came from and how it was placed.

B   Concerning removable antiquities it will be useful (if possible) to investigate empty Turkish fortresses and mosques, especially those in which they have never allowed foreigners. In these buildings very beautiful reliefs and other pieces have often been used as building stones.

C   Concerning the acquisition of vases it is requested not to look for small and ordinary objects, which the museum now owns in considerable measure. But the desired ones are specifically:

    a)   large vases with important drawings such as the ones found in Aulis and owned by Gianachi Logotheti, primate of Levadia, and published by Millin, *Vases*, tom. II, pl. 55–56. Confer Dodwell *Travels* I, p. 301.

    b)   vases with figures or floral patterns in relief, some of which come from Melos (if I remember correctly) and owned by Mr Durand in Paris.

    c)   vases with white ground and red figures; but not washed with any liquid. The only means of discovering if there is a drawing beneath the dirty crust is to remove the crust with utmost care using a sharp pen or razor. But this should be done only on a small part and only inasmuch is necessary to see if a decoration is hidden.

D   Greek, Latin and old Eastern manuscripts, especially to be found in Greek monasteries. Of course those of classical authors are highly valued. But old books, the Church Fathers, homilies, missals, etc. should be inspected to see if they were copied (*palimpsesti*), if the parchment, on which an older writer had written, was scraped off to write the later text across it. In that case they have much value.

E   Samples of the different varieties of stone and especially marble in the quarries on the isles, with notes from where the samples have been taken.

F   Specific astronomical observations at all locations, if time allows it. Detailed maps of those places, where antiquities have been found, will be most welcome.

G   Botanical information, drawings, etc. as much as is possible for the traveller.

H   Buying medals and gemstones need not be mentioned: this goes without saying. But one should take notes about the places where certain types of medals occur frequently, because

such notes can be useful for tracing the origin of question-
able coins.

P.S. Clearing the ruins of collapsed temples, digging in and
around them and also digging in old wells seem to promise
good results.[24]

A month later Reuvens had a meeting with Rottiers, who said he had
hopes of excavating on the island of Delos and even included the coasts of
Syria and Egypt in his plans. Reuvens was flexible: 'It is certainly desirable
that the colonel visits those places which he claims to know best.'[25] At the
end of October 1824 Rottiers left Antwerp in the company of his youngest
son Victor and the painter Petrus-Joseph Witdoeck, who was asked to make
the archaeological drawings during the expedition. On 14 January 1825
the company sailed from Marseille to Minorca, where they embarked a
Dutch warship. Ten days later they reached the coast of Algiers, where
the vessel was nearly shipwrecked during a storm. In the harbour of
Algiers Rottiers spied on the Algerian fleet, which was about to be deployed
in the Greek–Turkish war. He sent his report to the Dutch embassy in
Constantinople.[26]

Via Malta, Melos and Mykonos, Rottiers arrived in Smyrna, from where
he wrote to Reuvens for the first time on 27 April: he was irritated by the
bad weather, the dangers and the discomforts during the fruitless first months
of his journey. The commanding officer had shown more concern for the
condition of his ship and crew than for excavations on Delos: Rottiers saw
his mission endangered by external factors. He wrote:

If everything had gone better, and the gentlemen officers of the
Royal Navy had had more concern for my mission, then I could
have done much more. I am fully prepared to sacrifice my time for
the good event of my mission and to also stay in the Archipelago
next winter, but then other measures must be taken. I see with grief
that Englishmen and Frenchmen export objects, which they have
bought, while I have to ask permission for everything first and
while they take their antiquities out of the country. Mr Fauvel
leaves for Santorini in the next few days to inspect some statues
which were found there, but I hope to be ahead of him. And as that
purchase is my responsibility, I have cashed some money here, and
together with the money I still have on me I will try not to lose this
opportunity to buy, and if the Department disapproves of my conduct, then I shall keep everything I can buy for my own account, in
these strange days when everybody seems to be alert and is competing
with each other! Why not entrust a few thousand guilders to a loyal
officer, a real Dutchman, who now always has to account for such
purchases and for every delay in his expedition?[27]

From these rather confused words it becomes clear that the start of the expedition had not been favourable: bad weather, financial problems, competition and alleged poor co-operation from the navy. Rottiers' remarks about his lack of available money did raise a few eyebrows in The Hague. When Van Ewijck, the responsible administrator at the department, read this letter, he wrote a confidential note to Reuvens:

> Rottiers does not seem to be the suitable man. His words are untrue. First, before his departure, the whole sum for purchases was put at his disposal. He has not bought anything, so he must have money. Second, he complains wrongfully about the navy, because I have proofs of the good disposition of the commanding officer. That is all.[28]

Doubts arose about Rottiers' credibility. Quite a few things went wrong from the start in Rottiers' bookkeeping and in his communication with his principals. Rottiers had spent quite some money on matters other than purchases of antiquities: he had had high accommodation expenses in Marseille, waiting for his transfer to Minorca, and he had bought a number of rifles, which he intended to use as business gifts. He used the money he received from the department without realizing these funds were earmarked for antiquities. Better arrangements before departure about the spending of money might have prevented much displeasure. The department decided to write a letter to Rottiers through diplomatic channels to request him to respect the rules and not to spend money on other matters than antiquities. Rottiers called this warning 'preposterous'.

From the archives of the Dutch embassy in Constantinople it becomes clear that Rottiers was not short of new ideas, although his projects seem a bit fantastic and deviating from Reuvens' instructions. In the correspondence between the Dutch ambassador and the Ministry of Foreign Affairs there are documents which mention Rottiers' wish to receive a *firman* permitting him to start excavations in central Anatolia and Ephesus.[29] All these projects had never been discussed with Reuvens or the department.

EXCAVATION ON MELOS

During the summer of 1825 the Dutch ships in the Aegean were hindered by the increasing violence and danger of the Greek–Turkish conflict. After a few abortive attempts to leave Smyrna Rottiers finally succeeded in starting an excavation in Greece in August 1825. The Dutch ambassador in Constantinople needed an escort from Melos to Smyrna, and Rottiers' ship was chosen to perform this task. During the wait for the arrival of the ambassador's ship there would be time on Melos for a small excavation.

Figure 5.3 Marble portrait of a priest from Melos, first century AD. National Museum of Antiquities.

H.M. frigate *Diana* sailed from Smyrna to Melos, the island which had become known to every antiquarian through the find in 1820 of the above life-size statue of Aphrodite. Allegedly in the vicinity of the findspot of this Venus de Milo a few years later a late-Hellenistic head of a priest was found, which was bought by Rottiers on arrival on the Greek island (Figure 5.3). Rottiers decided to start his excavation in the field where this head had been discovered. He succeeded in leasing the terrain and started to work on 2 August. The captain of the *Diana* noted in his logbook:

> Put ashore the colonel with three men belonging to him and ten sailors with rations for eight days, and sent a fatigue-party of fifty men to Colonel Rottiers, to spade a piece of land. The fifty men returned to ship in the evening. Gave some of the ship's provisions to the Colonel to use ashore.[30]

Rottiers started digging in an area, enclosed by low dividing walls, next to the ancient road from the harbour Klima to the city of Kastro (the modern Milos), in the centre of the ancient town of Melos, which was destroyed by the Athenian army in 416 BC. Near this terrain ancient

Figure 5.4 Mosaic floor from Melos. Watercolour by P.J. Witdoeck, August 1825. Archive, National Museum of Antiquities.

remains were visible: a theatre, a Byzantine church, a baptismal font and some marble seats, which had probably stood on the ancient agora of Melos. Rottiers and his men worked for nine days in the walled field. During the night he, his son Victor and the painter Witdoeck kept watch in a tent under an olive tree. Every morning some twenty sailors climbed to the terrain to help the colonel. On the last day of the campaign eighty-five men were needed to carry the crates with antiquities aboard the ship. In his memoirs Rottiers claimed that he ended his excavation to obey the Greek authorities, which by legislation put an end to the export of antiquities:

> My activities were disrupted by the archon of Milo. This magistrate informed me of a decree by the Greek Government, which forbade every foreigner, from every country, to carry out excavations and appropriate pieces of antique monuments. All these objects belong to the state. Once the Greeks have finished a heavier task, they want to place them in a Hellenic Museum. With pride they will show foreigners what is left to them by their ancestors, by those men who gave Europe its art and civilization. I obeyed the orders of the archon, although I myself had bought the terrain of the excavations. It meant taking leave of grand projects. I sacrificed my sincere hopes to the young legislation of a suffering country and I do not believe that I should feel sorry for that.[31]

Rottiers portrayed himself too noble: the real reason for leaving Melos was the arrival of the Dutch ambassador. Legislation concerning the export of antiquities did not come into being before 1826 and could not have played any role during Rottiers' stay on Melos.

The content of the crates can be found in Rottiers' notes and in the inventory lists of the museum. Apart from the usual finds like sherds, coins and oil lamps Rottiers discovered a complete mosaic floor, of which he lifted seven parts. On a watercolour by Witdoeck (Figure 5.4) the whole floor is depicted after its discovery. On the central panel Dionysos is represented with thyrsus and ivy. This *emblema* was surrounded by four panels with heads of satyrs and birds. Below the Dionysos a panther was portrayed, licking up wine from a *kantharos*. Around these panels fish and geometrical motives were depicted. The decoration suggests that the floor once adorned a Roman dining room.

A second find was a Roman altar, decorated with bulls' heads, birds and garlands. Rottiers had hoped to find more parts of the statue, of which he had bought the head, but no other important finds were made. Rottiers ordered his painter Witdoeck to make a plan of the whole area, which is very detailed and allows the spot where Rottiers excavated to be identified without any doubt.

In his fear of critical questions about the results of his expedition, Rottiers started to make the utmost use of the finds on Melos. Without consulting his principals first, he sent a letter to the journal *Courier des Pays-Bas*, which was published on 28 December 1825. Reuvens read the following news about his agent in the Mediterranean:

> It is reported from Corfu (Ionic Isles) that during his travels in Greece Colonel Rottiers has unearthed on the island of Melos (in the archipelago) four feet below the earth a mosaic of very high antiquity. The piece can be dated two centuries before the Peloponnesian War. The style, which has something hieroglyphic, shows that the Greeks copied this art from the Egyptians. Antiquarians and art lovers will be grateful to Mr Witdoeck from Antwerp for the beautiful drawings which he has made (with all the proportions) of the piece and which will be published by Colonel Rottiers with a detailed description, upon return to the Low Countries. This beautiful antiquity, snatched away from the earth that has covered it since the destruction of Melos by the Athenians, resurfaces after more than 2,000 years to take its place among the mosaics of Palestrina in Italy and of the Praetorium of Pilatus in Jerusalem. With the aid of some good workmen among the crew of HM frigate *Diana* the most important pieces of the mosaic were salvaged and put in plaster. The portrait of Bacchus is considered the oldest picture that exists. It is beautifully preserved.[32]

The colonel's fantasy used to overtake him more than once, which was pardoned by Reuvens as long as these remarks remained behind closed doors. But the fact that Rottiers, without consultation, had allowed this tall story to be published in a journal which was widely read throughout Europe was too much for him. He informed the department that 'such expressions do a lot of harm to the honour of the Netherlands in the Levant'.[33] Rottiers had based his dating on the destruction of Melos by the Athenians in 416 BC. He argued *a priori* that the mosaic had to date from before this destruction, and was therefore the oldest known example of this art. Reuvens commented:

> It is not known from history that the art of mosaics is older than the flourishing of Pergamon, three or four centuries later, but it is a known fact that it was practised mainly during the Roman period. Moreover, one must have very little knowledge of art to consider this piece older than the works of Phidias.[34]

THE MONUMENTS OF RHODES

After his adventures on Melos Rottiers cruised the Aegean on different Dutch vessels and visited Athens, where he bought some antiquities and had the Theseion measured. His most interesting acquisitions were a monumental head of a kouros from Santorini, cycladic marble vessels from Mykonos and two geometric vases, belonging to a class of objects which was later named after Rottiers by J.N. Coldstream.[35]

In January 1826 he arrived on the island of Rhodes. Here he started to work on a project which for him became the most important part of his mission: for five months he stayed on the island to study, describe and draw the medieval architecture of the old city and the fortifications of the Knights of St John. Rottiers gained permission to make drawings of the Rhodian monuments by offering extensive gifts to the local ruler, the Turkish bey. Only the church of St John, converted into a mosque, remained forbidden terrain for him for fear of riots if it became known that a Christian had entered the holy place. Rottiers bribed the mullah with an old Koran and subsequently spent seven hours in the church with his painter. Together they made drawings, took a piece of wood as a relic and even said a prayer.

In 1830 Rottiers published the results of his stay on Rhodes under the title *Description des monumens de Rhodes*, with seventy-five plates engraved by Witdoeck. In the book his five months' stay on Rhodes is reduced to two weeks, in which he tours the island and has many adventures, escorted by a Greek *cicerone* Dimitri, who tells him about the past and present of the island and the city. The stories 'Dimitri' tells his audience are no new surprises: most of the information is easily traceable to facts from the eighteenth-century publication about the Order of St John by De Vertot d'Aubeuf.[36] The importance of Rottiers' publication lies in the quality and detail of Witdoeck's plates. Nowhere else is this amount of information to be found about the Rhodian medieval architecture as it looked around 1826, when most of the monuments were still intact. Thirty years after Witdoeck's activities a powderhouse in the centre of the medieval town exploded and ruined large parts of the city. The engravings of the *Monumens de Rhodes* are a reliable source for the study of these monuments and were used in the twentieth century to restore and rebuild parts of the centre. Also Witdoeck's rendering of the Rhodian Colossus became very popular and still enjoys a long after-life (Figure 5.5).

In the meantime the only news Reuvens received was one letter, telling him that an altar and an inscription had been stolen. In May Rottiers left Rhodes for Smyrna and sailed to Minorca a month later. On this voyage he bought an Egyptian mummy in three cases, which he provided with a remarkable but highly improbable background.[37] In September 1826 he reached Antwerp, the terminus of this expedition to the Mediterranean.

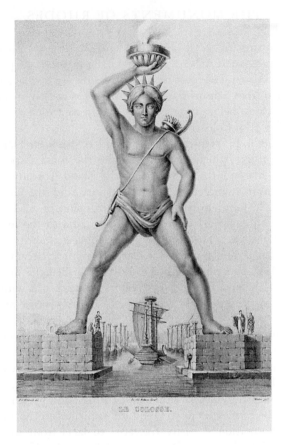

LE COLOSSE.

Figure 5.5 The Colossus of Rhodes: reconstruction by B.E.A. Rottiers. Engraving by P.J. Witdoeck. From Rottiers' book *Description des Monumens de Rhodes* (1830).

EVALUATION OF THE EXPEDITION:
'MUCH AND UNGRATEFUL WORK'

The antiquities collected by Rottiers were sent to the Netherlands in two different cargoes. The first sixteen crates arrived in Leiden in March 1826. These were mainly the finds from Melos and some other objects. A month later Reuvens gave his reaction in a report to the department. He was pleased with the finds:

> The altar is a fine piece. The mosaic good of style and drawing, but the colours are badly preserved. The largest part is missing, and probably destroyed during the excavation. Specifically the panther

and birds are missing. However the collection of mosaics in Leiden now has a very important acquisition.[38]

Reuvens was less pleased with the other aspects of Rottiers' travel: 'Mr Rottiers seems until now not to have fulfilled the other part of his instructions, which are aimed at the archaeological aspects.' Plans and drawings were lacking, although mention of them was made in the article described above. About Rottiers' wish to publish his drawings himself Reuvens remarked:

So it is highly probable that the drawings desired by me have indeed been made, but that Mr Rottiers considers them his own property. Considering the issue of property I have the following remarks to make. After sending you my draft instructions of 3 August I had an interview with this gentleman on 4 October, about which I wrote to you on the 5th: 'The Colonel, considering that his draughtsman travels at his expenses and receives from the state nothing else but the ship's victuals, which otherwise would have been used for a servant of the Colonel, holds the view that the drawings which he will bring back shall remain partly or entirely his property.' If Mr Rottiers has not repeated his objections to you, it can be deduced that he has silently accepted these instructions as a condition for his journey, and then it is natural that the property of the drawings belongs to the financial entrepreneur of the mission, namely the State. The circumstance if Mr Rottiers makes these drawings himself, or his son the lieutenant or he wants to have them made by a paid draughtsman, is for the question of property indifferent. He is obliged to supply them, because he must fulfil the condition, and he cannot claim any indemnification.[39]

From these rather juridical remarks it once again becomes clear that during the preparations for the expedition two different points of departure were used. Rottiers saw the journey more or less as a private enterprise, with some financial support from the government. He himself wished to decide when and where to make use of Witdoeck's talents for his own lucrative publications. Reuvens and Van Ewijck considered themselves in charge, responsible for the expedition and its results. Reuvens was facing accomplished facts.

On 19 September another eight crates arrived from Greece with the rest of the antiquities which Rottiers had acquired for the museum. The mummy in three cases was sent to Leiden last. After the inspection of this final shipment and the deciphering of Rottiers' travel account, Reuvens wrote a long report to the ministry. It comes as no surprise that the tenor of his report is very negative. Only six pieces were of value, but even these were no first-rank acquisitions:

The conclusion is that there is not one exquisite antiquity in this collection: on the whole this is a very poor result of such an expedition and such preparations. I have to add that the value of many objects would probably rise, if the place and way of finding or buying in all detail were known and elucidated by drawings. But this information is lacking to such an extent that I know absolutely nothing about quite a number of crates, and I have only general and hardly intelligible information about the others.[40]

Reuvens was not pleased with the smaller objects either, especially the unimportant lekythoi. If those pieces had come to light during excavations, then they would have had an added value, but he had warned explicitly against buying such items at random. Moreover, the boasting comments of Rottiers did not do much good to his temper: a small Hellenistic grave relief representing a funerary banquet with a reclining man, a seated woman and two adults and a child in a worshipping pose was described by the colonel as 'Isis and Osiris having a meal, made by one of the three Rhodian artists in Athens.' Reuvens commented:

It is a small funerary relief: the deceased is depicted as Serapis, not Osiris. I would kindly regard this as a mistake, but why should this piece of rubbish have been made by one of the three famous sculptors from Rhodes, who created in Rome or on their native island the Laocoon?[41]

The report continues in this style, summing up all the mistakes and inconsistencies in Rottiers' notes and earlier letters. Reuvens ended with an evaluation of the three most important targets of the expedition: excavations, documentation and acquisitions:

The acquired objects seem to me a poor result of such an undertaking. But my judgement would be different if there were proof of the undertaking of excavations, even if they were fruitless. These are uncertain enterprises and if the result is negative, nobody is to blame. But leaving apart Smyrna, a large town where most of the ancient material was used for rebuilding, Mr Rottiers has been on Tino, Miconi, Stancho and four or five months on Rhodus. On Santorin he writes that nothing can be done there; but why did he not do anything on those other islands I mentioned? To be on Miconi is as good as to be on Delos, the main target of his voyage. And during this or another excursion there seem to have been workmen, because two of them ran away in Athens. On Rhodus there would have been possibilities in the ruins of Lindos, Jalysus, maybe Camirus and even the whole surroundings of the town of

Rhodus. All this did not take place: because of some unwilling captain? Lack of money? Or other circumstances? And was Mr Rottiers forced to use ships of the Dutch navy to such an extent, could he not have used small Levantine vessels, like everybody else?

Regarding the drawings allegedly made I cannot say anything before I have seen them. But of ancient buildings only mention is made of the temple of Theseus at Athens, which I called rather superfluous in my letter of 29 July. The drawings of Rhodus, if they are good, may be of importance for the so-called gothic architecture of the Middle Ages. Not much is known, but not everything is unknown. But these are all matters of secondary importance. Why of all the places I mentioned for excavations no drawings of antiquities or at least locations, plans? Why from Smyrna, where Mr Rottiers has been six times, and very often many weeks, no drawings of the stadium, the theatre and the antiquities in the neighbourhood, ruined as they may be?

Finally regarding the purchases, it is indeed impossible to ask for specific objects, because everything depends on chance. But if I may say so, Smyrna is the centre of the antiquities' trade, at least for coins and engraved stones. And if you are planning to buy cheap, it is not very wise to blaze about an official archaeological expedition in the journals of Belgium and France. Only the Dutch consuls and their staff should have been told about this endeavour, and maybe not even all of them.[42]

Reuvens' final report is clearly very negative. It was clear to him that Rottiers could and should have done more. Especially the five months on Rhodes were spent solely on Rottiers' project of drawing the medieval architecture, which was maybe the main hidden goal of his journey and the reason for bringing Witdoeck with him. But the department and Reuvens could have been more alert from the beginning of the project. Also Reuvens committed the mistake of giving the colonel too much free rein in choosing his destinations. His words 'It is certainly desirable that the colonel visits those places which he claims to know best'[43] must have been interpreted by Rottiers as a *carte blanche*, of which he made extensive use, but not for the benefit of archaeology.

Rottiers' reaction to these harsh words is not known, but can be deducted from his reaction when he received a rebuke concerning his handling of the expedition's finances. In a letter to the ministry he speaks about a 'disgraceful circular letter from the Foreign Office', which reached him in Smyrna. He was very angry:

Because I demand satisfaction about such a thoughtless and disgraceful measure, I expect you to ask our Ambassador in Constantinople to obtain from all consulates information about how I generally behaved in the Levant. I do not know why, but so much is true, that in every aspect they tried to do harm to me, and often as if I were a foreigner.[44]

Back in Antwerp he tried for the last time to reconcile himself with Reuvens by sending the professor a book, which was returned the same day with a short note: 'I give no opinion on the question if it is befitting to send me a gift (be it small or large), when I am in the middle of writing a report about your affairs. But it is certainly unfitting for me to accept it. In future I wish to be spared such offers.'[45]

But he was not spared the colonel's attentions. In 1827 the museum received a Moorish gravestone form Minorca (which went to the ethnographical collections) and paintings by Witdoeck of the temple of Athena Parthenos and the so-called Theseion in Athens. Reuvens immediately thought them another reconciliatory gift and made preparations to send them back, but was informed by the department that these paintings had been offered by Rottiers to the king, who in turn had donated them to the archaeological museum. The paintings remained in Leiden, although not in Reuvens' room.

Rottiers continued to send small items to the museum and later curators had interviews with him when they were working on the first catalogue of the Greek collection. He died in Brussels in 1857 aged 86, and was buried with military honours. With his death ended an eventful episode in the pioneering years of the museum, which can be said to be characteristic of the difficult relation between impetuous dynamism and scholarly consciousness.

6

JEAN EMILE HUMBERT

The quest for Carthage

It should also be recalled that the international scholarly
environment at the time was largely populated by 'amateurs',
princes and prelates, senior civil servants, aristocrats and
officers – a socially inhomogeneous group of enthusiasts. But
these men were the pioneers behind many of the great European
collections of today. The sciences and arts [. . .] were at that
time only just starting on the road to professionalism.

> Anders Monrad Møller, 'What the collections meant
> to Christian VIII', in *Christian VIII and the*
> *National Museum*, Copenhagen 2000, p. 98.

DUTCH ENGINEERS IN TUNISIA, 1796

In February 1821 Reuvens had a meeting with Jean Emile Humbert, like
Rottiers another officer who had returned to his native ground after the
long years of political unrest.[1] This meeting led to more than fourteen years
of intense co-operation between the scholar and the officer and opened new
prospects for the development of the museum. Humbert was born in 1771
in a family of Swiss Huguenot origin, which had come to the Netherlands at
the end of the seventeenth century. His father was a well-known portrait
painter in The Hague. Emile's brother David received an education as an
artist in Rome. Later he taught Italian and art history at the University of
Leiden and became the first director of the university print collection. He
received international renown for his publication *Sur les signes inconditionnels
dans l'art*, a brilliant theoretical work which received too little attention
from his contemporaries.[2]

Jean Emile Humbert was trained as a military engineer in 's-Hertogenbosch
and Maastricht. The artistic vein of his family was apparent in the fine
drawings he made, not only of military installations, but also of his friends,
romantic landscapes and buildings. Judging from his letters we can say he

Figure 6.1 Portrait of J.E. Humbert. Drawing after an engraving by Boggi, *c.*1810. Prentenkabinet, Leiden University.

was a typical representative of the romantic wave that went through Europe in this period: Humbert indulged in passion, friendship and patriotism. He wrote poetry, composed songs and fell in love intensely. At times he could be extremely cheerful, only to be drowned in melancholy the next moment.[3] As far as we can judge, many of these emotions were genuine and sincere, although in some cases there is evidence that his behaviour was insincere and that he was trying to use his romantic *bonhomie* to cover up for some of his less commendable actions.

After his training as a military engineer and his promotion to the rank of lieutenant, Humbert faced unemployment because of his refusal to serve the Batavian Republic, which was created in 1795. Together with two other officers, Colonel A.H. Frank and his son Captain C.F. Frank, he replied to an advertisement which invited engineers for a project in Tunisia. The local ruler, Hamouda Pacha Bey, was looking for Dutch officers to construct a new harbour for his fleet. In 1796 his life as an expatriate in North Africa began. Humbert was lodged in the house of the Dutch consul, Antoine Nijssen, whose family had served Dutch interests since 1756. He met the other members of the family: Antoine's brother Charles, Dutch consul in Algiers, César, son of Antoine and vice-consul, and

Thérèse, the daughter who stole Humbert's heart and whom he married in 1801.

The start of the Tunisian mission, which was led by Colonel Frank, was initially obstructed by a French diplomatic offensive, directed against the influence of consul Nijssen at the Tunisian court. A special French envoy tried to dissuade the bey from accepting the proposals of Colonel Frank and offered another project instead: moving the city of Tunis to the shores of the sea on Cape Carthage.[4] After nine months of intriguing and forced rest, the proposals of the French were dismissed and a new harbour came into being based on the designs of the Dutch engineers. They planned their harbour in the middle of the tongue of land that separates the Lake of Tunis and the Mediterranean Sea. To reach the city of Tunis a canal had been dug across this spit of land in the sixteenth century, which was called La Goulette (bottleneck). The entry to the lake was defended by a fortress and redoubts. The Dutch engineers deepened and broadened the existing canal, constructed sluices and designed a large harbour inside the lake with all the necessary buildings. In 1798 the harbour was inaugurated and adorned with a Latin commemorative inscription.[5] After eight years of increasing tension between the members of the expedition 'in a country far away from their relatives, where they have to suffer daily the insults and the contempt of the local population',[6] Colonel Frank left Tunisia for good. Humbert was asked by the Tunisians to take over supervision of the works and was promoted to chief engineer. He completed the harbour of La Goulette and also carried out other military and civil projects in Tunisia.

From the start of his stay in Tunis, Humbert had become interested in this exotic land with its rich history. Tunis was a cultural melting-pot, where Muslims, Jews and Christians lived together with their own dress codes, languages and customs. Humbert began to compile an encyclopaedic collection of notes about ethnology, history, languages and curiosities. He also started collecting antiquities, mostly coins and medals, but his main interest focused on the peninsula, only a few miles from La Goulette, where in antiquity the city of Carthage had been situated. Many mysteries surrounded the topography of the site. The Roman destruction of the Punic town in 146 BC and the subsequent rebuilding, which started some one hundred years later, of the *Colonia Iulia Carthago* had been so drastic that no Punic remains had been found on this spot and the exact location of the Punic town remained a point of scholarly debate. The problem centred around the question which hill was the *Byrsa*, the centre of the Punic town where Queen Dido had founded her 'New City'. Eighteenth- and nineteenth-century travellers[7] described two hills as possible candidates: in the north, Cape Carthage, overlooking the Mediterranean Sea, and the lower '*prétendue Byrsa*', on which some Roman remains were visible. The location of the Punic double harbour was connected with this problem. During the third Punic War in 146 BC, Roman troops led by General Scipio had conquered the harbours first, then the agora and the hill Byrsa. The central hill and the harbours formed a topographical unity and making a choice for one hill or the other immediately had effects for the location of the harbours. Archaeological investigations and measurements were forbidden by the authorities for fear of espionage, but Humbert's special position at the Tunisian court gave him ample opportunity to study the terrain. His engineering capabilities enabled him to make a detailed drawing of the peninsula, the best map available at the time. He became an authority on topographical questions concerning Carthage.

Many travellers who visited Tunisia in this period were escorted by Humbert during their visit to Carthage. These long trips were often enlivened with a lunch in the subterraneous vaults of the Roman cisterns, where Humbert 'full of gaiety and classic wit' sang songs of his own composition about Dido, Aeneas and the tragic faith of Sophonisbe during the fall of Carthage.[8] Humbert's name is mentioned in letters of English ladies, memoirs of American generals, books by German scholars and a literary work by the French romantic writer François René de Chateaubriand, who mentioned Humbert (although misspelt as Homberg) in his *Itinéraire de Paris à Jérusalem*. In this book a scholarly dissertation is given about the topography of Carthage, which can be traced back directly to the theories of Chateaubriand's Dutch informant.[9]

ANTIQUARIAN INTERESTS: AN EXILED COUNT IN TUNIS

The defeat of Napoleon Bonaparte and his associates brought a new influx of immigrants to the shores of North Africa. One colourful example was the Italian Count Camillo Borgia, born in Velletri in 1774, nephew of the influential Cardinal Stefano Borgia. The private 'Museo Borgiano' in Velletri contained an impressive collection of classical, Egyptian and oriental art, which made a lasting impression on the young Camillo. After a military career in the armies of the Papal State and Austria, he became enflamed with the changes which were taking place in France. Accused of sympathies for the French revolutionary ideas, Borgia was imprisoned two times, first in Vienna and later in the Castel S. Angelo in Rome. Borgia took revenge for this treatment in 1809, when he was appointed by Napoleon as head of the police force in the department of the Tiber. After the fall of Napoleon, Borgia went to Naples, where he was appointed by King Joachim Murat as *camerlengo* (chamberlain) and general of his personal staff.[10] After the execution of Murat, Borgia had to leave his family behind in Naples and fled to Tunisia, where he was housed by the Danish consul, Andreas Christian Gierlew, because of old ties of the Borgia family with the Danish community in Rome. He was sentenced to death in his absence by the Papal court in Rome.

Borgia decided to make the best of his period of exile in Tunis: he started working on a description of the history, antiquities, customs and traditions of Tunisia.[11] Of course he came into contact with Humbert, with whom he established a good relationship in spite of their differences in rank and political ideas. In the autumn of 1815 they made three expeditions in the interior of Tunisia, to El Kef and Zaghouan (12 October–10 November 1815), to El Djem (26 November–20 December 1815) and again to Zaghouan (26–29 December 1815). Among other places, they visited and described the ruins of El Kef/Sicca Veneria, Henchir Mest/Mustis, Dougga/Thugga, Teboursouk/ Thubursicu Bure, Oudna/Uthina, Zaghouan/Ziqua, Hergla/Horraca Caelia, Sousse/Hadrumetum, El Djem/Thysdrus and Lamta/Leptis Minor: Borgia kept a diary with notes and sketches. Humbert made drawings of the ruins, inscriptions and antiquities they encountered. Topographical measurements of the places they visited completed this large description and *corpus* of archaeological notes, which Borgia planned to catalogue and publish. Some of Humbert's and Borgia's drawings were engraved and made ready for publication.

Borgia also obtained permission to excavate in Utica, the Roman harbour town north of Tunis. Here he organized a reception for Caroline of Brunswick-Wolfenbüttel, the princess of Wales, who preferred a semi-permanent cruise in the Mediterranean to the company of her husband, later King George IV. Seated on a mule, the princess was guided through the ruins of Utica, discussed with Borgia the brave suicide of Cato Uticensis and bought some antiquities from the Tunisian children who had come to see this exotic princess. In Tunisia Caroline furthermore managed to free some Italian maidens from the harem of the bey and was negotiating the liberation of more slaves when Admiral Exmouth arrived with his fleet, threatening to bombard the city of Tunis.

In Utica Borgia unearthed an above life-size statue of a woman ('Flora', now lost), with an inscription on the base, but interrupted his activities when in 1816 he received news that Pope Pius VII planned to organize a crusade against the Barbary states. Borgia sent a long letter to Rome, offering his services to the good cause of the faith. In 1817 Borgia received a free pardon and returned to his native land. The crusade never took place, so Borgia continued his antiquarian work in Naples, where he started with the preparation of his publication. His health, already bad, had been worsened by the excavations at Utica, and this interrupted his projects. Borgia fell ill and died in the middle of arranging the enormous amount of papers concerning Tunisia's history, at the age of only 44.

BETWEEN HOPE AND FEAR: REPATRIATION AND NEW PROSPECTS

In the same year as Borgia's untimely death, Humbert made the discovery of his life: he found four Punic stelae on the peninsula, and two fragments,

with inscriptions in the yet undeciphered Punic language. During the ploughing of a piece of land near the village of La Malga the two fragments had
come to light, upon which Humbert decided to further investigate the
terrain. His workmen removed some 1.5 metres of ground before they found
the first complete Punic remains to come to light since the destruction of
Carthage. Humbert decided to keep his find a secret until his return home
to the Netherlands. The Borgia diaries remaining unpublished, Humbert
rejoiced at being the first to enter the debate about the topography of Punic
Carthage with proof in his hands. He prepared detailed drawings of the four
stelae and the two fragments, which he published in 1821 with a short
description of the circumstances of finding them.[12]

After the fall of Napoleon and the creation of the Kingdom of the
Netherlands under King Willem I, Humbert had wished to return to the
Netherlands, but the bureaucratic complications were difficult to solve. His
long stay in Tunisia in the service of a foreign ruler had made him almost
disappear in the state's archives and miss the normal promotions in the
Dutch army (officially he still retained the rank of captain). The vice-admiral
of the Dutch fleet in the Mediterranean came to his aid and pleaded his
case in The Hague. The Ministry of Defence looked into the case, decided
to promote him to the rank of major and give him a new assignment in the
Dutch Indies. This was much to Humbert's dismay after his long and harsh
years in Tunisia. In 1819 he decided to travel to the Netherlands with a
twofold aim: first, to try to alter his assignment in the Indies and, second, to
sell his collection of antiquities and notes concerning the history of Carthage
and Tunisia. First he travelled to Italy, where he stayed for a few weeks with
his friend from his army days, Johann Reinhold, who had become the first
Dutch ambassador to the Holy See in Rome. In Rome Humbert lived with
the Reinhold family in their apartment at the foot of the Capitoline Hill,
where he met many of his host's acquaintances. He was consulted by the
German scholar B.G. Niebuhr, who was working on his *Römische Geschichte*,
in which he cited Humbert in the chapters about the topography of ancient
Carthage.[13] He also had meetings with the Bavarian antiquarian Johann
Martin von Wagner and the Danish sculptor Bertel Thorvaldsen, whom
he saw working on the restoration of the Aegina pediment groups for
the museum in Munich. It must have been an exciting time for Humbert,
after the hardships in Tunisia. But these happy days did not last long: in
mid-November he received news from his family that his daughter and son-
in-law had succumbed to the plague, which had ravaged the African coast.
Humbert had abruptly to return to Tunis to assist his wife in these dramatic
circumstances. The hygienic measures in Tunis dictated that the whole
inventory of his house, including all his belongings, had to be burned.
Suddenly he was ruined and bereaved, with only his wife's jewels and a
collection of antiquities as possessions.[14] After arranging his affairs in Tunis
and selling his wife's jewellery, Humbert travelled again to the Netherlands,

Figure 6.2 One of the four Punic stelae found in Carthage in 1817 by J.E. Humbert, third–second century BC. National Museum of Antiquities.

determined not to be employed in the Indies, and with the faint hope of selling his antiquities to an interested buyer, although 'the Dutch had more interest in cinnamon and sugar than in the fine arts' as he remarked to his friend Reinhold.

Friends were needed. Reinhold informed Minister Falck about Humbert's valuable collection. Falck in his turn wrote to Reuvens with the suggestion that he meet Humbert and assess the value of the Punic collection for the archaeological museum. In February 1821 Humbert had his first meeting with Reuvens, who was stunned by the detailed plans and drawings and

Humbert's amount of knowledge about Carthage. The meeting lasted a couple of days, during which they discussed the problems surrounding the topography of the peninsula, Humbert's finds and the history of investigations in North Africa. Another meeting was planned for April, when the antiquities were due to arrive. Reuvens saw the chance of a life-time: with the aid of Humbert he could establish his name by being the first to publish a scholarly work on the topography of Carthage, a city which had played a role comparable to Rome and Athens in antiquity. Together with Humbert he discussed the possibilities of organizing an expedition to Carthage to clarify the topography and to carry out new excavations. Reuvens' enthusiasm made Humbert see his future in a different light. The Dutch Indies could be exchanged for a new stay in Tunisia. A publication by Reuvens could also establish his name as the explorer of Carthage. At once his future became linked to that of Reuvens'.

The change of climate, the tension of the preceding months and the new prospects made him fall seriously ill. In March 1821 Reuvens wrote to Minister Falck:

> Major Humbert has had a serious illness due to the change of atmospheric conditions, affecting his imagination. Worrying about the delay of his affairs and the absence of his wife has caused him to stand with one foot in the grave. Half delirious he was continually shouting 'Carthage' and my name. Now the gentleman is recovering and if this continues he will be better soon.[15]

In April the antiquities and coins arrived, which were inspected by Reuvens and his colleague De Jonge of the Royal Coin Cabinet in The Hague. In his report to the ministry Reuvens highly praised the collection, especially the four Punic stelae: 'I consider the import into our country of four such highly unusual objects to be an honour, and when the possession of these pieces in any museum becomes known to the scholarly world, the fame of that museum will be established.'[16] In addition, the drawings were very valuable, especially the plan of the Carthaginian peninsula: 'Truly a unique and elsewhere unobtainable aid for planning excavations, which the Government may want to carry out.'[17] The drawings of antiquities and inscriptions made during the travels with Borgia were also useful, even if the texts were known from other publications. The fact that Humbert had copied the form of the letters with great care had an added value for dating the inscriptions: 'Today we are not content any more with mere copies of the old inscriptions, if the shape of the letters is not precisely rendered: this is necessary to judge the date of the stone.'[18] The Punic stelae with inscriptions were, according to Reuvens, the most important acquisitions and made the collection worth 17,000 guilders. The decision to send Humbert to the Dutch Indies was reversed. Instead he received a major's pension and was free to offer his service to archaeology. The happy conclusion of his journey to the Netherlands had created a bond between Humbert and Reuvens. When Humbert had read a copy of Reinaud's description of the coin collection of the Duke of Blacas, he returned the book to Reuvens with the following note:

> You have without doubt remarked that Colonel Rottiers, much less a good Dutchman than Major Humbert, has enriched the cabinet of a French ambassador, while the latter considers it a pleasant duty to offer the poor things he has collected to his native country. Forgive me, dear Sir, a small amount of *amour-propre*: I'm entitled to have some, because the wish to offer all to the country has conquered over the mere desire of selling at the highest price. This proves that when you live amidst the Arabs and camp in their tents it is easier to preserve your patriotism than when you lie comfortably between the beautiful *Géorgiennes* [from Georgia, South Russia]![19]

FIRST ARCHAEOLOGICAL EXPEDITION TO NORTH AFRICA, 1822–4

For the first time since his appointment Reuvens had the vision of a grand project, which he could realize with the aid of an archaeological agent in Tunisia. The topography of Carthage would form the core of his publication, but he wanted to add chapters about the history, ancient topography, antiquities and even aspects of the Islamic history of Tunisia. For this last subject he tried to interest in the project H.A. Hamaker, professor of oriental languages at the University of Leiden.

Humbert's expedition to Tunisia focused on four points. First, to enrich the museum with statuary from Utica, which could be bought at La Goulette from the Tunisian minister of marine. Second, excavations at Carthage to get more information about the topography of the ancient Punic settlement and maybe to find objects for the museum. The drawings were the third point of interest. Humbert had to complete some plans and make new drawings and sketches of antiquities in the interior of Tunisia. Also, corrections were needed to sketches made during the travels with Count Borgia. Last but not least, Reuvens mentioned the acquisition of Punic material. He was interested in the style of the ancient Carthaginians: were they influenced by eastern, Egyptian or Greek art? Statuary, vases and architecture could give information about this question. Reuvens also needed more written documents, preferably a bilingual inscription 'for example with Punic and Greek, or Punic and Latin, this being the most certain way to gain more knowledge about the Punic language'.[20]

To start this endeavour, Reuvens asked the department to organize an expedition to Tunisia, which would last three years and have the dual aim of

Figure 6.3 Marble statue of Trajan from Utica, second century AD. National Museum
of Antiquities.

enlarging the museum's collection by excavations and purchases and of
investigating the topography of Carthage. Minister Falck, the driving force
behind the growth of the archaeological museum, proposed this project to
the king and arranged a sum of 10,200 guilders for a three-year expedition
to Tunisia. Humbert was allowed to buy antiquities and carry out excavations with a maximum of 1,500 guilders yearly. For larger expenses he had
to ask permission first. His major's pension of 1,500 guilders was raised to a
sum of 3,000 guilders yearly. For his travel expenses he could spend 1,200
guilders.

The ministry decided also to award Humbert the Order of the Dutch Lion for his past services and willingness to help with this scholarly project. Earlier Humbert had pointed out that a royal decoration would help considerably to impress the authorities in Tunis and could be useful in obtaining the permits needed to excavate in Carthage.

As a parting salutation Humbert composed a romantic song 'Le Voyageur', which he had printed and distributed among his friends and relatives (see Appendix 4). In January 1822 he left the Netherlands. In February he celebrated the *Carnevale* in Livorno in a way that was uncommon for the usually phlegmatic northerners, which earned him some reproaches from his travel companions.[21] In particular, a supposed love affair with a lady from Livorno was commented upon in various letters.

In May 1822 Humbert arrived in Tunis, where he offered presents to the bey and obtained permission to collect antiquities and start excavations. The bey did have some wishes in return. First he offered Humbert a new position at his court. When Humbert politely declined this offer the bey had another proposal: in exchange for the permit to investigate the Carthaginian peninsula, Humbert had to promise to do some engineering work on the harbour of La Goulette. This meant spending quite some time in the neighbourhood of Tunis, which conflicted with the time available for his travels in Tunisia. Humbert faced the necessity to humour the Tunisian ruler for fear of losing the permission to start his archaeological activities, and agreed. For the whole period of his mission Humbert had to serve two masters, a fact which in the Netherlands did not become known.

Humbert's first concern was the purchase of nine monumental Roman statues, which were found during excavations in Utica. Six of the statues had been excavated around 1800 and described by Count Borgia in September 1815. They were in possession of the Khaja (governor) of La Goulette. Three more statues were added later to this collection. The masterpieces were an above life-size statue of Emperor Trajan in armour (Figure 6.3), a headless, draped statue of a woman, a half-draped statue of the Emperor Tiberius and a statue of Jupiter. Three more draped female statues, an imperial statue and a marble head completed this collection. Apart from the statue of Trajan, the largest female statue was of special interest to Humbert. He described it as follows:

> Perfectly draped: the folds of the drapery on the right leg are exceptional, but still look natural. The soft contours and the modest attitude distinguish this statue especially. The bosom and hips are covered by a thin and somewhat stretched fabric, which accentuates the nude. The foot is charming.[22]

It was a blow to Humbert to notice on his return to La Goulette that this masterpiece of Roman sculpture was missing. During his absence it had been acquired by the Danish consul and antiquarian Christian Tuxen Falbe in 1820, the successor of Andreas Christian Gierlew, who had been helpful to Borgia during his period of exile. In turn Falbe had donated the statue to the Danish king Christian VIII.[23] The fact that Falbe had acquired this very statue was probably the reason for a life-long feud between the two anti-quarians, which led to some remarkable incidents, as shall be described later.

The price asked for the eight remaining statues was 8,000 piastres, about 6,400 Dutch guilders. The department tried to dissuade Reuvens from buy-ing the statues by pointing out that the price was high, in view of the allowed yearly sum of 1,500 guilders for antiquities. Moreover, there was not enough room in the small museum in Leiden for statues of that size. Reuvens argued that the price was not too high for European standards and that space was available: the moment these statues arrived in Leiden, less elegant sculptures from the Papenbroek collection could go to the depot:

> There are some open spaces and also many with rather mediocre pieces, which until now I have left standing in deference to Papen-broek's name and to cover the bare walls, but which should give their places to other less shameful pieces as soon as those arrive, as happens in all museums.[24]

There was considerable competition in Tunis. The English consul Alexander Tulin had offered 5,000 piastres for only two of the statues, and his Danish counterpart Christian Falbe was willing to pay 12,000 piastres for the whole collection. When Humbert received authorization to offer the price of 8,000 piastres, he immediately closed the deal and was able to inform the department on 9 September 1823 that the eight statues had been bought. Earlier he had admitted that one piece had gone to Denmark: 'A statue without a head and fortunately the less interesting one from an artistic point of view', he wrote to the department, always eager to please.[25] Without doubt Humbert's special relations with the officials at La Goulette and his secret service to the bey had secured the collection for him.

Apart from this fine collection of Roman statuary, Humbert also bought other items in Tunisia. Besides innumerous small objects like oil lamps, *terra sigillata* and coins, he managed to acquire a collection of sculpture from El Djem/Thysdrus and fourteen votive reliefs from the vicinity of El Kef/Sicca Veneria, in the interior of Tunisia. They were made in a rough, local style with depictions of gods, worshippers and sacrificial animals. These interesting reliefs dated from the Roman imperial period, but honoured the old Punic deities Baal-Hammon and Tanit, Romanized as Saturnus Africanus and Dea Caelestis. As such these Romano-Punic reliefs were a valuable addition to the Punic votive stones which Humbert had discovered in 1817 and also illustrated Humbert's broad interest, which did not merely focus on the elevated art of antiquity.[26]

EXCAVATIONS IN TUNISIA

One of the targets of Humbert's expedition to Tunisia was the excavations on the Carthaginian peninsula, aimed at clarifying the topography of the Punic city. The organization of excavations in this period can be read in a report by Humbert about Borgia's excavations in Utica in 1816. Most probably Humbert had to obey the same conditions set by the Tunisian government. In his report about the possibilities of starting excavations in Tunisia he appeared optimistic:

> But what Doctor Shaw has described, the inscriptions he has mentioned, the few things that I have found, the objects Count Borgia has excavated and everything that Fortune offers daily to the Arab farmers, everything points towards the brilliant success of future excavations in Carthage, if based on scholarly principles. During the past Government of Hamuda Pacha no excavations were permitted, but under the present rule of Mahmoud Bey it is possible to obtain this favour. These are the conditions under which Count Borgia was granted the permission to investigate the soil of Utica:
> — He paid the workmen in the excavations 8 till 10 caroubes each day, which amounts to about 45 Dutch cents;
> — The overseers who managed the excavations and paid attention that no objects were stolen by the workmen were paid 80 cents each day; the number of overseers was calculated on the number of workmen;
> — A Mamelouk, or officer of the Bey, needed for keeping order, was paid one guilder and 60 cents each day;
> — The gold and silver objects which were discovered in whatever form, were estimated and the countervalue of the metal was paid by Count Borgia to the Bey;
> — Copper, bronze and all terracotta objects could by law be kept by Count Borgia. But when statues were discovered, their value had to be estimated by an artist and half of their value was paid to the Bey.[27]

Payment of workmen and surveyors was thus organized. Transgressions of the rules immediately led to the withdrawal of the permit to excavate. Although the rules were simple, it was clear that the Tunisian government did not allow uncontrolled loot of cultural property.

Humbert did not excavate on a grand scale. Most of the excavations consisted of long trenches in the terrain, dug in a few days by workmen, to look for topographical elements like roads, gates and walls. The longest excavation took two weeks and was made on the spot where Humbert had found the four inscribed stelae. Humbert made detailed notes of each excavation and noted the place on his plan of Carthage. The finds were small in number and interest: mostly grave gifts like oil lamps, small pottery, coins and skeletal remains. Between La Malga and Sidi Bou-Said he discovered two Punic objects: a fragment of a Punic inscription and a stone with the symbol of Tanit. Outside of Carthage Humbert also organized small excavations near Portefarine (Ghar el Melch), Utica, Mehamdia, Béja and Sursef. A good example of his excellent archaeological drawing technique is the plan of a Roman mausoleum, discovered in 1822 north of Tunis: the details and various cross-sections (Figure 6.4) show that he used fully the techniques which he had learned as a military engineer, but now for archaeological drawings.[28]

He earned less sympathy from his role in preventing other archaeological activities in Carthage. Christian Falbe, the Danish consul and antiquarian, was also studying the topography of Carthage and had obtained permission to excavate on the peninsula. Humbert contacted one of his Tunisian friends and told him that somewhere in Falbe's excavation (where a Roman mosaic was discovered) a lead coffin was hidden, full of silver and golden coins. A detachment of soldiers was sent to the spot and before the eyes of the consul the whole excavation area was destroyed: a clear warning that Humbert was ruthless in ensuring his monopoly on investigating the topography of Carthage. Falbe never forgave Humbert this episode, which he made known to the public in his publication on the topography of Carthage of 1833.[29]

Humbert, with his emotional character, had difficulties coping with the daily confrontation with the ruined past, as it compared with the soft life he had experienced in Livorno. He wrote weekly to his girlfriend in Livorno, sending African gifts such as aloe-wood, ostrich feathers and fine perfumes. On the wall of the Roman cisterns he left poems in honour of his *amabile donna Italiana*, stressing the merits of memory above temporary pleasures.[30] He had attacks of melancholy and longed for life amidst his friends in Italy. In his letters he described himself as *Le solitaire des ruines* and he pictured himself in his watercolours as a small lonely figure, surrounded by imposing North African nature. He described his feelings of depression as follows:

When one passes most of the time between the ruined remains of temples and palaces, when one is constantly busy reading rusted coins and grave inscriptions, is it then surprising that one's mood gets a bit lugubrious? Every step I take and every object I touch reminds me of the transience and futility of human endeavours. These sad examples of the past are serious lessons for the future. From what has been, I learn what shall be: ambition, fanaticism, intolerance, despotism and prejudice will continuously injure, harm and shame the human race![31]

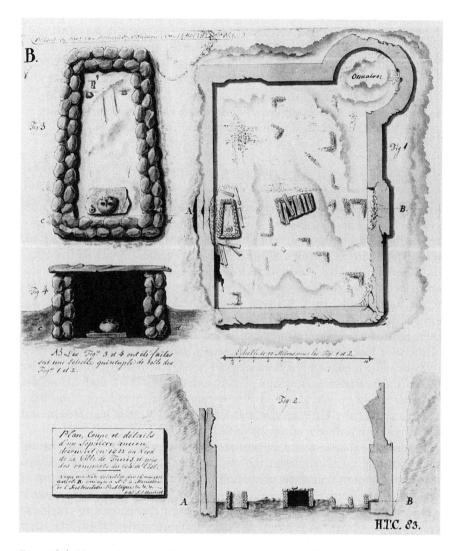

Figure 6.4 Plan and sections of a Roman mausoleum near Tunis. Coloured drawing
by J.E. Humbert (1822). Archive, National Museum of Antiquities.

Humbert had a close encounter with the underworld, when he was nearly
killed by a fall in an ancient tomb. He described the episode with gusto:

> Yesterday a new discovery nearly cost me my life. A Moor had
> informed me about a souterrain, where human remains had been
> found. I went there immediately and I decided to descend into the
> cavern by means of a ladder, which I had ordered from a neighbouring

village. But the stability of the ladder was diminished by my weight and my impatience to see the antique tomb, so I went down a little bit too fast. Fortunately I fell on soft earth, otherwise I would be lying now with a broken back besides the remains of an age-old skeleton, and that would certainly have displeased my wife: the fair sex does not want one to break one's neck for something as unimportant as archaeology. A small contusion on my arm was all the damage I sustained from my descent into the Realm of Death.[32]

CARTHAGE REVISITED?

In September 1824 Humbert arrived in the Netherlands aboard the marine vessel H.M. *Middelburg*, a real African explorer: with him were sixty-five crates filled with sculptures, ceramics, coins, medals, manuscripts, skeletons, seeds, spices, stones, fossils and hides of exotic animals. When all the crates had arrived in Leiden, Reuvens started the inspection of these objects, and asked permission to divide the material among various institutions. In his report to the department, Reuvens showed himself pleased with the results, especially with the statues from Utica. The topographical research left much to be desired: the excavations had been small in number and scale, and most of the sites had already been investigated. A second expedition was needed to make more topographical drawings and to do more research in the interior of Tunisia. Reuvens was especially pleased with the new Punic finds: 'Humbert outrivals all his predecessors in discovering Punic monuments, the bone and marrow of the Carthaginian soil, of which all Roman inscriptions and buildings form only the outermost rind.'[33]

It was clear that a second expedition to Carthage was needed to clear up the remaining questions about the topography. For the first time Reuvens thought of chemical analysis of the soil to distinguish the original form of the peninsula from the later alluvial deposits. Apart from this research and new excavations, he desired expeditions into the interior to check the descriptions of Shaw and Borgia and to collect antiquities. Third, the coast of North Africa could be explored with a navy vessel. On his way to the Mediterranean Humbert could make purchases in France and Italy. Professor Hamaker added some wishes for his department: questions about linguistic problems and anthropological aspects of life in North Africa.[34]

As can be expected, Humbert was reluctant to return to Tunisia. He had hoped to be employed in Greece, but learned that Colonel Rottiers was already active in those areas. The department had suggested an expedition to Egypt, but Humbert told them that this country was in possession of England and France, and their consuls would not allow any competition.

Reuvens had the best arguments: Humbert had to go to North Africa, the area he knew best, in view of the forthcoming publication: 'Babylon and

Persepolis, Thebes and Memphis, Athens and Rome have been investigated with pugnacity and clarified: Carthage, which played no less an important role in history, has not been found yet and is an empty place in history.'[35]

Humbert's reluctance to go to Tunisia also had other reasons, which were unknown to his principals. In Tunis Antoine Nijssen was seriously ill and had asked to be relieved of the consulate. In Tunis serious rumours circulated that Humbert was lobbying in The Hague to obtain the consulate, at the expense of his brother-in-law César, who eagerly wanted to succeed Antoine. Humbert's wife Thérèse, who had fallen fatally ill in 1825, had warned her husband in one of her last letters that César had publicly threatened that he and his brothers would shoot down Humbert 'the moment he set foot on African soil'. These strained relations with the Dutch consulate were of course a serious impediment to the success of an archaeological expedition.

Nevertheless, preparations went ahead, and on 22 June 1825 a royal decree was passed for an expedition of four years with a budget of 2,500 guilders for excavations and purchases. Humbert was promoted to the titular rank of lieutenant-colonel as a reward for his efforts during the first expedition.

THE BORGIA INHERITANCE

After the death of Camillo Borgia in 1817, his widow Adelaide was left in dire circumstances. She had been forced to sell the diary, sketches and notes of her late husband to Count Alexandre de Laborde, a French author who specialized in travel descriptions.[36] In the sales document Borgia's widow stipulated that de Laborde was obliged to publish the material within a certain period of time, but de Laborde was faced with a number of problems. Borgia's handwriting was nearly illegible and the text was teeming with orthographical and grammatical mistakes. De Laborde had the text copied by an Italian, Giuseppe Longo, who rendered the manuscript legible but by misreading added quite a number of mistakes of his own. This corrupted version was then translated into French by a certain François Zingaropoli, who copied Longo's mistakes and added new slips of the pen and mistranslations of his own. The result made de Laborde's head spin: he himself had never been in Tunisia and the result of all the copying and translating had made the text incomprehensible. He decided to put an end to the project and sell the documents.

For the forthcoming publication of Carthage, Reuvens tried to get hold of Borgia's manuscripts, which were very valuable as an addition to Humbert's drawings and plans. A period of difficult negotiations with Alexandre de Laborde and Adelaide Borgia began.[37] The difficulties focused at first on the title of the work. Reuvens wanted to include the Borgia material in his study and use it where possible, mixed with Humbert's and his own observations. In the subtitle of the work the names of Humbert and Borgia could appear. Adelaide stipulated that her husband's material should form the core of the publication, and that his name should be most prominent on the frontispiece.[38] Further disagreements occurred concerning the number of free copies and the price for the documents and the new (but useless) French translation. After agreeing to publish the work within four years and to give thirty free copies to Adelaide Borgia, Reuvens became the owner of the manuscripts: 'Better bad conditions than no contract at all.'[39]

On 30 June 1830 the manuscripts were handed over to Reuvens, but the negotiations were not complete. Adelaide Borgia started to write letters to Reuvens pleading again for him to publish the manuscript separately under her husband's name, and offering other material from her legacy: three Arabian manuscripts, bought in Tunisia. Reuvens decided to buy these manuscripts as well, but with a new stipulation that he could use the Borgia material as he wished, that there would be no time limit for the publication and that the widow should be content with twenty free copies of the publication. In August 1831 this new contract was signed: Reuvens finally had his hands free to start working on the publication of his *Borgiana cum annexis*.

7

STATION LIVORNO

The Etruscan and Egyptian collections

If one is to understand the supremacy of the Greeks, then
something is needed to contrast them with.

> Anne Haslund Hansen, 'The needs of a
> gentleman: the Egyptian antiquities in the
> collection of Christian VIII', in *Christian VIII and
> the National Museum*, Copenhagen 2000, p. 114

Vir illustris et de studiis Archaeologicis bene meritus, I.E.
Humbert.

> L.J.F. Janssen, *Musei Lugduno-Batavi
> Inscriptiones Etruscae*, Leiden, 1840, p. 1

ETRUSCAN URNS FROM VOLTERRA

Italy was Humbert's second homeland. The Italian way of life, the mild
climate and the pleasures of food and company made him feel at home. His
personal circumstances had much to do with his love for Italy: in Tunis he
had always had the reputation of an upstart, especially in consular circles:
the poor lieutenant-engineer who had made good by marrying into the
family of the Dutch consul. In the Netherlands, after an absence of more
than twenty years, he no longer felt at home: there he was regarded as an
uprooted, adventurous expatriate who did not fit in the indolent atmosphere
of *Biedermeier* society. In Italy he could enjoy life in relative anonymity, and
in the literary salons of Livorno he enjoyed the reputation of the *Colonello
Olandese* who had excavated in Carthage, had bought impressive collections
and now worked as an archaeological agent for the king of the Netherlands.
His prolonged stay in Livorno, though contrary to the plans and wishes of
Reuvens, was an active period of his life, with very important consequences
for the collections of the archaeological museum in Leiden.

In the spring of 1826 the second mission took Humbert to Livorno,
where he had to embark for the North African coast. In his first letter to
Reuvens, Humbert asked for a postponement of the journey to North Africa

for a few months: summer in Tunisia would be too hot to start excavations, pirates were active on the Mediterranean, and the hatred of Christians in Tunisia had reached a new peak since the Greek–Turkish war: outside the city walls the bey could not guarantee the safety of European residents: 'Shooting down a bird or a Christian is all the same to them,' Humbert repeated in his letters. In Italy there were ample opportunities to buy antiquities for the museum. Reuvens agreed to a delay of four months. Humbert started collecting in Italy with zeal.

Humbert had ample opportunities to buy Etruscan antiquities, which at that time were not much known outside of Italy. The so-called 'Etruscan taste' which had been popular in the applied arts of eighteenth-century Europe had little to do with Etruria: it had been inspired by the publications of Greek vases by Sir William Hamilton, British ambassador at the court of Naples.[1] These popular and precious vases were commonly called *vasi Etruschi* but stemmed originally from Greek workshops in southern Italy and Greece itself. Real Etruscan artefacts could be admired in the palazzi of collectors, for example in Volterra, Florence, Arezzo, Siena, Cortona and in the papal collections in Rome. The most important pieces from these collections were published between 1737 and 1743 by A.F. Gori in his *Museum Etruscum*. The Etruscan antiquities from the environs of Florence were published separately by him in his *Museum Florentinum* (1731–52). Museums in Europe turned their attention to Etruscan artefacts relatively late. Although earlier attempts were made by Champollion le Jeune, it was in 1827 that the Musée Charles X bought five Etruscan urns from Volterra. In 1861 parts of the enormous Campana collection were also acquired by Paris.[2] In 1830 the Royal Museum in the Lustgarten in Berlin counted only four Etruscan pieces among approximately 900 antique statues. Thanks to the activities of Eduard Gerhard, the founder of the Istituto di Corrispondenza Archeologica in Rome, its collections were augmented and placed in a separate Etruscan gallery in 1844. The exhibition in London in 1837 of the Campanari collection with reconstructions of painted tombs was a great success. The British Museum bought large parts of the Campanari collection and public interest in the Etruscans led to more tourism and travel accounts of visits to the cities and cemeteries of Etruria.[3]

On 26 May 1826 Humbert wrote from Livorno that he had bought six Volterran cinerary urns, five made of alabaster, one of tuff. The pieces had belonged to the collector Antonio Giorgi, who around the mid-eighteenth century had accumulated a collection of approximately forty-five urns. The most important piece, called *Il Polifemo*, depicted Ulysses' departure from the island of Polyphemus, with the giant (two-eyed in this *Interpretatio Etrusca*) throwing stones at the departing Greeks (Figure 7.1). The other urns had representations of Ulysses and the suitors of Penelope, the recognition of Protesilaos by Laodameia, Paris threatened by his brothers, the killing of Myrtilos by Pelops, and an unidentified scene of six persons around an urn on a pedestal.[4]

Figure 7.1 Etruscan cinerary urn from Volterra: Ulysses and Polyphemus, second century BC. National Museum of Antiquities.

In 1822 the Giorgi collection was sold. A certain Nicolo Viti bought twenty-eight urns, and resold them to other dealers. Six of these pieces, among which *Il Polifemo*, were bought by Humbert in May 1826, to the displeasure of Champollion le Jeune, who had wanted to acquire the objects but had not received authorization from Paris in time.[5]

SUPPOSED FORGERIES: 'RESIGNATION, PATIENCE AND PHILOSOPHY'

In July 1826 the six urns arrived in Leiden. Together with his colleague David Humbert de Superville, Humbert's older brother and reader of art history at the university, Reuvens inspected the antiquities. The reaction of both scholars, who were not familiar with the special character of Etruscan art, is very interesting. The 'primitive' character of the anthropomorphic lids, in the shape of reclining men and women with large heads and short bodies, in combination with the frontal reliefs, executed according to classically ideal proportions, was 'very suspicious'. A draft has been preserved, on which Reuvens jotted down his first thoughts about the urns. Reuvens considered

91

the anthropomorphic lids 'totally childish in design: big heads, wrong contours of muscles, or without muscles, wrong proportions of hands, etc.'.[6] They contrasted remarkably with the reliefs, in which there were elements of a far later period of art: '. . . almost free-standing reliefs, a kind of work that belongs to a later period. The style seems a bit French. Strange bend in a left leg above the ankle. In another an arm is resting on a hip, totally in the French theatrical proud attitude.'[7] Three of the urns were declared eighteenth-century fakes, 'produced to deceive Gori and other Etrusco-maniacs'.[8] About *Il Polifemo* Reuvens and Humbert de Superville had doubts. In November Reuvens informed Humbert about this supposedly bad bargain. He wrote that the lids of the urns were possibly genuine, and two of the urns also:

> But (forgive me for saying so) the three urns with other subjects seem to be fakes, made in the time when Gori thought he could recognize the secrets of Mithras in those representations. It seems to me that the urns have been copied after others (which have to be explained quite differently), with slight modifications. About the one with Ulysses I am a bit less sure, but this one, too, is suspect. I have decided to inform your brother about these doubts and have asked his opinion as well. In the meantime I consider these purchases of interest, because they serve to distinguish certainty from doubtfulness in archaeology. But only if they are not bought for too high a price, which I gather is not the case with these urns. In this sense I will write my report to the Department.[9]

Humbert was shocked by this verdict. He considered this incident an intolerable loss of face before Reuvens, before the department (on which he was dependent financially) and before his learned brother, with whom his relationship was difficult. He needed all his 'resignation, patience and philosophy' to avoid asking his immediate dismissal, but finally decided to use attack as the best defence. With the help of Italian archaeologists he produced a dossier about the urns, in which the authenticity of the pieces was declared and proven with various arguments.[10] First, the discovery of all six urns was fully documented. Second, it would cost more money to make a counterfeit than to buy an original urn, the price of alabaster being very high. Third, no lumps of alabaster *of this size* had been found for ages in the surroundings of Volterra: it was therefore impossible to fake these urns in this precious material. Humbert asked for an official reaction to this dossier and even requested to have the urns returned to Italy for an exhibition and a public debate about their originality. He wrote to Reuvens:

> I throw down the gauntlet and I declare here, in front of scholarly Europe, that the urns I sent to Leiden are fully antique and that the Homeric chest is and will be above suspicion, for now and for ever.[11]

The good relationship between Reuvens and Humbert suffered a blow as a result of this incident. Things got worse when Reuvens heard rumours about the prospect of a marriage between Humbert and a lady from Livorno. The letters became formal and mutual reproaches were made, especially about the main object of the mission: the expedition to Carthage. Reuvens refused to answer officially to the questions in Humbert's dossier, but conceded that he had judged *Il Polifemo* too quickly. He remained doubtful about the three other urns. For Humbert this was enough to end hostilities, and 'the sweet title of friend' was used again in the next letters. In February 1827 he bought twenty more Volterran urns from the former Giorgi collection, all with certificates of authenticity by the Florentine archaeologist Francesco Inghirami, who had also assisted Humbert in compiling the dossier about the previous shipment.

THE MUSEO CORAZZI IN CORTONA

'La ville de Cortone, depouillée du Musée Corazzi, perd ainsi son plus bel ornement et cesse d'être, au profit de Leide, le sanctuaire Etrusque'
Désiré Raoul Rochette, *Journal des Savants*, 1835, p. 397

In the same year as the purchase of the six urns from the Giorgi collection, Humbert informed Reuvens that in the town of Cortona, near Lake Trasimene, an Etruscan collection, the Museo Corazzi, was being offered for sale. Cortona had been an important centre of collecting and studying Etruscan antiquities from the sixteenth century onwards. As the seat of the Accademia Etrusca, which organized lectures, fostered Etruscan studies and published important volumes on the history of the region, the town of Cortona was renowned in the world of antiquarians, collectors and scholars. Moreover it housed two of the most important Etruscan collections in Italy, the Museo Venuti and the Museo Corazzi, both private collections in the hands of privileged Cortonese families.[12]

The Museo Corazzi was a collection of more than 500 pieces, formed by Count Galeotto Ridolfini Corazzi (1690–1769), which consisted mainly of bronzes, found in the surroundings of Cortona, the *agro cortonese*. The bronzes were divided by Corazzi into three classes. The first section comprised the 114 most beautiful and important pieces from the so-called *scuola toscanina*. The 191 bronzes of the second class were smaller in size and not all of Etruscan manufacture. The third class of bronzes comprised 233 non-figurative bronzes such as weapons and utensils. Apart from the bronzes there were several other 'curiosities' such as vases, cameos, jewellery, reliefs and Renaissance majolica.

Many pieces had been published by Gori in his *Museum Etruscum*. Although the asked-for price of 60,000 guilders was very high, Reuvens was interested

Figure 7.2 Bronzes from the Corazzi collection, found in 1746 near Castiglion Fiorentino (Montecchio, Arezzo province, Tuscany). National Museum of Antiquities.

in entering into negotiations. Etruscan material was not widely known in western Europe, but therefore not without value for his profession. He wrote to the department:

> Studying Etruscan objects is highly important. The language of this powerful nation is still enigmatic, but there are enough remains, both of this language and of the early established art of the Etrurians, to expand the oldest history of Italy remarkably if only one could sufficiently understand everything. But in archaeology no study is aroused or vigorously continued without the objects themselves: therefore it would be useful as well as glorious to have an adequate amount of them in Leiden's museum.[13]

Establishing the pecuniary value was more difficult. The scarcity of Etruscan objects at auction made comparison with other pieces impossible. Reuvens suggested valuing the objects as if they were Roman and doubling the price because of their 'rareness and higher importance'. But even then the price sought for the Corazzi collection was far too high. In this private museum there was no highlight like the *Arringatore* or the *Chimaera* of Arezzo. Humbert got orders to go to Cortona and provide information about the size of the pieces, possible fakes, and the number of Etruscan inscriptions.

Humbert travelled from Livorno to Cortona, visited the collection anonymously and reported to the ministry a few days later. In his report he stressed that the museum was one of the last coherent private collections in the region: '. . . the only private museum, because professor Reuvens does not know yet that the Museo Venuti from the same city does not exist any more but has been transferred partly to Rome. The Museo Guarnacci in Volterra has been taken over by the municipal museum in that town.'[14] The price asked for the collection had been lowered to around 38,000 guilders.

But Reuvens faced a dilemma. The target of Humbert's second expedition was Tunisia. Was it wise to start buying collections for huge amounts of money in Italy? This question was connected with another: in which direction should the Museum of Antiquities develop? If one wanted to compete with the national museums abroad, every ancient culture should be represented in the collection with a sufficient number of pieces. If one desired a study collection for the university only, then it was not necessary to buy these amounts of Etruscan antiquities. A small sample of Etruscan pieces could be sufficient. The decision was not his. He wrote to the department:

It is a question which I am not allowed to answer: is the Government willing to spend such an amount of money on a branch of archaeology which cannot be considered indispensable for a good museum? If I am allowed to express my feelings straightforwardly without taking a side, then I would let the decision of this question depend on another: does the Government have it in view to expand the Museum of Antiquities in such a direction that it not only fosters archaeology among our compatriots, but also nourishes and extends it generally to achieve honour and foreign glory for our country? And does the museum have to have only enough antiquities to cultivate an *elementary* knowledge of archaeology for the natives? In this last case, although the possession of some Etruscan artefacts as *examples* is indispensable, the purchase of this collection would be too heavy for the use and pleasure it could give; these kinds of objects will not be held in high artistic esteem, and will not be used as a subject of scholarly investigations by most students. But in the first case a good Etruscan collection (which as I have said cannot be found on this side of the Alps) will increase the renown of the museum considerably, and the richness of the whole museum will encourage and foster the study of each separate subject, including the less known and abstract ones like the Etruscan antiquities. The study of Etruscan artefacts will specifically stimulate interest in Roman antiquities and the study of ancient history to a considerable degree.[15]

The decision about buying the Museo Corazzi for 38,000 guilders was left to King Willem I, who asked advice from the ministers of the interior and of finance. The first, who was also responsible for the Department of Education and Culture, advised buying the collection, especially 'in consideration of the benefit of Ancient History and in consideration of the renown which will be awarded to the collection in Leiden'.[16] His colleague in finance was more tentative and preferred to have Reuvens' questions about the desired cultural policy answered first. If necessary the sum of money could be found in the Contingency Fund for 1826, although this was generally reserved – as has been noted – for catastrophes such as floodings and dam-bursts.

The correspondence between Leiden, The Hague, Livorno and Cortona continued. In the middle of these considerations about finances and cultural policy came the dénouement in Cortona. On 9 November financial difficulties led to a turbulent Corazzi family meeting, with the outcome that Count Corazzi lowered the price immediately by more than 5,000 guilders, provided that the buyer could pay immediately in cash. Humbert decided not to wait for yet another letter from Holland and gave the order to his intermediary to close the bargain. He suddenly became the owner of a splendid collection of Etruscan antiquities, but had to face the delicate task of informing his principals about this turn of events.

Humbert was not a man to mince matters. To the department he wrote that he had greatly exceeded his authority, but that he hoped to have acted in accordance with the intentions of the department, namely to obtain the collection at the lowest possible price. He could also inform his employers that a day after his action the city of Parma had offered a much higher price for the collection, but Count Corazzi was already bound by the contract with Humbert. The department could not do much else but give permission for the purchase *post factum*, adding 'that it must be made clear in strong terms to the above-mentioned Colonel Humbert that his way of acting was highly irregular'.[17] When the collection arrived in Livorno, and Humbert could inspect all the bronzes in detail, he was not too repentant of his conduct and wrote to the department:

> I confess, dear Sir, that today I am proud of all the reproaches for having gone too far in my zeal of obtaining for the Government a collection of Etruscan antiquities, which rivals that of the city of Florence and has not got its equal in the other museums of Europe![18]

As mentioned before, the special value of the Corazzi collection lay not only in the considerable quality of the individual objects. Most other private eighteenth-century collections of Etruscan antiquities had been dispersed among various museums and other collections. The Corazzi collection, together with its valuable archive material, entered the Dutch archaeological museum intact, and became available for study in its entirety, except for the Renaissance ceramics, which were transferred to the Rijksmuseum in Amsterdam. Together with Humbert's other purchases of Etruscan material, namely the collection of Clemente Santi, bishop of Sovana, the Corazzi collection became the starting point of Etruscology in the Netherlands.[19] *Factum ita est, ut copiam monumentorum Etruscorum haberemus eximiam, cis Alpes unicam fortasse* (And this is the reason that we possess an excellent number of Etruscan antiquities, which maybe is unique on this side of the Alps).[20]

The Corazzi collection was shipped to the Netherlands together with some Egyptian, Punic and Roman antiquities bought from the British consul in Malta, Alexander Tulin. Tulin had been active as an antiquarian in Tunis and as such had become acquainted with Humbert. When Tulin moved to Malta, he took his collection with him. The negotiations about acquiring his collection were carried out by letter and in November 1826 Humbert received the antiquities in the harbour of Livorno. A sum of 8,500 guilders was paid for the collection, which was renowned especially for a splendid Punic stela with a Tanit-symbol and a long inscription.[21]

EGYPTIAN ANTIQUITIES ON THE EUROPEAN MARKET

A quite unexpected result of Humbert's prolonged stay in Italy was the purchase of an Egyptian collection, which changed the character of the archaeological museum in Leiden considerably. Other European nations had acquired Egyptian antiquities earlier as a result of the famous French expedition in Egypt and the political changes after Napoleon's campaign. Egypt's new ruler, Mohammed Ali Pasha, tried to foster contacts with the European powers by opening up trade and establishing new consulates. The influence of the French and British consuls on Ali Pasha was great. They used this influence to collect antiquities, which were sold to European museums. The methods they employed for collecting were unscrupulous and reminiscent of the battles fought earlier between French and British troops in Egypt. The main players were Bernardino Drovetti, consul-general of France, and his British counterpart Henry Salt, who was escorted by the colourful bruiser Giovanni Battista Belzoni, who had started his career in a circus.

The first of the collections was put on sale by Drovetti in 1816. It comprised around 5,000 objects, with a large number of well-preserved papyrus scrolls. After years of negotiations the collection was sold to the archaeological museum in Turin for 400,000 francs.[22]

The British Museum already had some Egyptian antiquities from the collection of Sir Hans Sloane. The French defeat in Egypt brought more important pieces to the museum, such as the famous Rosetta stone. In 1818 Henry Salt offered for sale a collection of twenty monumental statues which had been excavated by his companion Belzoni. The trustees, who had already bought the colossal head of Ramses II from Salt, eventually acquired this 'first Salt collection' for only £2,000, a price that was lower than Salt had paid for acquisition and transport.

A few years later the British consul-general had further success in Paris. Champollion le Jeune became interested in the 'second Salt collection', which was on sale in Livorno in 1825. After a year of negotiations it was bought for France for 250,000 francs. The 'second Drovetti collection' was also bought by the French government in 1826. London, Paris and Turin had taken the lead in acquiring Egyptian collections. The Netherlands were to follow with the purchase of the collections of Maria Cimba and Jean d'Anastasy.

'EGYPT ALONG THE RHINE': THE CIMBA AND D'ANASTASY COLLECTIONS

Egyptian antiquities were self-evidently included in Reuvens' collecting policy. In his view as described earlier, all cultures that were known or influenced by the Greeks and Romans had to be present in an archaeological museum. In 1821 a few Egyptian antiquities from the university collection came to the museum, which had been on show in the Theatrum Anatomicum; they had served as a *memento mori* for the students as they watched the dissections performed here. In 1826 Reuvens acquired more pieces at an auction of Egyptian antiquities from the Delescluze collection, the same Bruges shipowner whom we encountered earlier in connection with Rottiers' second collection. Now an important addition was made to these pieces: the antiquities of Signora Cimba from Livorno, acquired in 1827.

Maria Cimba was the widow of Henry Salt's personal physician, who, on a smaller scale, had also been a collector of *Aegyptiaca*.[23] In 1824, after the death of her husband and children, Maria Cimba left Egypt and returned to her native Livorno with her late husband's collection, which she offered for sale. On 26 May 1826, shortly after his arrival in Livorno, Humbert sent a catalogue to Reuvens with a description of the 335 pieces, for which 14,000 guilders were asked. Champollion le Jeune, following Humbert like a shadow, was interested as well, but lacked the funds after the Salt purchase a year earlier. He tried to buy the most important pieces, but the widow refused to split the assembly: without the top pieces it would be hard to sell the remaining part.

After answering Reuvens' questions about sizes, hieroglyphs, length of papyrus scrolls and number of pharaohs' names to be found on objects for sale, Humbert was given permission to start negotiations with a bid of 8,000 guilders. A month later he had to write to The Hague that the collection had been sold for 9,000 guilders to 'an English gentleman'. After the Corazzi affair Humbert had not dared to act on his own a second time, with the result that the collection went to another party. Three months later the tide had turned: the Englishman had not been able to assemble the amount of money in time, and Signora Cimba now asked Humbert if he was still interested. Humbert declared his interest, but knowing the difficult financial situation of the vendor, did not hurry. He told Cimba that the Dutch government could raise a fair amount of money very quickly, but only if she was willing to lower her price considerably. Signora Cimba agreed to sell her collection for only 5,000 guilders.

The same year Humbert received news about another Egyptian collection that was offered for sale. His subsequent purchase of the collection of Egyptian antiquities of Jean d'Anastasy was the largest in Humbert's career. The collection comprised over 5,600 objects, and the negotiations took more than a year. The sum spent by the Dutch government on this purchase was the largest ever for an archaeological collection. The importance of the purchase was also cause for involving the Ministry of Foreign Affairs: the ambassador in Rome, Johann Reinhold, was asked to supervise the transaction.

Jean d'Anastasy (1780–1857) was the son of a Greek merchant from Damascus, who had made a fortune by supplying Napoleon's troops in Egypt. The withdrawal of the French from Egypt was a setback for the business, but Jean started a new trading firm in Alexandria, which became the biggest in Egypt. He held the monopoly of the grain trade during the reign of Mohammed Ali Pasha. He served as a consul for various Scandinavian countries, and used his influence to start collecting Egyptian antiquities. For sixteen years he bought and traded antiquities, mainly from the surroundings of Saqqara, the ancient Memphis. He did not take part in the cloak-and-dagger expeditions of his French and British counterparts, and as a result enjoyed a reputation of fairness and reliability.[24]

Shortly after acquiring the Cimba collection, Humbert informed his employers that a collection of Egyptian antiquities had been offered for sale by Costantino Tossizza, a Greek merchant of the trading firm Fratelli Tossizza in Livorno. Rumour was that this collection could compete with those of Drovetti and Salt: a catalogue of more than 110 pages was being prepared. Over a month later Humbert was able to inspect the collection, which was spread over various storehouses in the city. He saw beautiful objects: monumental statues, sarcophagi, mummies, bronzes, jewellery, glass, vases and many papyrus scrolls. The owner turned out to be Jean d'Anastasy from Alexandria, who had left the care of the negotiations to the Fratelli Tossizza.

With only the catalogue in hand, Reuvens had the difficult task of assessing the value of this collection. First of all he wanted to involve more people in the valuation of the Egyptian antiquities, in particular the Dutch ambassador in Rome ('a man of classical knowledge') and possibly also an Italian scholar well versed in Egyptology. In this matter he did not trust the capabilities of Humbert, whom he described as:

> An amateur without classical education, who has developed himself
> by some reading of modern authors and by seeing many antiquities,
> but only in a small circle in Tunis. I am convinced that everything
> which is not Roman or Punic is more or less strange to him. A
> remark which, I think, does justice to the truth and no injustice to
> the man's merits and zeal.[25]

It is obvious that the affair of the Etruscan urns had left its mark on the
relationship between the colonel and the scholar. Being too busy to travel to
Italy himself, Reuvens asked ambassador Reinhold which Italian scholar would
be capable of valuating the collection. Reinhold advised Ippolito Rosellini,
but this recommendation was rejected because of the narrow ties between
Rosellini and Champollion le Jeune, who was in Livorno at the time.[26]

In August 1827 negotiations started in Livorno. Ambassador Reinhold
was officially in charge, with Humbert as a legal representative in Livorno.
Humbert was aided by the merchant Giuseppe Terreni, who knew the circles
in Livorno more than anybody else. Jean d'Anastasy was represented by
Costantino Tossizza, the American François Barthou and, at a later stage, the
Italian Francesco de Castiglione. The last two traded in Egyptian antiquities
and some of their pieces came to the collections in Leiden separately from
the d'Anastasy collection. The price asked for the whole collection was
400,000 French francs, about 200,000 Dutch guilders.

REUVENS' FIRST VALUATION: 'BELOW THE
SALT COLLECTION'

After having studied all available information and the catalogue with supplements of the d'Anastasy collection, Reuvens tried to give a first tentative
valuation on 21 September 1827. He tried to compare the collection with
those of Drovetti and Salt. The Drovetti collection was conspicuous for its
colossal granite sculptures. Salt had a smaller number of granite statues.
D'Anastasy had fewer sculptures still, and the material was often limestone,
which was valued at much less than hard stones like granite or porphyry.
But d'Anastasy was richer than both others in papyri and thus had more
value for scholars. Also the number of mummies was higher than in either
other collection. Reuvens established an estimate for the pecuniary value by
looking at the number and the material of the statues. This meant a price
below the collection of Salt. He proposed to open negotiations with a bid
of 100,000 francs, with a maximum of 200,000 francs. This advice was put
forward to the king, who was not pleased with the first report: he asked for
much more information, including about the collections of Salt and Drovetti,
before giving his consent to start bidding. A month later Reuvens sent his
second report, which started with an important remark:

It would be unforgiveable for me as a Professor of Archaeology if such an important treasure of scholarship, which I would call *invaluable* if I did not fear to exaggerate (always to be avoided by judgement), fell into strange hands, only because supposedly the *pecuniary value* could not be estimated precisely. With due respect, I thought that in my last report I had come as close as possible to the question of the value, in general terms and without having seen the collection. Anyway, everybody must understand that the pecuniary value of such objects is totally fictitious: when the King of Sardinia bought the collection of Drovetti, there was no example of a large Egyptian collection on which the price could be based. The price was established by the demands of the seller and the negotiations of the buyer, in short by bargaining.[27]

Reuvens touched upon an important issue: Egyptian antiquities were relatively new on the international art market, and their prices could not be established by way of comparison, as was the case with the classical antiquities. The prices for the Drovetti and Salt collections were not based on objective comparisons, but on the hazardous ways of the market. Reuvens had been asked by the king to give a detailed report about a very important collection, but all the information he had was second-hand. He was seriously considering asking permission to travel to Livorno himself.

Time was running short. Reuvens suggested an opening bid of 100,000 francs and waiting for the asking price to be lowered: 'Haggling about Italian and Levantine prices is much more common than feelings of honour would permit us to do. Mr Kerfbyl[28] writes not to know much about the trading house Fratelli Tossizza, but remarks that "he is a Greek", which words are certainly not mentioned without reason.'[29]

The department agreed to start bidding at 100,000 francs and set the maximum bid at 200,000 francs, less than the Salt collection (250,000 francs) and half the asking price of the d'Anastasy collection. Humbert offered Tossizza the opening bid, which was instantly rejected, and then 140,000 francs. Tossizza reacted by leaving the room 'angry and disappointed', declaring himself free to start negotiations with other parties, namely Russia and Sweden.

REUVENS' SECOND VALUATION:
'THE COLLECTION HAS RISEN IN VALUE'

The sellers of the collection did not break off negotiations completely, but made a masterly move. It was very clear that the valuation of the collection was done by Reuvens, and not by Humbert or Reinhold. Instead of waiting for Reuvens to come to Livorno, they sent a representative to the Netherlands to talk with the scholar. In November 1827 François Barthou arrived in Holland, where he had talks with Van Ewijck and with Reuvens at Arentsburg, an excavation site between Leiden and The Hague (see next chapter). Barthou showed himself a perfect diplomat. During his conversation with Reuvens he admitted some weak points in the d'Anastasy collection and even mentioned some faults which Reuvens had not noticed. His approach had the desired effect. Reuvens wrote to the department that the collection had risen in value because of more confidence in the negotiators and valuable information about alabaster urns, small pyramids, bronze statues, mummies and papyri. Barthou had clarified catalogue statements about the collection which Reuvens had earlier disqualified as 'downright charlatanry'. He admitted that d'Anastasy's collection was less important than that of Drovetti, but said it had to be placed above Salt's because of the unique collection of mummies, the number of papyri (126 against 98) and the total number of pieces (5,600 against 3,000). Reuvens began to think of placing d'Anastasy on a level with Salt.

In the meantime in Livorno, Humbert had become angry with the delay and the amount of mistrust Reuvens showed towards the vendors. Bargaining with d'Anastasy was not easy: both Corazzi and Signora Cimba had been short of money and had lowered their prices considerably for this reason, but this was not the case with the wealthy merchant in Alexandria. Prices could be lowered, but the real value of the collection should always be the starting point for good negotiations. He wrote to Reuvens:

> I admit that Tossizza is a Greek, and in this respect I distrust him as well. But it is often too simple to say of a person 'he is a Jew' or 'he is a Greek' and then never change one's opinion again. And furthermore, in the case under discussion, we must not dwell too long on the question of whether Mr Tossizza is asking too much, but must give the price that this collection is worth with regard to its artistic and scholarly value.[30]

Humbert and Reinhold were in an awkward position. From their correspondence it is clear that they did not agree at all with Reuvens' valuation of the collection, but they were forced to use his arguments in their dealings with Tossizza. Humbert had even called the Dutch bid 'ridiculous'. Words of this kind were not used by the diplomat, but he too found it unbelievable that Reuvens, with all the information at hand, did not place d'Anastasy above Salt: 'So he has made a terrible mistake! It is annoying, but what can we do? The admission of his error has to come from himself . . .'[31]

In the meantime the bid was raised to 165,000 francs, which was rejected immediately by Tossizza. Humbert informed the department about this news, and once again added his thoughts about the whole matter:

The essential difference that exists between Greek, Roman and Egyptian antiquities makes it very hard to determine the objective value of the latter. And without going into details I want to point out that from this difference emerges the principle that one should not measure the monuments of Egypt with a Greek or Roman ruler.[32]

In the last days of 1827 Humbert offered 180,000 francs. Some movement was made by Tossizza, who rejected the bid but lowered the asking price to 350,000 francs. Humbert became agitated and suggested to Reinhold writing to King Willem I personally, but this was going too far for Reinhold: 'Resign yourself to our national phlegm! For you this may be more difficult than for me: I have not passed a great part of my life under the burning sun of Africa!'[33] But neither did Reinhold remain totally phlegmatic. He wrote to his ministry that in his view the collection was in all aspects superior to that of Salt. D'Anastasy was a bit unlucky that his collection had arrived last of the three on the market and that competition was low. Reinhold estimated that the d'Anastasy collection could be acquired if the same price was offered as for Salt (265,000 francs). However, this letter had no effect either. The minister answered that Reinhold was to wait calmly and to report if the final offer was rejected. He had to be careful that no other party bought the collection for 200,000 francs. Now Reinhold's phlegm disappeared. He wrote to Humbert:

> Patience again, and do not let the collection slip away for 200,000 francs!! And now, do not go through the roof when reading this: 'My dear Sir, remember the composure, which is an innate characteristic of the Batavian offspring: once it brought us triumphantly into the river Thames. Those times are over, but I hope that it will now succeed in uniting the rivers Nile and Rhine.'[34]

In February Humbert reached his limit: he offered the final 200,000 francs. Again this offer was rejected, but Tossizza lowered the price to 300,000 francs. As an incentive twenty silver statuettes and a papyrus were added to the collection. He gave the Netherlands forty days to consider this offer. After this period the price would rise again to 320,000 francs.

REUVENS' THIRD VALUATION: 'THE PRICE HALF-WAY BETWEEN SALT AND DROVETTI'

The stream of new information about the d'Anastasy collection with its supplements forced Reuvens to reconsider his earlier valuations. When he heard that the last offer of 200,000 francs had been rejected, he wrote a new report, in which he valued the d'Anastasy collection above that of Salt.[35] In

his report he gave two reasons for changing his view. First, the new information added much to the value: there appeared to be more pharaohs' names on
the objects than mentioned in the catalogue, a great asset for the historical
value of the collection. Another drawback had been the material of the larger
pieces of sculpture. They were made of 'soft Egyptian limestone, which can
be carved with a pocket knife' and not in costly materials like 'granite,
porphyry or basalt, elements so hard that Dutch chisels are bound to bounce
off it'. But the condition of many of the limestone statues was perfect, according to Reinhold and Humbert (see for example Figure 7.3), and this could
be said of only three large statues in the Salt collection. Finally Reuvens used
an argument which he had also stressed during the negotiations over the
Corazzi collection: this was probably the last opportunity to buy a large collection of Egyptian antiquities. Drovetti and Salt did sell pieces occasionally, but
not in these numbers. Reuvens' conclusion was that the d'Anastasy collection
could be compared with the Salt collection in large statuary, and was better
in all other categories. In his report he proposed to offer the 'middle price
between Salt and Drovetti': 300,000 francs, or about 150,000 guilders:

> The best reason to bid the middle price between Salt and Drovetti
> is that d'Anastasy's collection, although of less artistic value, offers
> much more interest for Egyptian history and archaeology than the
> Salt collection, and that in all probability there is no chance that
> such a splendid assembly will ever be created again.[36]

THE BREAKTHROUGH

Reuvens had been forced to revise his valuation three times, first because of
lack of information, and later due to mistrust of the reports he was receiving,
and of the selling party. Amid all his other occupations he had had to buckle
down to very intricate comparisons and conflicting information from letters
and catalogues. In his own perception he had given a good explanation for
his different valuations and the resulting difficulties. The ministry brought
his proposal to offer 300,000 francs without comment to the attention of
King Willem I. His majesty was not amused at all: he had agreed to spend
the maximum amount of the first valuation (between 80,000 and 200,000
francs), and now had to learn that this maximum was by far not enough:

> From your report of the 20th of this month His Majesty concludes
> that now a sum of no less than three times 100,000 francs is being
> asked. The King does not find any liberty to spend such an amount
> of money on this collection, although he is disappointed that this
> will end the prospect of enriching the cabinet of antiquities with
> this assembly.[37]

Figure 7.3 Limestone statue of Maya, minister under the pharaohs Tutankhamun and Horemheb, and his wife Merit, from Saqqara, *c.*1300 BC. National Museum of Antiquities.

As a proof of his good will, the king did give permission to raise the bidding one last time, by a further 30,000 francs. If this offer were rejected, the negotiations would have to end. Nobody believed in a positive outcome any more.

In this atmosphere of dismay the correct procedures were not even observed. The department instructed Humbert directly about the final bid and the end of the negotiations, without a formal letter to Reinhold first. When Reinhold asked Humbert about the state of affairs, he had to read the letter twice: the final bid of 230,000 francs had been accepted and the d'Anastasy collection was now the property of the government. He complimented Humbert with the words: 'I congratulate you on this interesting acquisition and I am convinced that the government will do justice to all the pains you have spent upon this affair.'[38]

With this unexpected turn of events ended a period of more than eleven months of negotiations. Why D'Anastasy accepted the last offer of 230,000 francs can only be guessed at. Probably he had become aware of the absence of other European competition and preferred to be sure of a buyer, even if this meant receiving less than he had hoped for. The Dutch government was lucky that the big players, especially France and Britain, had been well provided with these kind of antiquities only a few years earlier.

EPILOGUE: THREE GIFTS AND AN UNRELIABLE MERCHANT

The rest of the year 1828 was spent by Humbert on the logistics of packing and shipping the enormous number of antiquities in the harbour of Livorno. The heavy weight of many objects and the fragility of others posed problems for the ship's crew. The ship had to be smoked out to destroy all mice and rats, which otherwise would have devoured the delicate mummies. In October 1828 the HM *Zeemeeuw* left the port of Livorno for her journey to the Netherlands. After a near shipwreck in the Bay of Biscay, the ship arrived in the harbour of Hellevoetsluis on 1 December 1828. The antiquities were delivered in Leiden on New Year's day 1829: the Nile had indeed now been connected with the Rhine.

In the meantime Humbert had his last dealings with Tossizza. During the negotiations D'Anastasy had written a *triplicata* to his three agents that the future buyer of his collection should receive a bonus, consisting of three objects: a Byzantine bronze helmet (said to have been found on a mummy), a Greek manuscript and a bilingual papyrus in Greek and Demotic. D'Anastasy had hoped to speed up negotiations with the prospect of this gift. Tossizza, the main negotiator, had not mentioned this information to Humbert, and even after the closing of the deal remained silent about the three gifts. Barthou, in every respect a gentleman, informed Humbert about this misconduct of Tossizza before leaving for Alexandria. Humbert confronted Tossizza with this news, but the merchant denied any knowledge about three presents. When Humbert engaged a lawyer and threatened legal proceedings, Tossizza's memory suddenly came back to him: he admitted having read the *triplicata*, but claimed that Jean d'Anastasy had changed his mind later in view of the stinginess of the other party. Humbert made preparations to start a lawsuit against Tossizza, when a letter from Alexandria arrived, signed by Jean d'Anastasy. The consul-general had had a talk with Barthou about the recent events in Livorno, and was angry with Tossizza's free interpretation concerning the meaning of the *triplicata*. He apologized for his agent's behaviour and ordered the three objects to be given immediately to the new owner of his collection. Humbert experienced one of his finest hours when he received a letter from The Hague with compliments about the way he had concluded the negotiations, although he did not receive the high military decoration he had hoped for. Reinhold explained to him that his actions were certainly a solid proof of loyalty to his country, but could not be regarded as a military exploit.

END OF THE EXPEDITION: THE NANI-TIEPOLO AND PACILEO COLLECTIONS

The acquisition of the d'Anastasy collection marked the peak in Reuvens' collecting policy, but also the end. Reuvens realized that the chances of Humbert going to North Africa had become very small, but there was still a year and a half left of the time allocated to the expedition. He also realized that the purchase of a collection of Egyptian antiquities of this size and quality made the gaps in the other departments look more prominent than ever. In various reports to the ministry he stressed the importance of making use of Humbert's prolonged stay in Italy to fill the lacunae in the collection. The museum now possessed an Egyptian collection, which Reuvens considered to be third in importance in Europe, after those in Turin and Paris. Academic use of the collection was still limited, because students lacked the basic knowledge of Egyptology, but the general public would be very impressed by the admirable products of Egyptian art. Reuvens stressed the fact that Egyptian monumental objects such as obelisks and large sarcophagi were still missing. With regard to Greek and Roman antiquities, these 'appealed directly to the sense of beauty' and were very useful for students because of their direct bond with the classical authors. Through the study of Greek and Roman art, archaeology could gain its place in society. But the collections were far from ideal and the museums of Paris, Berlin, London and Munich were all much better equipped than that of Leiden: 'Now that our Egyptian collection stands equal in stature with the best museums, the imperfection of the classical sculpture gallery is an abuse in the eyes of travellers and our own public.'[39] The same was true for the collection of Greek ceramics, of which the museum possessed only mediocre pieces from Rottiers' collections.

Reuvens tried to convince the department to use the presence of Humbert in Italy to buy monumental Egyptian sculptures, Greek and Roman statuary and Greek vases: collections of these kinds were still available, but the possibility of buying them 'hung by a silken thread' and could be gone within the next years. Humbert got permission to make two journeys to Italy in search of these collections, but it was made clear that he was only allowed to express interest in the collections, and not to start negotiations.

In search for ancient sculpture Humbert travelled to Venice, where a part of the Nani-Tiepolo collection was still for sale.[40] With the aid of the Dutch consulate he made contact with the owners of this collection of Greek and Roman statuary, and promised to keep in touch with a view to the possible purchase of the collection.[41] During his travels he bought some antiquities and received a medal which was struck in 1822 in honour of Giacomo Tommasini, professor of medicine at the University of Bologna. The medal was offered to the University of Leiden.

After the short trip to Venice Humbert travelled to Naples to investigate the possibilities of buying a collection of Greek ceramics. The journey took him also to Florence and Rome. In Florence he visited the Uffizi Gallery and studied the 800 recently excavated vases from Sarteano. He also made coloured drawings of the Egyptian rooms in the archaeological museum, which were designed by Rosellini and Champollion le Jeune.[42]

In Rome he met Eduard Gerhard, the founder of the *Istituto di Corrispondenza Archeologica* with whom he visited the exhibition of 1,500 Greek vases, which had been excavated near Vulci on the estate of Lucien Bonaparte, the prince of Canino. A selection of these vases came to the Leiden museum in 1839, as shall be described later. In Rome Humbert also met an old acquaintance, Johann Martin von Wagner (see Chapter 6, page 76), who had been responsible for the acquisition and restoration of the archaic sculptures from the temple of Aphaia on Aegina. Humbert ordered a set of casts of these sculptures, which arrived in Leiden in November 1830.

On 22 December 1829 Humbert left Rome and he arrived in Naples three days later. His main interest was in the collection of vases owned by the company Pacileo, Gargiulo and De Crescenzo. The collection comprised over 1,500 Greek and south Italian vases of different epochs and sizes, 250 terracotta statuettes, 467 bronzes, 223 pieces of jewellery, 35 glass vessels, 40 marble sculptures (of which 19 were modern) and 15 models in cork of ancient buildings. The price asked for the whole collection was 85,450 francesconi, the equivalent of around 240,000 guilders: 120,000 guilders more than had been paid for the d'Anastasy collection!

The catalogue of the collection was written by Raffaele Gargiulo, who combined his post as *professore* in the Royal Museum in Naples with his activities as antiques dealer in the Pacileo firm. The chronological system Gargiulo used (see Appendix 2 for the full text) is interesting.[43]

In his catalogue Gargiulo divided the *vasi Italo-Greci* into six chronological classes: the *lavoro greco remotissimo* (Corinthian ware), the *vasi dipinti con figure nere graffite sul campo giallastro* (Attic black figure), the style of *dipingere il campo nero, rilasciando le figure del color dell'argilla cotta* (Attic red figure), the period in which *l'arte del disegno incominciava a deteriorare* (late Attic and south Italian red figure), the style with *poco di cambiamento, decadimento del disegno* (late south Italian red figure and some Etruscan red figure). The last category comprised objects *di cattivo stile nel dipinto, imitando anche le tre prime originali epoche*. Judging from the illustrations, this section treated the Etruscan imitations of Corinthian and Attic black- and red-figure wares.

Humbert sent the catalogue of the Pacileo collection to Leiden, together with 243 drawings of the most important vases in the collection, which were especially made on his orders.[44] He also sent imitations and forgeries of Greek vases to Reuvens. A very interesting report concerning the trade in antiquities completed this dossier about the collection of Onofrio Pacileo. Humbert provided a good insight into the legal, semi-legal and illegal ways of exporting vases from the kingdom of Naples. Some countries used the diplomatic bag:

> A commission has been established by the Government of Naples, which considers all antiquities one would like to export. A high degree of rareness prohibits the object from leaving the country. There are, however, ways to export rare vases from the Kingdom of Naples, and these are related to considerations of rank and influence. Foreign diplomats attached to the Court of Naples can obtain, through the service of the Foreign Office, a permit to export a certain number of crates, thus avoiding a visit by the Customs Office, if they are labelled *oggetti d'uso* or 'domestic objects'. In reality these crates are filled with antiquities, mostly vases. The Minister of Foreign Affairs is aware of these practices, fully knowing the meaning of the term *oggetti d'uso*, but pretends not to. This favour, however, is not offered in the same way to every foreign diplomat. There are preferences.[45]

Humbert was not able to buy much in Naples. Apart from the imitations of Greek pottery, he acquired books, engravings, two cork models of Greek graves (from Santa Agata de'Goti and Paestum), some weaponry and a model of a column from the temple of Neptune in Paestum. On his way back to Livorno he had a meeting in Rome with Anton Reinhard Falck, who had retired from politics. Humbert discussed with him the idea of founding a Dutch cultural institute in Rome on the model of the *Istituto di Corrispondenza Archeologica*, with Humbert as its secretary. Falck was enthusiastic about the idea and did his best in The Hague to find support, to no avail. It was not until 1904 that the Dutch Historical Institute in Rome came into being.

Humbert was facing the end of the expedition. For the future he saw two possibilities: either a third expedition to Italy to resume the negotiations in Venice and Naples, or an active role in the founding of a new permanent institute in Rome. Carthage was further away than ever.

On 27 April 1830, four days before leaving for the Netherlands, Humbert made his last purchases in Livorno: an Egyptian stela and seven fragments from a decorated Egyptian tomb. The vendor was Francesco de Castiglione, one of the former agents of d'Anastasy. Once in Leiden, the fragments turned out to belong together and had once decorated the tomb of Horemheb, general under Tutankhamun, and later a pharaoh himself (see Figure 7.4).[46] Another piece of the same relief in the possession of De Castiglione was later sold to the Kunsthistorisches Museum in Vienna.[47]

In June 1830 Humbert arrived in Leiden, where he was instructed by Reuvens to start working on the Borgia manuscripts bought by the government in

Figure 7.4 Relief with the honouring of General Horemheb, from Saqqara, *c.*1330 BC.
National Museum of Antiquities.

1829. Humbert had to go through the corrupt text, make amendments
and corrections and complete the plans which he had made in 1822–4. In
1831 Humbert was free to leave Leiden. Because of the political situation
a third expedition was not possible and without payment he was not willing
to continue working in Leiden on the Borgia manuscripts. He decided to
return to Livorno, where 'at least he could live pleasantly' on his meagre
military pension of 1,500 guilders.

Humbert's final years in Italy were not easy. He noticed a certain decline
in Reuvens' interest in the publication of the Borgia manuscripts, especially
after C.T. Falbe's outstanding monograph on the topography of ancient
Carthage, which was published in 1833.[48] Reuvens was concentrating more
and more on the catalogue of the Egyptian antiquities and on the publication
of his excavations at Arentsburg/Forum Hadriani (see next chapter). In 1834
Humbert once more travelled to Leiden and tried to renew co-operation with
Reuvens on the Borgia manuscripts. However, bad health prevented him
from doing much work: in five months he received 152 visits from his doctor,
who tried to ease his stomach aches and attacks of rheumatism. Reuvens did
his best to arrange compensation for Humbert's travelling expenses, and in

May the colonel left the Netherlands for good. His prospects of marriage with Margherita Terreni (see Chapter 6, note 21) were thwarted because of serious difficulties in Italy with the church, which did not permit a union between a Protestant and a Catholic. Their affection and friendship did not survive these setbacks.

In 1838 Humbert tried to travel to the Netherlands a last time, but before he reached the Alps he had to return because of a sudden illness. He was taken to a hospital in Pisa, and later to Livorno, where he died after a long period confined to his bed, in February 1839. He was buried in the Cimitero della Nazione Olandese-Alemanna in Livorno. In his will Humbert had ordered the following text to be put on his gravestone:

Ci-gît
Jean Emile Humbert
Qui fut utile aux sciences
Par ses découvertes sur les ruines
de Carthage
Né à La Haye le 28 Juillet 1771
Mort à Livourne le 20 Fevrier 1839[49]

In his will Humbert bequeathed his private collection of antiquities to the museum in Leiden. Five Egyptian statuettes, some scarabs, amulets and two Attic red-figure lekythoi were the last pieces of a long series in the museum which was inventoried with a capital H for Humbert.

8

FORUM HADRIANI
Digging behind the dunes

Thus we got three distinct terms, Barbarians, Philistines,
Populace, to denote roughly the three great classes into which
our society is divided.

Matthew Arnold (1822–88)

THE SEARCH FOR FORUM HADRIANI

As in most countries, the history of excavations in the Netherlands starts
with painful stories about the destruction of archaeological sites during
digging activities without any scholarly aim, documentation or record of the
finds. Before the creation of an archaeological chair in Leiden many archaeological sites in the Netherlands had been excavated with the sole aim of
finding either 'curiosities' or building material. Sites were pillaged in search
of the valuable tuff (a rock formed of consolidated volcanic ash), which the
Romans had imported and used in constructing their fortresses and cities.
Such sites often carried toponymical elements in their name that marked
them as ancient 'castles' (*burchten*), like Brittenburg at the coast near Katwijk
('British castle'), Roomburg near Leiden ('Roman castle') and Voorburg near
The Hague (derived from the Latin name Forum Hadriani). Due to the
scarcity of natural stone in the Netherlands, the foundations of these forts
and cities had been excavated thoroughly from medieval times onwards.

Reuvens was very interested in archaeological excavations, which, as he
pointed out in his inaugural speech, were useful in solving problems concerning the ancient topography of the Netherlands. Archaeology could shed
light on questions which could not be answered by studying the ancient
writers alone.[1]

The first excavations directed by Reuvens were made by Colonel Humbert
during his stay in Tunisia in 1822–4. Although Reuvens had not been able
to act as a field director *in situ*, he was very specific in his instructions
and methods. He emphasized the need for plans, drawings and notes. Grave
contents needed to be inventoried and kept together, with a specimen of the

112

skeleton (if possible the skull). He also desired to have earth samples to make a chemical analysis of the soil of the Carthaginian peninsula: in this way it would be possible to distinguish the soil of the peninsula from the later alluviations and deposits of the river Medjerdah, which had altered the original coastline of the peninsula.

Rottiers, too, had been asked to excavate in Greece and provide plans, notes and measurements from his travels in 1824–6. On the island of Melos he worked according to these instructions, and he made quite accurate plans of the excavated area, which allow us to identify with certainty the place where he and his crew excavated in August 1825.

The first excavations in the Netherlands with Reuvens as a field director started in 1827 on the site of the ancient Roman settlement of Forum Hadriani. The *Fossa Corbulonis*, constructed by the Roman general Corbulo around AD 47 between the river Rhine and the *Helinium* (the estuary of the Meuse) used a number of natural creeks and newly dug canals to create a passage between the two important rivers, behind the dunes and the North Sea. Alongside this canal lay the town Forum Hadriani, the political centre of the tribe of the *Cananefates*. The native settlement of the *Civitas Cananefatium* was elevated to the status of a Roman marketplace by the emperor Hadrian, when he visited the northern frontier in AD 120–21. The town was promoted to a *municipium* by Antoninus Pius before 162 AD: the name then changed into *Municipium Aelium Cananefatium*. Some hundred years later the city was destroyed by German tribes during the disorders and the collapse of this part of the Roman border (*limes*) around 270 AD.

Forum Hadriani is mentioned on the late Roman Peutinger Map, south of the river Rhine, which formed the border of the Roman empire: the exact location of the Roman town had aroused scholarly interest since the seventeenth century. Near the village of Voorburg, Roman finds were unearthed on a somewhat higher ridge of sand, which was known as the *Hooge Burg* ('the high castle'). It was speculated that this could be the site of Forum Hadriani. Alongside the modern canal De Vliet, the successor of the *Fossa Corbulonis* between the Rhine and Meuse, a number of luxurious country seats had been built, especially in the neighbourhood of The Hague. Near one of these houses, the country seat Arentsburg, an important find was made in 1771: a more than life-size bronze hand, which had been part of a Roman statue (see Figure 8.1). The hand was exhibited in The Hague, where it aroused international interest. The Russian diplomat Prince Gallitzin obtained permission to borrow the hand and take it with him to St Petersburg, where it was used by E.-M. Falconet as a model for the hand of Peter the Great on the equestrian statue of the czar in that city.

In January 1826 Reuvens received a letter from his colleague de Jonge, director of the Royal Coin Cabinet in The Hague, informing him about two important issues: the bronze hand was for sale and there were plans to sell the country house of Arentsburg with its estates: 'Arentsburg is being sold

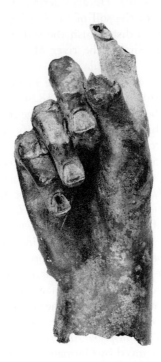

Figure 8.1 Bronze hand of a Roman statue, found in 1771 at Arentsburg (Forum Hadriani), second century AD. National Museum of Antiquities.

this spring. It would be desirable that the government bought that piece of land and let you excavate it properly. Who knows, you could find the whole statue! Talk about it with Ewyck. Vale!'[2]

On 10 February Reuvens wrote a letter to the department, starting with a eulogy of archaeological fieldwork in the rest of Europe. The Netherlands were now offered a chance to investigate one of the most promising sites in the country, 'the only place in the province of Holland which offers a possibility of finding Roman antiquities, and important ones too. [. . .] The chance of finding the statue (although it could have rusted away or been destroyed in antiquity) nevertheless exists, and the discovery would be marvellous.'[3]

Reuvens proposed that the department buy Arentsburg with its estate for archaeological investigation. After the excavations, which would take at least two years, the ministry could sell the country house again: the costs would be limited to the campaigns during the summer months. The project was approved by the department and in April 1826 Arentsburg was bought for excavations, which were to start in the summer of 1827. Reuvens was asked to write a report with an estimate of the yearly costs of the excavations.

The year 1826 was extremely busy for Reuvens. Rottiers had returned from Greece and a report about these travels was needed, based on the chaotic notes of the colonel. Moreover Reuvens had to compile a list of instructions for Humbert's second expedition to Italy and North Africa and he was busy with the project for a new museum building. When the department warned Reuvens in December 1826 that they had to have a financial overview of the following year's excavations, the professor broke down. On New Year's day 1827 he wrote:

> You have already asked me for a swift reply. When this letter reached me, I was busy with other work, which you stressed was also very urgent. And you will remember the other intricate reports which I had to write, with no time for other important work, about the collections of Cimba and Lescluze; about the journeys of Mr Rottiers, and the next expedition of Mr Humbert, and only yesterday about a project for a new museum. It is not possible for me to finish all these reports in time: I have to prepare my lectures and exams with time for study and correction. The exams have been very busy during the last term and the Department is asking me to hasten my plans for publications and to write reports on various subjects, which I have to study thoroughly. What is thus to become of normal study? What is to become of the career of a professor who has to give up normal research? I believe study and research are the main source from which all other activities must stem. To prevent them is to cut down the tree in order to pick the fruits.[4]

Reuvens estimated the costs for the campaign to be 5,000 guilders. But the complaints about his workload, combined with this high estimate of the cost of the excavation at Arentsburg, now turned against the project. The department began to question the whole project. Was a sum of 5,000 guilders needed to excavate a piece of land, without the certainty that precious antiquities were to be found? Obviously in the view of Reuvens' principals the main interest of excavations lay in finding valuable ancient objects. For them excavating was equivalent to treasure hunting and it could be

> very foolish to spend so many thousands on a very uncertain chance of finding something substantial. With that amount of money one could buy a whole collection. Is it not wiser to do exactly that? Moreover, the excavations will keep you away from useful studies. Maybe these thoughts have crossed your mind too, and I would like to hear your private opinion before we carry on. The saying goes that it is better to stop now than to err later. It seems that this also applies to this case.[5]

Again Reuvens had to explain the real importance of archaeological field-work. In his reply he summed up the reasons why other countries in Europe invested in excavations. He did not shrink from some exaggeration: 'The political tide could turn against the government', if it continued not to be interested in archaeological fieldwork:

> I cannot say it too often, although I have to repeat it every time when the shipments from Rottiers and Humbert arrive: archaeology does not benefit from a single pot, a coin or even a statue, but from the consequences of these finds for the study of ancient topography and history. The question of Voorburg, of its possible identification with Forum Hadriani, is one of the main issues in the debate about the ancient topography of our country. Will foreigners not say that the Dutch Government speaks a lot about fostering archaeology, but when things get serious steps back with its usual parsimony? I am convinced that not to start the excavations would be a major scholarly and administrative lapse. It would set back the budding profession more than acquiring many collections has made it grow, and it would generate a general distrust about the Government's sincerity as regards scholarly endeavours. All the absolute sovereigns in Italy, France, Austria, Prussia and Russia spend money on such enterprises. Is a Constitutional State unwilling to give funds for such things? Will not all ultra-monarchists in and outside our country say that indeed such endeavours are unthinkable in a Constitutional State, and will not the Belgians, who have more feelings for such things than the Dutch, have one more reason to wish back the French or the Austrian Government? I will spend my time on this subject, as well as on others. I am able to treat one subject without neglecting others. This opportunity is unique, and will not return for the country or for me.[6]

By royal decree of 4 February 1827 a sum of 5,000 guilders was reserved for the excavations at Arentsburg. A fence was placed around the estates and Reuvens got permission to take up his residence in the country house to conduct the excavations. The owners of the neighbouring houses looked askance upon these activities. In particular H.J. Caan, who worked at the Ministry of the Interior and owned the country estate De Hoekenburg, was very interested in the developments on the other side of his fence. At first he offered his help with the financial administration of the excavations, but soon it became clear that he had only his own interests in mind. He objected to fencing the ground, which would obstruct one of the footpaths (he had the right of way), and he also protested against the cutting down of trees, necessary for the digging and to provide wood for the fences. After months of exchanging legal correspondence it was decided that Caan would have access through the fence around Arentsburg and that twenty-three trees adjoining his property would be for the time being left standing. As soon as Reuvens moved into Arentsburg he took over the financial administration from Caan, feeling that this was just the beginning of a complicated relationship with the esquire.

START OF THE EXCAVATIONS: 'SHERDS OF TILES, POTS AND URNS'

On 22 June 1827 Reuvens began the excavations, assisted by his students Pieter Otto van der Chijs and Conrad Leemans. Reuvens had decided to start on the spot where the bronze hand had been found in 1771.[7] The site had been established by interviewing witnesses of the find, who could give such directions as 'twenty or thirty paces from the old entrance of the wood, and then two or three paces somewhat eastward'.[8] Reuvens knew that the department and society in general viewed his endeavours very critically. It is not unlikely that he wanted to impress public opinion about archaeology with a spectacular find, which coming at the start of his excavations would do no harm to the image of archaeology. In other respects, too, he remembered public relations: during the first season of the digs he organized public viewings and conducted tours, which attracted more than 600 people. However, although expectations were high, the bronze statue never materialized. On the chosen spot the first finds consisted of 'sherds of tiles, pots and urns etc., found at the depth of 2 and 3 feet'.[9]

Reuvens spent all summer on the estate. He lived at Arentsburg with his family, the students Van der Chijs and Leemans and two draughtsmen, W.J. Gordon and T. Hooiberg. When the university term started in September, he travelled to and fro to Leiden five times a week by boat. From the neighbouring villages he hired personnel to do the digging, by preference 'fathers of large families', who were the most reliable. Finding an object was worth a bonus of ten cents, which made for healthy competition. Girls helped with washing the sherds. At the height of the season forty-two men were working in the field in two shifts.

The first preliminary report of his findings was published in the *Nederlandsche Staatscourant*, the official gazette, of 12 October 1827. Reuvens started his article by summing up the achievements of other European nations in the field of national heritage, and praised the Dutch government for the fact that archaeological fieldwork had started in the Netherlands too. Reuvens called the results of the first campaign 'already very important and interesting for the ancient history of the land, and for archaeology in general'.[10] Foundations of a building had been found, with the walls still intact to a height of half a metre. Other walls had been dug out, recognizable only from a 'faint discolouring of the earth'.[11] Reuvens interpreted two lower rooms as cellars, both with a well. A long, broad foundation nearby these

Figure 8.2 C.J.C. Reuvens and Conrad Leemans at the excavations at Arentsburg. Drawing, probably by T. Hooiberg, *c.*1829. Archive, National Museum of Antiquities.

rooms was described as possibly the remains of the city wall. Tiles with legionary stamps were also found. In his diary Reuvens mentioned examples of the 10th, the 16th and the 30th legions, and of the army of Lower Germany (*Exercitus Germaniae Inferioris*). And of course loads of sherds, pottery and glass: 'Very much broken glass surfaced, which, judging from the ears etc., belonged to medium-sized vessels.'[12] Metal utensils and jewellery had come to light, and many bronze and copper coins. The most interesting object was a small bronze statuette of a dog. The building with cellars was tentatively interpreted by Reuvens as a villa. As long as the weather permitted, Reuvens continued his digging: 'We will try to keep the excavations open and visible, as long as the season permits. Amateurs of antiquities, who would like to see the excavations, can present themselves at the estate on all days between 12 and 1½ hours, stating their name and capacity.'[13]

In 1828 Reuvens continued the work, searching for the remains of the building. In spite of 'enormous downpours in the months of July and August', he was not dissatisfied with the results. He changed his earlier interpretation of the remains as belonging to a Roman villa: the emerging plan looked like a series of buildings rather than one coherent edifice. He was especially pleased with two finds: a building with the Roman heating system (hypocaust) and an enigmatic skeleton of a woman:

> We have found various rooms, which were heated by furnaces below ground level (called *hypocausta* by the ancients), of which the lower floor with the small pillars (on which the ground floor rested) was very well preserved. Many of the tiles, of which the small pillars were made, had the stamp EX GER INF (Army of Lower Germany). Last year we suspected the existence of *hypocausta* from the shape of some of the bricks, but we did not find one intact.
>
> But the most important find of all is without doubt a skeleton, of which the upper part has been preserved perfectly in its original position. It seems to be female, oriented with the head towards the East. The left arm is placed with the hand on the stomach, as if the arm had been wrapped in a piece of clothing. The right hand rests on the chest. At the height of the neck, between the clavicles, a clothing pin (fibula) of normal Roman shape has rusted onto the bone. On the left wrist there is a double bracelet, and at the height of the left breast two other fibulas have been found. The head and the elbows rest on loose pieces of brick. This discovery is very remarkable, because the body was found inside the buildings, near the best-preserved hypocaust of the main building. There are some indications that there may have been cinerary urns, which we will examine with chemical tests.[14]

Reuvens was intrigued by this find. In his view the fibulas and bracelet pointed to a Roman burial, but one inside the city walls. The amount of care in the burial (the head and elbows resting on bricks, and the arms folded) ruled out a violent or illegal interment. Reuvens ordered detailed drawings of the half corpse, and engaged a sculptor to make a series of plaster casts of the skeleton, which he intended to present to archaeological museums and societies in Europe:

> The discovery of the skeleton must have a prolonged use for the study of antiquity and ethnology: I have succeeded in making a plaster cast of it, under the supervision of the sculptor Royer. This cast, which has only touched the uppermost part of the bones, has to be touched up by the artist, for which he has not yet had time. Once this work is done, I intend to send copies of the cast as a gift to Dutch public museums and to some of the most important archaeological museums abroad.[15]

Reuvens presented casts of the skeleton to museums in Paris, Berlin, Munich, Breslau and Stuttgart. His successor Leemans later offered copies to the British Museum and the Society of Antiquaries. To date only the cast in the collections of the Muséum d'Histoire Naturelle in Paris has been recovered: the piece was found in the depots of the associated Musée de l'Homme in February 2002, splendidly preserved with the original colouring of the bones and the bronze jewellery (Figure 8.3).[16] Most probably the skeleton belongs to the period after the destruction of Forum Hadriani (c. AD 270). There are indications that tribes of German origin had lived inside the ruined city walls and may have used part of the site as a burial ground.

During the excavations Reuvens was assisted, as stated, by his students Pieter Otto van der Chijs and Conrad Leemans. Van der Chijs had studied classical languages but an interest in numismatics had taken him to the lessons of Reuvens, who recognized a sharp intellect and tried to help his career. But the rough life in the field did not appeal much to the classicist. He was assigned to keep the diary of the excavations, but already the first pages show that he lacked an archaeologist's eye. Every evening Reuvens had to change in red ink large parts of the diary '. . . especially because my notes are an improvement of the earlier remarks of Mr vdC, which otherwise would be unintelligible'.[17] At the end of August Reuvens took over the diary completely. During the following season in 1828 he gave the task to Leemans. The months in Arentsburg led to an estrangement between Reuvens and Van der Chijs, who was well aware that he could not meet the high demands of his professor.[18] Van der Chijs returned to his numismatic studies and became the leading expert on medieval coins of the Netherlands. As the director of the university's coin collection he joined rooms with the archaeological museum in 1837, by then under the guidance of Conrad Leemans. The renewed acquaintance of Reuvens' former pupils was not made without problems, as shall be described later.

Figure 8.3 Plaster cast of a female skeleton, found at Arentsburg, donated by Reuvens to the Muséum d'Histoire Naturelle in Paris in 1829. Paris, Muséum d'Histoire Naturelle.

INVENTING ARCHAEOLOGY: FIELDWORK AND DOCUMENTATION

Digging in the Dutch soil and interpreting hardly recognizable vestiges of human activity was not an easy task for the pioneers. The diary of the excavations reads like a voyage of discovery with new challenges daily. Very often the tuff foundations had been dug out, and only the discolouring of the soil indicated the original outline of walls. To distinguish these discolourations from the adjoining soil, Reuvens gave orders to level the soil with sharp spades ('to skim off the ground'). Reuvens was the first Dutch archaeologist to discover techniques by trial and error. To help future generations of archaeologists he made a list of advice at the end of the diary. On interpreting colourations he wrote, for example:

A long trench is often needed to start the research, but there is the danger of losing the coherence. When workmen find a few stones in a trench, they often throw them out, because the foundation is so weak that they do not recognize it as such. Digging a trench to pursue a foundation is not advisable because you miss all kinds of small peculiarities. Thus we would never have noticed the foundations of columns and the wells. [. . .] Foundations of one and the same building do not appear at the same level at different places. The workmen must be instructed not to throw away stones which

121

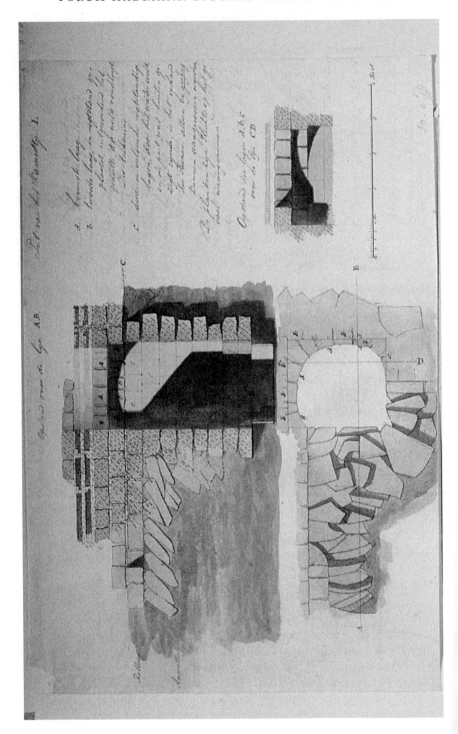

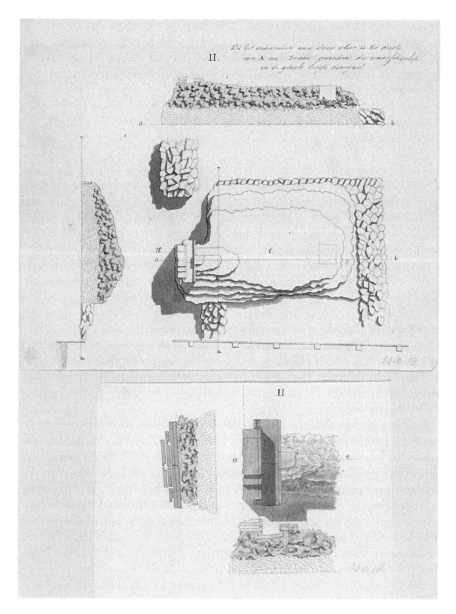

Figure 8.4 Plans and sections of the excavations at Arentsburg, 1827–30. Drawings by T. Hooiberg and W. Gordon. Archive, National Museum of Antiquities.

they find in the upper layers. [. . .] However, much is lost by the investigation itself, before one recognizes what is in front of him.

The deep traces of black ground, which one can see sharply against the untouched soil, are without doubt the result of human activities, and nearly always foundations. If those have been dug out, they are still recognizable by small remaining pieces of stone. If small stones are missing, then they are probably conduits for water, for example for leaden pipes.[19]

The drawings during the excavations were made by two young draughtsmen, Timen Hooiberg and the Englishman William Gordon. Reuvens ordered three types of field drawings: drawings of the horizontal plane, vertical sections and three-dimensional perspective elevations. The importance of profile drawings was stressed by Reuvens. On some three-dimensional drawings small trenches can be seen, perpendicular to the foundations. By using this technique, the foundations remained in contact with the surrounding soil, which could give dating elements for the constructions. Other drawings show sections and profiles (Figure 8.4). It is clear that the excavator Meadows Taylor in 1851 was not 'the first man to hint implicitly at the true function of the excavator and recorder with a technical competence far in advance of the time'.[20]

It is quite possible that Reuvens was inspired to use sections and profiles by the drawings which Humbert had made during his campaign of 1822–4 in Tunisia, as shown in Figure 6.4. In his diary he mentions Humbert as one of his main advisors on excavating techniques. The skills of the engineer could also be used for archaeology.

Reuvens intended to use the modern printing process of lithography for the final publication of the finds at Arentsburg. This new technique was known to Reuvens from the experiments of Dominique-Vivant Denon, who had worked with lithography around 1817, dissatisfied as he was with the quality of copperplate engravings. A year later a handbook of lithography was published by Aloys Senefelder, the man who had invented the technique some twenty years earlier.[21] In Leiden Humbert de Superville had also worked with lithography and may have acquainted Reuvens with his results. During the summer months Reuvens' draughtsmen Hooiberg and Gordon made sketches and water-colour drawings in the field. In the winter they reworked these drawings and created coloured lithographs for the final publication.

END OF THE EXCAVATIONS: 'THE OLD STATE OF STAGNATION'

Reuvens had hoped to finish the excavations at Arentsburg in two years, but due to the bad weather he had lost a lot of time during the first campaigns. In 1829 the department took steps to put an end to the digs, much to the distress of Reuvens. Reuvens asked the department for at least another campaign: to stop now would mean a terrible loss of face and 'many reproaches of objective foreign judgements, and aversion if not contempt, to say the least, of civilized travellers'.[22] He felt that he had to convince his critics and not give in against all 'prejudice, laziness and interference'. Excavations were new in the Netherlands and the first results had not impressed Reuvens' critics, who jeered about his 'science des pots cassés'. The department proposed to let the excavations continue till 1831, but with a yearly budget reduced from 5,000 to a mere 1,600 guilders. On this low budget Reuvens excavated again during the seasons of 1829 and 1830, but after the uprising in Belgium in 1830 the whole budget was cancelled. Reuvens asked the permission of the king to continue the excavations using his own money to pay the workmen.

In the meantime Mr Caan, owner of the neighbouring estate, was developing his own ideas about the future of Arentsburg. He made a proposition to the department to buy the country house as soon as the excavations ended. To establish an objective price for the house he stipulated that during the period of taxation all archaeological activities should stop to prevent further damage to trees and meadows. In exchange he suggested the possibility of some research on his estate De Hoekenburg, which could be interesting for the interpretation of the buildings already discovered. A period of negotiations, taxations and reappraisals started, during which Reuvens had to remain idle: time was on Caan's side and department officials were more interested in selling the country house at a good price than in the results of the excavations. Impatient about the delay, Reuvens tried to persuade the minister with a confidential letter, in which he complained about Caan's behaviour and the influence of wealth, power and nobility at the cost of his profession:

> I hope that I am allowed to formulate a few thoughts of a general nature. The masses are self-seeking and not interested in noble feelings. But in this country there are a few, otherwise very honourable, citizens who try to strangle everything including sciences and the arts in order to let avarice prevail in our nation, and to return everything to the old state of stagnation (if I may call it thus). It is this spirit that now scorns the new scholarly endeavours. But I think it is in the interest of the Government and eventually in the general interest of all citizens that this spirit does not gain too many victories over the better judgement of the High Government. It is true: an archaeological excavation does not have the immediate benefit of a beautiful collection or a rich library. But the unique opportunity which will never return, and the strong willingness of His Majesty to let this endeavour end properly, are very serious reasons to regard the interruption of the excavation as a new victory of certain classes and their spirit.[23]

In a later letter Reuvens gave Caan's reasons to prevent him from excavating:

> I dare notify Your Excellency that the reason for Mr Caan's behaviour and deliberate lingering seems to be one of these: either to prevent me from excavating on his fields during the winter months, because maybe he fears for more damage during the wet season – something that he has accomplished perfectly, or to let the deal fall through, so as to prevent me from digging on his field as well as to prevent expanding the excavations at Arentsburg. When the country estate is later put up for auction he will be able to buy it cheap, less disturbed and without any damage to his own fields.[24]

The ministry decided to act upon Reuvens' information: by royal decree of 24 September 1833, negotiations with Caan were officially put to an end. Reuvens had only a few months left before the final auction of Arentsburg. In a last desperate effort he started new excavations: he planned to remove the trees which earlier had been spared at his neighbour's instigation. At once he received a letter from Caan:

> The decision to let the trees stand is now being revoked by you. I warn you from my side, that the moment one tree is pulled down at your request, I will immediately claim the exertion of my rights, as described in the ministerial disposition you mentioned earlier, and this with all the facilities which I and my predecessors formerly enjoyed.[25]

The next morning Reuvens travelled to The Hague for a private interview with the minister, who sent his secretary-general to Caan to settle this new dispute. Caan would not give in, and both sides engaged lawyers. In the meantime the excavations were limited to other areas, where Reuvens tried to make the best of the situation, awaiting the selling of the country house. The auction took place on 1 April 1834. Caan became the new owner of the house for 14,500 guilders, with the trees intact and without any more interference from troublesome archaeologists.

SMALLER EXCAVATIONS AND SURVEYS

The results of the excavations at Arentsburg were limited by financial setbacks after the events of 1830 and by the machinations of the neighbouring squire. They did not justify the publication of a monograph, but Reuvens saw possibilities of including the report of his excavations in a larger work: a description of all Roman remains in the Netherlands. This 'topography of the Roman Netherlands' became the third publication Reuvens wanted to complete, besides the catalogue of the Egyptian collection and the publication of the Borgia manuscripts *cum annexis* concerning the archaeology of North Africa.

In 1833 and 1834 Reuvens surveyed the provinces of Drenthe, Gelderland and Zeeland. Travelling by stagecoach, boat and on foot Reuvens spent months in the barren countryside of the remote provinces. His notebooks are full of observations about the visible archaeological remains around 1830. In the northern province of Drenthe he studied the so-called 'Roman army camps', systems of earthen walls in the landscape, which for ages had aroused the interest of local antiquarians. In his description Reuvens rejected the possibility that these walls had once had a military function. He came very near the truth by suggesting that they might have been connected with farming activities, for example, as 'meadows for sheep breeding'. The wall systems are in fact prehistoric ploughlands, now generally known as 'Celtic fields'.[26] During his survey Reuvens made notes and drawings of fifteen 'camps'. He did not close his eyes to the other archaeological remains: the prehistoric megalithic *hunebedden* and tumuli, ancient graveyards and medieval churches. He began a documentation, which may be called the start of the first archaeological database in the Netherlands.

In Gelderland he started an excavation near Nijmegen (*Noviomagus*), the most important Roman settlement in the Netherlands. During the construction of the military fortress *Krayenhoff* some Roman finds were reported, which Reuvens bought for the museum. In September 1834 he obtained the opportunity to carry out excavations in this area together with Leemans, and they discovered the remains of a large rectangular building, which he interpreted as a bathhouse.[27] He further investigated tumuli and earthen structures at the Grebbeberg and Uddel, of which he made descriptions and ground plans.

In the province of Zeeland, too, he travelled in search of Roman remains. He studied the altars dedicated to the local goddess Nehalennia, which had been found in this province since the seventeenth century. Reuvens corresponded with the Royal Academy of Arts and Sciences about the project of a publication of the altars. It is possible that he envisaged including this publication as a chapter in his larger work about the Roman presence in the Netherlands. In Zeeland he documented the altars which were kept in the church of Domburg (later destroyed by fire), but, as in Drenthe, he also described all other archaeological monuments which came to his attention. With the aid of local antiquarians and burgomasters Reuvens compiled a dossier on the province with drawings, notes, letters and extracts. He paid special attention to the so-called *Vlietbergen*, artificial mounds in the otherwise flat landscape, which were surrounded by mystery and local folklore. To determine the antiquity of these mounds, he dug trenches and tried to date the pottery which came to light. His untimely death prevented the publication of the results of his investigations, but the dossiers of the excavations and the diaries of his different travels show that he can deservedly be called the first field archaeologist of the Netherlands.

9

THE IDEAL MUSEUM

Dreams and reality

We have come to rely upon a comfortable time-lag of fifty
years or a century intervening between the perception that
something ought to be done and a serious attempt to do it.

H.G. Wells (1866–1946)

THE ARCHAEOLOGICAL CABINET

The housing of the collection of antiquities in Leiden has a troubled history, in which Reuvens, the university trustees, the Ministry of the Interior and the king of the Netherlands were involved. Reuvens had the ideal of a national museum, with an adequate and worthy building. Long before the plans for such a building came into being he had begun collecting zealously, with finances from the government and the approval of the king. Officially the acquired antiquities were added to the university collection, but university trustees lacked funds to house and maintain the museum: they considered the antiquities merely as one of the manifold academic collections. Conservation and management of the 'archaeological cabinet' were, of course, the task of the trustees, but its development into a large, money-consuming institution was not the intention of the university. With the growth of the collections the trustees were forced time and again to offer solutions, which at best can be called emergency measures. No general strategy for the university collections underlay the various actions that were taken to tackle the problems.

The sculptures of the Papenbroek collection were still in the orangery of the botanical gardens when Reuvens was appointed in 1818. Climatological conditions in this damp building were far from ideal for the sculptures and their restorations held together by rusting iron. Larger statues had been placed outside, where they suffered the influence of the elements. One of Reuvens' first concerns was to find a decent location for the collection placed in his trust. In 1821 a solution was offered by the university. The Museum of Natural History was situated on the Rapenburg canal; it was a large

128

building with a seventeenth-century core and later additions. Four small houses adjoining this museum were bought by the university to make room for a new wing. The new wing with two floors and an attic was built on a sidestreet off the canal. The trustees decided to place the antiquities on the ground floor of the building and the collection of prints and plaster casts of the department of art history on the first floor. Although the idea of placing three university collections together in a kind of 'museum quarter' testifies to a certain vision, the different lodgings were much too small to develop into real museums. Three years after moving into this 'cabinet', Reuvens deplored ever having accepted the location, at a time when he was hampered by his 'young years and newness at the Academy'. The rooms had serious disadvantages: low windows, which provided awkward lighting and reduced the possibilities of placing statues against the walls, a damp atmosphere and steep stairs. The two large rooms (each 15 by 5 metres) and the four smaller ones (5 by 3 metres) were instantly filled with the statuary from the Papenbroek collection and the Parthenon and the Phigaleia plaster casts from the British Museum. Yet Reuvens tried to make the best of the situation. By a lucky chance the draft sketches of this first museum have been preserved, which enables us to reconstruct the arrangement of the available antiquities.[1] Some Egyptian and Persian antiquities from the Theatrum Anatomicum of the university were placed in the first room. The next hall housed the plaster casts of the Parthenon and Phigaleia sculptures, which Reuvens had bought in 1819 during his visit to London. The third room was dedicated to Roman funerary reliefs, urns and altars. One of the walls was shaped like a Roman columbarium with niches containing marble funerary chests. In the next room the Greek and Roman inscriptions and coins were placed. The fifth hall showed the larger statues from the Papenbroek collection. The last room contained Greek funerary art.

When examining this arrangement, two observations can be made. First, it is clear that the arrangement is made according to category and material: there are different rooms for plaster casts, inscribed objects, Roman and Greek funerary art, statuary, etc. In this arrangement chronology did not play a role, probably because relative and absolute archaeological dating was still in its infancy. The principle of placing categories together and not mixing the material remained predominant during most of the nineteenth and twentieth century.[2] The second interesting element is Reuvens' aim at 'contextualization' of the objects: an impression of the original surroundings and function of the antiquities. The reconstruction of a Roman columbarium, a wall with niches for funerary urns, is a good example. In Reuvens' diary of his visit to England in 1819 can be found a sketch of such a columbarium in the British Museum. In the same diary he wrote of being very pleased about the placing of statues in niches, as in the arrangement of the sculptures in Cambridge.[3] As a practical disadvantage of creating niches he mentioned the amount of space thus lost: this, combined with the awkward placing of the windows, is the reason why he did not create more context for his objects in the first archaeological museum in Leiden.

TOWARDS A NATIONAL MUSEUM:
'A PONDEROUS AND STATELY BUILDING'

Because of the growth of the collections due to the activities of Rottiers and Humbert, the trustees in 1824 offered Reuvens more room after a number of complaints on his part: by moving part of the collection of the Museum of Natural History a new wing could be given to the antiquities. But Reuvens refused: this small enlargement offered no solution for the future. In addition to more space for his antiquities he needed room for other facilities: a lecture hall, a restoration department, a store, and a locality for documents and models. He proposed to design a new building, which could combine all functions and put an end to the continuous problems with arranging and rearranging the antiquities after each new shipment.

This new building became a symbol of Reuvens' ideas about the place of archaeology in society. In his view one of the most important roles of archaeology was to improve contemporary art and architecture, by giving insight into the achievements of ancient Greece and Rome. Archaeology could create a taste in the Netherlands for the real classical architecture, as it had previously done in England and France: 'Archaeology is in one aspect the coadjutor of all scholarly knowledge, but it has also a very important effect on the elevation of the non-scholarly classes and on the promotion and the improvement of contemporary art.'[4] In May 1826 Reuvens was asked to give 'a rough sketch and estimate of such a building, with a proposal for where in the city the museum could best be built'.[5] The first requirements for such a building were, according to Reuvens, beauty, symmetry, adequate lighting and good architecture. The latter, especially, had been neglected during the previous centuries:

> Architecture and sculpture in our northern provinces are in decay, only partly because of the economizing spirit of our ancestors (who were very luxurious in other areas), but mainly because of the general lack of acquaintance with the beautiful examples of antiquity. Sculpture and architecture began to flourish in France during the reigns of François I and Louis XIV. But both sovereigns had imported the taste for those arts from Italy, the storehouse of beautiful antiquity, together with the ancient examples themselves. Architecture is taking a very high profile in England nowadays through the manifold travels to the beautiful ruins of Greece and the former Greek colonies. Travels which are made not only by the artists but also by the nobility and scholarly classes. Especially since the French

Revolution, the art of painting in that country and the taste in applied art and jewellery (which also had its influence on us) have been purified and improved. This can only be ascribed to the will (which in that period deteriorated into a passion) to imitate antiquity in everything.[6]

Building an archaeological museum in classical style could give a general impulse to architecture in the Netherlands, which was badly needed: 'Although we have two Royal Academies of Art, the museums in Leiden are disgraceful examples of architecture in the northern part of the Netherlands, and this is especially a sad statement about a museum in which ancient architecture is going to be taught.'[7]

The sketch of the new building was commissioned to the architect Zeger Reijers,[8] who was ordered to design a two-storied building in Greek Doric style. His first sketch (Figure 9.1) showed a symmetrical building with a monumental staircase and four Doric columns. A figured frieze ran above the door and windows of this portico. The entablature had metopes and triglyphs in classical style. On both sides of the entrance were two wings with twelve large windows for the ground floor and twelve smaller ones for the first floor. At right angles to this main building a third gallery was designed behind the entrance. This groundplan in the form of a 'T' had the advantage that – if necessary – new parts could be built to the museum without harming the symmetry of the design. It was designed to allow for growth and expansion. Reuvens was not pleased with the first sketches. In his eyes the architect had 'totally misunderstood the spirit of the Greek order' by mixing elements of the Roman Doric (Tuscan) order with classical Doric architecture. The proportion between height of the columns and the entablature was incorrect. In Greek Doric temple architecture there were never two triglyphs between columns and, moreover, the columns lacked flutings. The horizontal ledge and the heavy cornerstones 'spoiled the perpendicular effect of the columns'. The overall impression was wrong: 'The whole substructure makes the building too tall, whereas it had to be ponderous and stately, and it is very costly.'[9] The reaction of Reijers to all these remarks is not known, but when presenting his sketches he had remarked that 'the Greek Doric order is much more applicable to a building without a second floor'.[10]

Much more difficult to solve were the financial consequences of such a building: Reijers had made an estimate of about 250,000 guilders for the whole building (exclusive of the costs for the land), a sum which was 'far beyond the expectations' of Reuvens and the department. The department could not do much but hope for the benevolence of the king. From the archives it is clear that Reuvens tried hard to lower the price of the building by amending the sketches, but he was not able to reduce the price below 200,000 guilders. The king refused to spend this amount of money and urged the trustees to look for other solutions, such as placing the collection

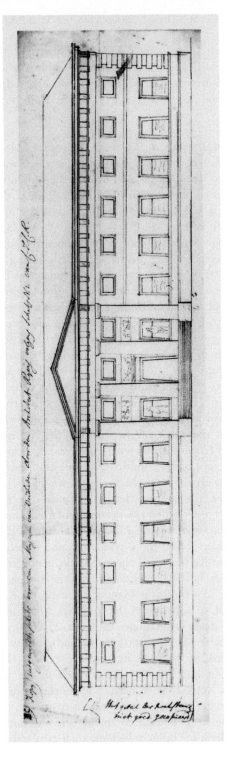

Figure 9.1 Project for an archaeological museum by Zeger Reijers, 1826. Archive, National Museum of Antiquities.

in an already existing building. The consequences of collecting had not been foreseen.

STATE OF AFFAIRS: 'GENERAL AND LOUD COMPLAINTS'

On 2 June 1827 Reuvens offered the king the printed version of his inaugural speech, which he had delivered nine months earlier at his appointment as *professor ordinarius* of archaeology.[11] In his speech about the connection between archaeology and contemporary architecture he had given an overview of the architectural styles in the Netherlands from the Middle Ages till the nineteenth century. His judgement was very harsh: after the Middle Ages Dutch architecture had lost its connection with the main developments in Europe and had not profited from the flowering of the Renaissance as had Italy, France and England. The French architects had reached great architectural heights by studying antique examples in Italy, but their Dutch counterparts had contented themselves with a second-hand imitation of the antique, an *imitatio exilis et misella*. Reuvens gave three reasons for this neglect of architecture and the poor appearance of Dutch buildings. First of all, the lack of stone in the Netherlands, which forced architects to import stone at high prices or to make use of cheaper bricks; second, the paralyzing effects of the eighty years of war against Spain in a period when other countries benefitted from the height of the Renaissance; and third, the influence of the Reformation with its Calvinist approach to luxurious display of wealth. He saw possibilities of turning the tide: with the chance to read archaeology at Leiden, artists and architects could now gain direct knowledge of ancient art, without having to travel to Greece or Italy. More attractive building material could be won in the quarries in the southern provinces (now part of the kingdom), which could alter the brick-dominated earlier architecture. The new building for the archaeological collection could be the proof of the realizability of his ideas. But first the king had to be convinced of the need for such a building:

> The idea of placing a Museum of Antiquities (i.e. of the best examples of the fine arts) in a building which offends all good taste, would be a horrifying prospect. The museums, Sire, which have been built for academic collections in Leiden during the past years do not add anything to improve public taste by any embellishment, but on the contrary are even the subject of general and loud complaints, because of their inefficient arrangement and outward ugliness.[12]

Reuvens gave an unflattering image of the organization in Leiden: the answer of the trustees to the increasing lack of space in the university museums consisted of rearranging, rebuilding and adding to the existing buildings, whenever a problem arose. Reuvens reproached the university for not wanting to formulate a clear policy for the collections: 'they are compelled to add to existing buildings when the need occurs, without surveying all those needs first, once and for all.'[13]

THE IDEAL SURROUNDINGS:
'THE SPLENDOUR OF A CAPITAL'?

The collections bought by Jean Emile Humbert in Italy between 1826 and 1830 made the already existing problems acute. Packing and shipping the more than 5,500 objects of the d'Anastasy collection had been a huge problem, but housing them in Leiden was a first-class logistic *salto mortale*. When Reuvens received the shipment he was out of funds and out of room for the numerous crates with their costly contents. The trustees decided to build a wooden barn in the botanical garden for the larger statues and to use the museum building as a storeroom for the more delicate objects: it was the only place where the mummies could be kept, because of the (limited) possibility of heating. A normal visit to the museum had already been impossible for years.

In the meantime other solutions were sought. A medieval church could house all antiquities, but the redecoration would cost more than half of the budget for a new building. A year later another solution was offered: the trustees had a project for a new Academy building, and offered Reuvens a few halls for his collection, which he refused. A few rooms in a building with a totally different function could not be called a museum. All the plans led to nothing, but did cost a considerable amount of time and energy. A highly placed civil servant at the Ministry of the Interior remarked: 'Personally I believe the archaeological museum belongs to the *septem cruces* [seven plagues] of the administration.'[14]

The continuing problems between Reuvens and the university in finding a solution for the archaeological collection led the department to interfere and look at the possibilities of separating the archaeological collection from the university and creating a museum outside Leiden in one of the larger cities of the Netherlands: Amsterdam, the capital of the kingdom, The Hague, where the government resided, or Brussels, the capital of the southern provinces and the alternate seat of government. In 1830 Reuvens was asked for his advice about the best possible place for the collection. He answered with a report of fifty-five pages, in which he gave an interesting analysis of the conditions a city should have to be a fertile place for an archaeological museum. Placing a national museum in the capital of a country seemed a logical step, looking at the examples of London, Paris and Berlin:

The example of the large capitals like Paris and Berlin is indeed tempting. The Museums of Art, ancient and modern, are placed in the middle of the lively movement at the centre of the state: they serve to ennoble the national taste, the arts and the industry, they diffuse essential knowledge about history and ethnology and stimulate further research. The Museums are also objects of national pride and are an essential support for patriotism. They attract visitors (in our country not an unimportant point) or serve to prolong the stay of civilized foreigners, of the diplomatic corps, of other nobility and the upper classes (for which the beautiful products of antiquity form the most attractive branch of study) and of scholars, men of renown, or youngsters at the start of their career. They contribute highly to the splendour of a capital, which in its turn is a source of prosperity and flourishing for the whole country.[15]

But for the benefit of a museum a fertile academic climate was also necessary. By exchange of ideas between museums, universities and art academies, the necessary progression could take place. Without a university, a museum would be forced to a standstill, and this meant decline:

It is part of human nature that everything which does not progress, recedes. Standstill is not possible, because if we stood perfectly still, all the others surrounding us would proceed. To benefit from a Museum, the arts and industry must also be supported by the continuous demands of theory, by the nearness of a centre of learning. Even the effect of a Museum on esteem abroad is more the result of publications than of the exhibition of the collection itself.[16]

Reuvens selected four criteria, to be used for choosing the right city for a national museum of antiquities. These were the presence of an art academy, trade and industry (factories), a renowned university, and a high rate of employment, wealth and affluence.

With this set of rules he subsequently measured the three 'capitals' of the Kingdom in comparison to the state of affairs in Leiden. Brussels was not suited for a museum, because the university lacked a faculty of humanities. The academic climate could be improved by moving the University of Louvain to Brussels, or by creating an athenaeum, where the humanities could be taught. Without such matters an archaeological museum in Brussels did not have a future: 'I believe that if we moved the museum to Brussels it would sparkle just for a moment like a novelty, but would then sink into deepest darkness.'[17]

In comparison with Brussels the possibilities for The Hague were even worse. There was no practice of the visual arts, hardly any economic activity, no academic climate and the educated residents were either diplomats or civil servants: 'The Hague lies as if it were in a sack, not on a road connecting it with commercial transit and domestic trade. Factories as far as I know do not exist, and there is even less trade.'[18]

Amsterdam was a more serious candidate, and in his report Reuvens treats this city with much more attention. At first sight the city had strong points: it had industries, a spirit of enterprise and a rich elite of educated citizens. The academic climate was fostered by the presence of the Royal Academy of Arts and Sciences and the Athenaeum Illustre. Also the Academy of Art was located in the capital. Wealthy citizens held memberships of learned societies and literary clubs. Yet, Reuvens mentioned some strong points against the capital. The first had to do with air pollution, which could damage the objects placed in his care:

> A first difficulty in Amsterdam, which is probably more important than one should think at first sight, are the evil fumes which traverse the city. If I remember correctly they cause all objects which cannot be cleaned with water, or which are not varnished or placed in airtight cases, to get tarnished and to decay. To such an extent that in a few years time all the plaster casts, all small Egyptian objects, maybe all painted mummies and (who knows) all objects of limestone will look dirty and black.[19]

But also the spiritual climate in the capital was a cause for concern. Amsterdam had a good number of wealthy citizens, but Reuvens doubted if they were really interested in an archaeological museum. The Athenaeum Illustre was in his view too weak in the humanities. The faculties of law and theology were very good, but in these circles archaeology and ancient history were still regarded as a 'fanciful pastime'. Moreover Reuvens had serious objections against Amsterdam on moral grounds. It was not a city where young students received a good example:

> A prolonged stay in this city causes serious damage to common decency, to which I would like to draw the Government's attention. It adds greatly to deep moral decay of a people, when the flower of the nation from all provinces is sent to a deeply degenerated capital for its education.[20]

Reuvens had an aversion to the 'contaminated spirit of the masses in the capital', which in his eyes could only lead to 'flabbiness, effeminacy and enervation' of the youth. These were drawbacks for Amsterdam and a reason for not transferring the study of archaeology and the Museum of Antiquities to the capital. In short, only one city was worthy of the archaeological collection: Leiden; but not the city as it was. The city could boast of a splendid university for the humanities and of a small art academy, but industry was in serious decline and a large part of the population lived in dire poverty. The two first assets could be enhanced by enlarging the art academy and by sending promising artists to Leiden to study the antique sculptures and follow the lessons of Reuvens. The academic climate could get a new impulse by transferring the Royal Academy of Arts and Sciences from Amsterdam to Leiden: as today, most of its members were working at the University of Leiden already. There was also a juridical problem when moving the antiquities to another city: the core of the archæological collection, the Papenbroek bequest, was the property of the university and the ministry could not alienate this part of the collection from Leiden. Reuvens ended his report with the following words:

> But even if the Government does not want to comply with any of my wishes and asks my thoughts about a fully unconditional choice between the four possible cities, then without any doubt I would vote for Leiden. Amsterdam and The Hague are quite out of the question, and judging between Brussels and Leiden I would say that it is better to let the Museum ennoble the nation gradually than have a short flicker by a superficial fashionable craze.[21]

THE DARKEST HOUR: ANTIQUITIES AND MUSHROOMS

On 25 August 1830 the celebrations for the birthday of King Willem I ended in turmoil: in Brussels riots broke out after the presentation of Auber's opera *La Muette de Portici*, the story about the revolt in Naples against the Spaniards in 1647. The following week the unrest spread through the whole of Belgium. Out of fear for a similar uprising in the northern provinces, factories, town halls and museums were placed under surveillance. In Leiden the professors were summoned to carry arms and guard their premises. The Dutch government decided to send troops to restore order in Belgium. Colonel Humbert, just returned from Italy, wanted to take up arms and join the military campaign against the Belgians, but his bad health prevented this plan. Reuvens' promising student and assistant Conrad Leemans left town with the Regiment of Leiden Chasseurs for Belgium, where he was wounded during the 'Ten Days' Campaign' of 1831. The consequences of the ensuing secession of the southern part of the Netherlands were grave. The economic uncertainty and the high costs of the armies in the field were reasons to be very cautious with non-essential spending. Of course these events had their effect on all projects Reuvens had in view: a third expedition by Humbert to Italy was cancelled, with the result that the start of negotiations over the collections of Greek and Roman statuary (Nani-Tiepolo in Venice) and Greek vases (Pacileo in Naples) was thwarted. The new

137

museum building now belonged to the realm of utopias, while the yearly subsidy for maintenance of the buildings and the collection was cut down to one-third of the already small amount of 1,400 guilders a year. The situation began to get out of hand. Three years after the arrival of the d'Anastasy collection the mummies were in danger due to the wet climate and the bad conditions in the museum. Reuvens began to develop feelings of despondency. He wrote to the department:

It is known from experience that mummies in our moist climate need very strict conditions for conservation. Already in 1829 a mummy's head began to putrify. I was forced to give it a coating of wax. A totally naked mummy started to show serious moist eruptions. At that time I followed the advice of some experts and placed the mummy in a narrow airtight chest with glass windows and put some *muries calcis* [a salt–chalk mixture] next to it. This remedy worked very well: the mummy is now dry and will be preserved, but it has to have special care by changing the *muries* frequently. This year during the spring, when I gave the collection an airing, I noticed that all the other mummies were beginning to get more or less humid. The most beautiful among them (I might say the most beautiful existing in Europe) have a very precarious appearance and I have to order, on my own account, such chests for all the mummies, to prevent the decay from being irreversible.

First one kind of object needs special care, then another, with bell-jars, airtight closing, spreading melted elastic gum or other measures or new experiments to fight the moisture and to prevent decay. Last year I noticed that the *muries calcis*, when it is saturated with moisture from the mummy, produces a poignant acid, which cannot be kept in wooden drawers. So I have to order glazed or glass vessels to put the *muries* in: this takes time and an amount of money which cannot be booked on this year's account.

I finish by stressing once again the importance of the study of antiquities and the museum. I have tried to stimulate the interest of the learned public for this study, but there is so much to do, and I cannot do everything at once. I have been treated with much respect by some of the Trustees, but I know that I will receive little appreciation from most of my compatriots. But there are foreigners who have done justice to my good intentions. In these circumstances it is difficult not to get down-hearted. Still it is necessary that the objects in the Museum are at least protected from decay, and small affairs can be continued, hoping that better times may arrive.[22]

But better times were further away than ever. While Reuvens was trying to fight the moisture on the mummies with all kinds of absorptive experiments, the sculptures encountered other problems. Five years earlier these had been put 'temporarily' in the wooden shed in the botanical gardens. The surface of the Egyptian statues, especially those of soft limestone, had been affected by moisture and cold and began to scale off. In August 1832 Reuvens had to warn the trustees:

> I am in the awkward position of having to tell you that mushrooms are now growing in the shed, which serves to house parts of the antiquities of the museum. I have to ask you to take measures against this intrusion and to restore the damage.[23]

CHOICE OF AMSTERDAM: 'THE LAST OF ALL CITIES WORTHY OF SUCH AN HONOUR'

In these circumstances it is not surprising that Reuvens reacted vehemently when in 1832 the last part of the history of Leiden University was published by Professor Matthijs Siegenbeek.[24] In his last chapters about the present state of the university, the author sang the praises of the 'Museum of Fine Arts' (the cabinet of prints and plaster casts) and of the Museum of Antiquities, which possessed 'a level of perfection which leaves nothing to be desired'.[25] Reuvens was irritated about the division of 'Fine Arts' from 'Antiquities', which could give the impression that archaeology had nothing to do with aesthetics. But he was really worried about the praise of perfection: by reading this bragging prose his principals in The Hague could get a totally wrong idea about his continuous complaints about the lacunae in the collection and the poor condition of the housing. If the subsidies ended, thanks to this book, then the museum would be in real danger. He asked the trustees to distance themselves from this publication in order to safeguard the study of archaeology, which was living through such difficult years.

The imminent danger for the collection and the failing prospects of finding a new building urged Reuvens to look again at other possibilities outside Leiden. From the archives it becomes clear that he made a choice to move the whole collection to Amsterdam, in spite of his earlier harsh comments about the capital. In June 1834 it was common knowledge that the antiquities would leave Leiden. The trustees accepted the alienation of the Papenbroek bequest and seemed pleased to be rid of a constant source of concern. One of the trustees even used rather undiplomatic words: 'Speaking for myself, I will see those puppets and sarcophagi move without shedding one tear.'[26]

Others were totally against the idea of moving the museum to Amsterdam. In particular the academics found it a disgrace that Leiden would be robbed of an internationally renowned treasure of scholarly material. Professor Hamaker 'flew into a temper' and did not even want to contemplate the idea of moving the collection away from Leiden:

Such a Museum belongs to a university, where a range of scholars takes interest in it. Not to a city of merchants, not near an Athenaeum, where nobody will look after it. With what right are they insulting Leiden and benefitting, mark my words, Amsterdam, which is the last of all the cities in the Netherlands to be worthy of such an honour?[27]

In view of these new difficulties and discussions, Reuvens wanted to speed up the process. The city of Amsterdam offered a suitable building for free, but for all other incidental and recurring costs an agreement had to be made between the city, the department and the museum staff. Reuvens proposed organizing a meeting of all parties involved to find a solution for the financial consequences.

This meeting never took place. In December 1834 the city's chief architect died and the negotiations were postponed until a successor was appointed. On 26 July 1835 the academic world was shocked by the death of Reuvens himself, the central figure in the development of the archaeological museum. The turn of events after Reuvens' death, the choice of a successor and the handling of the professor's scholarly legacy will be dealt with in the next chapter. For the time being the collection remained in Leiden in a worrying condition.

10

END OF THE PIONEER YEARS
1835–40

'If I should die', I said to myself, 'I have left no immortal
work behind me – nothing to make my friends proud of my
memory – but I have lov'd the principle of beauty in all
things, and if I had had time I would have made myself
remember'd.'

John Keats (1795–1821)

No great man lives in vain. The history of the world is but the
biography of great men.

Thomas Carlyle (1795–1881)

REUVENS' DEATH, JULY 1835

The three great projects on which Reuvens was working, the publication of
the Borgia papers *cum annexis*, the description of the Egyptian antiquities,
and the topography of the Netherlands in Roman times, were suddenly
thwarted by his death in July 1835. This tragic event was to transform the
future of the National Museum of Antiquities. The last days of Reuvens' life
are described by his pupil Conrad Leemans in an obituary, written in the
form of a letter to his colleague L.J.F. Janssen.[1] From this letter the following facts arise: the health of Reuvens had deteriorated in the two years before
his death. He suffered from headaches and spells of sleepiness at unusual
moments during the day. During all the years of his active life he had
allowed himself hardly any time to relax. Autumn, winter and spring, he
was busy with his teaching, exams and the administration of the museum.
During the summer months he either directed the excavations at Arentsburg
or journeyed to European museums and excavations. After the successful
purchase of the Cimba and d'Anastasy collections, he planned to publish an
illustrated catalogue based on the description of the collection in Paris of
Champollion le Jeune. To prepare this catalogue and to study the Egyptian
collection in the Louvre with Champollion's description in hand, he travelled

to Paris in the summer of 1829 with his student Conrad Leemans. In 1833 he had visited the Roman antiquities of Trier, and in 1835 he intended to make his long-awaited journey to Italy, which he had postponed several times due to political unrest and epidemics of cholera. Just before leaving for Italy in July 1835, he travelled to London because of the news that some important Egyptian antiquities from the Salt collection were being put on auction. Reuvens was especially interested in the Greek papyri, which from the description seemed to be related to pieces in Paris and Leiden. He suspected that some pieces belonged together and had been sold separately for lucrative reasons. On 13 July 1835 Reuvens and his wife Louise arrived in London by steamer and spent a few days in the capital. At the auction the greater part of the Salt collection was bought by colleagues of the British Museum, but Reuvens managed to lay hands on a papyrus which had escaped the attention of the other scholars because of the amount of dirt covering the text. After cleaning, the manuscript turned out to be one of the most important items of the Salt collection: the death book of the merchant Kenna, dating from the nineteenth dynasty, with a length of 17 metres.[2] Reuvens' star rose considerably: *Mirati igitur sunt docti Angli, qui venditione aderant, Reuvensii singularem sagacitatem et diligentiam.*[3]

In London Reuvens also bought other antiquities, including Etruscan artefacts from the collection of Lucien Bonaparte, and he copied Greek papyri in the British Museum. At the auction he met Eduard Gerhard, secretary of the *Istituto di Corrispondenza Archeologica* in Rome and an acquaintance of Colonel Humbert, who invited Reuvens to visit him in Italy later that year. After this short stay in London Reuvens and his wife travelled back to Rotterdam by steamer. They enjoyed the first hours of the trip 'with a splendid view of the meadows along the Thames', but once on the open sea, Mrs Reuvens went below deck because of seasickness. Reuvens dined on board in the company of a few gentlemen, but went to bed early in the men's dormitory because of headaches and nausea. The following morning Reuvens was seen on deck very early. He was staggering and uttered incomprehensible sounds. The British sailors mistook these sounds for Dutch and thought he was seasick. When the professor panicked and started asking (in broken English) for his wife, the sailors thought he was a grieving widower and tried to calm him, preventing him from going downstairs. A fellow passenger warned them that Mrs Reuvens was aboard and needed to be alerted as soon as possible. As the steamer entered the Meuse estuary, Reuvens was taken to his wife and with a last effort he tried to explain his condition *paucissimis tantum verbis, iisque male cohaerentibus.*[4] After his last words, 'Louise, I am dying,' he collapsed and remained unconscious. In spite of treatments with ice bandages and bloodlettings, he died in the hospital of Rotterdam on 26 July 1835, only 42 years old, in the presence of his wife, his father-in-law, Conrad Leemans and the family doctor. The symptoms seem to indicate that Reuvens had succumbed to a severe stroke. A few days later, after a quiet ceremony in the presence of his family and friends, he was buried in the public cemetery Groenesteeg in Leiden, where the family tombstone with the inscriptions *REUVENS* and *BLUSSÉ* (Louise's maiden name) can still be seen. After these tragic events Leemans was asked by the trustees to take care temporarily of the museum's administration.

Conrad Leemans was born in Zaltbommel in 1809. In 1821 the family moved to Leiden, where Leemans went to school and came into contact with Abraham Blussé, publisher, inspector of schools and father-in-law of Reuvens. Leemans started to study theology in 1825, but acquaintance with the family Reuvens and involvement in the first campaign at Arentsburg led to a passion for archaeology and a change of studies in 1828. Every summer he was present at the excavation at Arentsburg, where in the second year he was charged with keeping the excavation diary. Later Reuvens put him in charge of the excavations in Nijmegen. Together with Reuvens, Leemans visited the collections of the Louvre in 1829, where he received his training as an Egyptologist. Much to the discomfort of Reuvens, Leemans left the Netherlands in 1831 to join the military campaign against the Belgians. On 10 August 1831 his brigade was ambushed: Leemans was injured by a bullet in the arm. In September he returned to the Netherlands, where he recovered on the Arentsburg estate with Reuvens and his family. Leemans received his doctorate in 1835: his thesis treated the *hieroglyphica* of the AD fourth-century Egyptian author Horapollo.[5]

With the chair of archaeology vacant and without a new director, decisions concerning the archaeological museum were taken directly by the trustees and the ministry. Much of the correspondence which Leemans received during the first months of his temporary curatorship were copies of decisions taken by the trustees or the department. First of all he was asked to compile reports about the condition of the collection, the present housing and the state of affairs concerning the three publications on which Reuvens was working. Leemans started with the report about the condition of the collection. The stone monuments were in danger because of the moist conditions in which they were kept:

> A large number of them are losing their upper surface, which is gradually converting into a fine chalky dust. This dust falls down with the smallest movement, which causes parts of the contours to disappear or to be less visible. Total deterioration has been prevented until now by repeatedly covering most of the statues with elastic gum, dissolved in ether or *oleum petrae* [petroleum].[6]

The wooden shed in the botanical garden was beginning to subside. In winter the sculptures inside it were covered with snow, moss was growing on a Greek altar and a capital and the wooden floor was rotting and in places had given way under the weight of the statues. The wooden objects and mummies had been kept dry by placing them in the airtight chests with *muries calcis*, but 'devastating fungus' had ruined some of the paint on the wooden coffins. Foreign visitors complained about the state of neglect in which they encountered the antiquities. Leemans quoted the Italian Egyptologist Salvolini, who wrote about the museum:

> Its condition is deplorable, mostly because of the miserable housing in which it has been placed for too long. It would be shameful for Europe to witness in its heart the loss of precious remains, which Christian fanaticism and Islamic barbary have left untouched![7]

As regards the publications which had been planned by Reuvens, Leemans was careful. He suggested postponing publication of the manuscripts of Count Borgia *cum annexis* for a while, because of the amount of research and correction still to be done. He saw problems concerning the publication of the excavations of Arentsburg: although the finds were partly illustrated in lithographs and described, the rest of Reuvens' notes were fragmentary and dispersed: 'One might hope that the death of the professor will not lead to a total destruction of this work.'[8] A swift publication was not possible, but Leemans was willing to do his best for this part of the scholarly inheritance, if he were to be appointed as Reuvens' successor.[9]

Leemans saw more possibilities for the catalogue of the Egyptian antiquities. The description and lithographs of many objects were ready and Leemans had received good training in Egyptology during his visit to Paris with Reuvens. The long-awaited publication of the Egyptian treasures in Leiden could also be a lucrative enterprise. Leemans suggested giving priority to the catalogue of the Egyptian 'monuments' and to postpone the publications of the excavations in North Africa and the Netherlands for the time being. He asked for and obtained permission to widen his knowledge of Egyptian antiquities by a four months' stay in London, where he studied the collections of the British Museum in 1836. He took two plaster casts of the Arentsburg skeleton with him, which he presented to the British Museum and the Royal Society of Antiquaries. At the Society of Antiquaries he gave a lecture about the recent find of three Roman funeral inscriptions at Cirencester in 1835 and 1836, which had aroused his interest because of the mention of a Frisian mounted soldier.[10] He was introduced at the Athenaeum Club and in his correspondence noted meeting with leading scholars and collectors including Edward Hawkins, Wilkinson, Lee, Pettigrew, Birch, Henry Ellis, John Gray and Sir John Soane. This period saw the beginning of a long and interesting correspondence with scholars throughout Europe.[11] His English way of dressing earned him the reputation of a dandy among his friends, when he returned to Holland in the summer of 1836.

THE NEW MUSEUM: 'MUMMIES IN A DUTCH DRAWING-ROOM'

With remarkable speed decisions were taken about the archaeological museum. In November 1835 Leemans received his appointment as 'first curator' of the museum. L.J.F. Janssen, a former clergyman, was appointed 'second curator'. Janssen had been active in Dutch archaeology, mainly in the eastern part of the Netherlands, and had published articles in German periodicals on medieval architecture, prehistoric tumuli and Roman excavations. Also in November a building was bought by the university to house the archaeological collection: an eighteenth-century mansion on the central street of the city, Breestraat nr. 18. Although the architecture of the house was unsuited for a modern museum, Leemans had no choice but to accept the building and to arrange the collection as well as he could.

A month later, the appointment of P.O. van der Chijs, another former student of Reuvens, followed as professor of numismatics and director of the Academic Coin Cabinet, which comprised Reuvens' private collections. Leemans was ordered to reserve a few rooms in his new museum for the coin cabinet, much to his displeasure: he needed all the space available for his own collection, but more important was the fact that the coin cabinet also comprised modern coins and medals, which in Leemans' view did not belong in an archaeological museum. There were also problems regarding the shared entrance of both museums, the responsibility for the keys and budgetary arrangements. In short, the cohabitation of the two disciplines started with much animosity and dissent. Moving the antiquities to the eighteenth-century mansion aroused criticism not only in the Netherlands. When Colonel Humbert in Livorno heard about this news he commented ironically:

> So the decision has been made that the house of Mrs Van den Bergh will receive all the things Egypt, India, Greece, Carthage and Rome have given us after these long expeditions? Who would have said to an Egyptian princess, to Greek and Roman citizens, that after all these centuries her mummy and their skulls would be arranged in a *Dutch drawing room* by young professors? What is worse than seeing funerary urns in an ancient dining room? The Dutch Government has tried and succeeded in rivalling the most important European nations as far as antiquities are concerned. Now it is time to think about a decent placement of these objects. Not in Leiden, but in Amsterdam, the capital of the Netherlands. But for us a decision has been made: the statues of Jupiter, Augustus and Trajan, etc., etc., which I have found in the soil of Utica, will receive compatriots and foreigners in a Dutch mansion . . .[12]

Leemans' collecting policy included the following nine categories: Asian antiquities, Phoenician and Punic artefacts, Egyptian antiquities, Greek antiquities, Etruscan objects, Roman artefacts (no division was made between Mediterranean and provincial Roman antiquities), Germanic antiquities from the Netherlands, Germany and Denmark, American artefacts, and, finally, plaster casts, cork models and replicas of ancient coins and carved stones. The sketches for the arrangement of the new building show that Leemans arranged the antiquities by categories in separate rooms for sculptures, minor arts, inscriptions, funerary art and ceramics, but material was also placed together according to certain themes. In the first room the non-classical objects were arranged: the Asian, Persian, Babylonian, Phoenician, Punic and American antiquities. The second room housed the heavy Egyptian monuments, including the statues and shrines from the d'Anastasy collection. The third and fourth rooms (on the first floor) illustrated the funerary rites of the Egyptians (mummies). The fifth room was dedicated to Egyptian religion and daily life. Rooms 6 and 7 both had a columbarium: the former with Greek and Etruscan funerary monuments, the latter with Roman and Germanic sepulchral art. Room 8 (on the second floor) was dedicated to the minor arts of Greece, Etruria, Rome and the Germanic cultures. The cork models and plaster casts were placed in room 9. Rooms 10 and 11 (back on the ground floor) were reserved for the heavy sculptures from Greece and Rome, including the Greek collection of Rottiers and the statues from Utica. Leemans also took over the idea of contextualization: besides the two columbaria, a small 'Roman' building was constructed in the courtyard from stones found during the excavations at Arentsburg.

In January 1837 a start was made in moving the heavy sculptures from the shed in the botanical gardens to the new location. It was decided to transport the heavy objects on the canals of the city, but this was not without danger. After a few days a calamity occurred. Leemans wrote to the department:

> We have started the transportation of heavy objects to the new building, but this enterprise was interrupted two days ago by a most disagreeable incident. The most difficult object, a granite temple of about 25,000 pounds, had been transported with much difficulty half way from the shed to the vessel when it overbalanced and fell into the water of the canal. The means to lift it from the sludgy bottom were totally unavailable in Leiden, so I had to go to Rotterdam today, to find a solution to safeguard this object and to prevent further misfortunes.[13]

Leemans asked the advice of engineers of the Royal Navy in Rotterdam to save the massive Egyptian temple (*naos*) from the mud. The heavy object was sinking deeper with every passing day, and Leemans was afraid he might lose it altogether. The navy sent a detachment of nine men 'to rescue the drowning person'. The temple was saved. One of the seamen caught a heavy cold due to the 'extremely muddy work' in the icy cold weather: he, too, recovered completely.

Leemans had remarkable troubles with the organization and the finances of the move. Much of his correspondence with the trustees concerned budgetary problems and delayed payments to the workmen. More than once Leemans had to pay the men out of his own pocket to enable them to support their families. In the summer of 1837 the financial problems were such that Leemans sent all the men away and put an end to the rebuilding of the mansion. The trustees tried to lower the price for the building by sending an architect to Leemans to discuss cheaper solutions for plinths, pedestals and showcases. Leemans refused to let the architect interfere with his ideas about the museological arrangement, and the negotiations came to a standstill.

In December 1837 the matter was put before the king, who by royal decree donated 2,000 guilders for the renovation of the building. This stimulus had its effect: work continued and on 7 August 1838 the National Museum of Antiquities opened its doors for the public. During the first months only the halls with Egyptian artefacts could be visited, three days a week, 'for every visitor who presents himself, decently dressed'. The other three days were reserved for special visitors with a signed entry form. Foreigners were also welcome outside of normal opening hours. A soldier stood guard at the entrance to protect the collection day and night. The opening was a success: in the first few months between 250 and 300 people visited the museum daily. At the entrance they were asked to write down their name and profession, which gives an interesting insight into the social composition of museums' visitor groups in this period. Among the first day's visitors we encounter a baker, a drummer, a carpenter, a tailor and a barber, but also a German baron, a Bostonian gentleman, the editor of an Edinburgh journal, the ambassador of Prussia and one of the czar's ministers.[14] Between August and December the museum had a total of 2,944 visitors. In short, 'a constant use was made of the opportunity to enrich oneself with knowledge of the ancient civilizations amidst the products of art of the ancient peoples, and to cultivate good taste and a sense of beauty'.[15]

PRIVATE INTEREST: PURCHASES
AND DONATIONS

The large collections brought to the museum by Rottiers and Humbert had made the collection grow in an impressive but unbalanced way. In particular, the classical department looked poor in comparison with the richness of the Egyptian antiquities. Reuvens had tried to convince the ministry of the need to acquire collections of Greek vases and Greek and Roman statuary, but the purchase of the d'Anastasy collection had prevented the spending of money on other collections such as the Nani-Tiepolo antiquities in Venice or the Pacileo vases in Naples. Leemans understood that the high tide of purchases was over and that he had to find other ways to prevent a stagnation in the growth of the collections. He found a solution in a way which nowadays would be described as good public relations. He started yearly reports about the state of affairs of the museum in the official gazette, which Reuvens had used earlier for his reports about the excavations at Arentsburg. In his first article he made an appeal to Dutch ambassadors and consuls to keep a keen eye on antiquities which could be useful for the young museum. He also asked private collectors to consider the possibility of donations or loans to the museum. Some ambassadors and collectors reacted positively: they either sent objects to the museum or acted as intermediaries in purchases. They were thanked extensively by Leemans in the next edition of the official gazette for their interest and zeal to foster the arts. Other diplomats and collectors felt obliged to follow suit, and from 1835 a constant flow of antiquities came to the museum, especially from the Mediterranean area. Antiquities from the Greek colonies along the North African coast were donated by Consul J.F.H. Clifford Kocq van Breugel, Greek sculpture from the Cyclades was bought by Consul Chigi, and A.H. van Lennep, Dutch consul in Smyrna, took on the role of a mediator in antiquities, which was continued by his family throughout the nineteenth century. But antiquities were also sent to Leiden from the New World: the Dutch consul in Bogota, Van Lansbergen, donated American antiquities to the museum. Leemans started collecting and publishing pre-Columbian artefacts and in this regard he differed from his predecessor, 'who advised against the acquisition of these antiquities, at least for this museum'.[16] In Leemans' view, the American artefacts had ties with European prehistory, considering the similarities in form and function of, for example, stone axes, arrowheads and other utensils. In his annual report of 1839 he wrote about this new kind of objects coming to the museum:

> We have to speak finally about a collection of objects, which only last year gained admission in our Museum. We speak of the American antiquities, which earlier were not enclosed in the field of classical archaeology.
>
> In recent years the study of Northern artefacts, initiated and fostered by the Royal Society in Copenhagen, has focused its attention on America and the ancient remains of that continent. It is impossible to deny the similarities between the old artefacts there and the ones that are found on our continent. Scholars have discovered parallels and similarities especially in buildings, statuary and writing between the South American peoples and the oldest Asian and African nations.

In North America there are no less striking resemblances concerning the earliest weapons and certain customs, of which memories still remain, which have parallels with the earlier inhabitants of the northern countries of Europe. These and many other circumstances lead to the important decision, that the civilization of the New World originated with the other civilizations from one point. This supposition finds new corroboration from old stories of the early Mexicans.[17]

With these new fields of interest, the skyline of Carthage gradually faded away. With the passing of time Leemans began to doubt the need to publish the Borgiana manuscripts *cum annexis*. He argued that between 1820 and 1830 Leiden alone had possessed a richness of North African objects and documentation, but since then many other explorers had come and published the results of their travels, for example Christian Tuxen Falbe,[18] Sir Grenville Temple,[19] Dureau de la Malle[20] and Prince Hermann Von Pückler Muskau.[21] In 1837 Falbe was planning a new expedition to Tunisia together with Grenville Temple. Moreover, Leemans doubted his own capabilities to publish the enormous amount of scattered notes, bad translations and confused manuscripts: 'It is very difficult, if not impossible, to follow now the vast and all-embracing standards envisaged by the late Professor.'[22] Leemans urged the trustees to look for another home for the documents, drawings and manuscripts of Borgia and Humbert; and either to publish only the most important parts of the manuscripts, or to sell all the material to the French government: 'France is gradually gathering all the documents, from which it can elucidate the history of the Barbary States.'[23] Selling the material to France was in Leemans' view a better option than to let the pieces lie idle. Although a few talks took place with French editors, the Borgia manuscripts remained in Leiden, especially because of the difficulties concerning the contractual obligations with the widow Adelaide Borgia.[24] Meanwhile the relations with the former Danish rival Christian Falbe became better. Leemans provided plaster casts of the Punic stelae in Leiden for Falbe's studies, and Falbe organized the exchange of some prehistoric antiquities between the National Museum of Copenhagen and the museum in Leiden.[25] A start was made with a kind of 'collection exchange' in Europe.

VASES FROM VULCI

In 1839 an opportunity arose to fill one of the largest gaps in the museum's collection. In August of that year Leemans was informed that in Rotterdam a sales exhibition was being organized of antiquities belonging to Lucien Bonaparte (1775–1840), a younger brother of Napoleon with the title Principe di Canino after his estates on the Tyrrhenian coast.[26] In his book *Museum*

Etrusque Bonaparte describes how he became interested in ancient ceramics: in 1828 a farmer was ploughing the field known as Cavalupo near Vulci in Tuscany, on the estates which belonged to Bonaparte. Suddenly two oxen vanished into the earth and landed in an ancient Etruscan tomb, in which two fragmented vases were found. These first finds were sold off illegally, but when Bonaparte's wife heard about the discoveries, she took control of the matter and started thorough investigations. The areas of Cavalupo, Doganella and Cucumella were searched for ancient tombs, with astonishing results. In four months more than 2,000 ancient vases were dug up. Decorated pottery was restored in the prince's palace, coarse ware was thrown away. Needless to say, no notes were made about the provenance of the individual vases. Bonaparte, who until then had occupied himself with astronomical observations, began to take interest in these new acquisitions.

Bonaparte's unprecedented plunder of the necropolis of Vulci had been a thorn in the side of the academic world, and the publication of the excavations did not do much good to change the general opinion about him.[27] Among other curious statements about the *vasi Etruschi* and their inscriptions, Bonaparte argued that his discoveries were the ultimate proof of the Etruscan origin of this kind of pottery, the old antiquarian theory which since the days of Winckelmann had hardly had any serious supporters. His book is a sequence of 'scholarly' remarks, made with much bravado, which are mainly intended for the lustre of the author's own aureole.

In 1829, before selling off his collection, Lucien Bonaparte organized an exhibition of some 1,500 vases in Rome, where Humbert (then on his way to Naples) saw them in the company of Eduard Gerhard (see Chapter 7). Humbert wrote about the exhibition:

> This marvellous collection comprises more than 1,500 vases and has been brought to the Palazzo Gabrielli in Rome, where they are exhibited in six halls, which are open to the public. When looking closely at these vases I am convinced that the most beautiful ones are likely to come from Greater Greece, and some of them from Greece proper, although the Prince of Canino states explicitly that they are of Etruscan origin and manufacture.[28]

In the years following, large parts of the Canino collection were sold to private collectors and to museums like the Louvre and the British Museum. The collection on sale in Rotterdam in 1839 consisted of 105 Greek vases. Leemans inspected the antiquities and wrote to the department on 1 September that four vases had already been sold to the king of Bavaria, and five others to the Baron Van Westreenen in The Hague. For the rest of the collection a price was asked of 6,910 guilders. On 5 September 1839, after a few attempts to lower the price, Leemans received permission to buy the Canino collection with funds donated by the king personally. He also received the news about his official appointment as director of the National Museum of Antiquities. In October of the same year another twenty-eight interesting vases of the Canino collection arrived in Rotterdam. They were offered to the museum for 3,000 guilders, but no further actions were taken and the present whereabouts of these vases is unknown.

In the official gazette of 1840 Leemans described the important purchase, and gave a synthesis of the current classification of Greek painted pottery. The pots themselves could have been made by skilled workmen, but the decoration was without doubt the work of great painters, who from time to time practised this art form. The vases were exported in great numbers to Italy, but also manufactured in Italy by emigré Greeks. The oldest vases were 'Egyptian' in style and decoration (Corinthian and Italo-Corinthian wares). Next came the black-figure vases with 'rigid and stiff decoration', which were followed by the red-figure vases of a 'more perfect style'. These were the 'most beautiful ceramics from the ancient world that have come to us'. The fourth class of objects consisted of vases of lesser quality, 'awkwardly decorated with scenes from the realm of Dionysos, the funerary cult and marriage scenes' (fourth-century Attic and south Italian wares). Leemans ended the classification with an overview of the different shapes and their uses.[29] After this description Leemans ended his article by thanking the government '. . . due to whose constant strong and generous support the Museum of Antiquities has become a jewel of our native soil'. The king, the real benefactor behind this purchase, had asked not to be mentioned.[30]

Another jewel of the museum was published in the summer of 1839: the first part of the *Description raisonnée des monumens Egyptiens du Musée d'Antiquités des Pays-Bas à Leide*, prepared by Reuvens, edited by Leemans: the first scholarly catalogue of the museum's collections. The catalogue followed the example of Champollion's *Notice descriptive* of the *Musée Charles X*, which Leemans had studied in Paris together with Reuvens in 1829: the first section was dedicated to objects related to the Egyptian religion, the second part to objects of daily life and the third to the funerary cult. The plates were published separately and had to be bound in volumes by the buyer. The text was published in Dutch and French. A year later the Etruscan inscriptions of the museum were published by Leemans' colleague L.J.F. Janssen.[31]

Proud of this achievement, Leemans sent presentation copies to members of the royal family, the ministries and to Reuvens' son, who had just entered his first year at the university. Copies were also sent abroad to institutions like the Royal Society of Antiquarians (London), the Royal Numismatic Society (London), the library of the Athenaeum Club (London), the ministry of education in Paris, the Royal Society of Antiquarians of the North in Copenhagen, the Istituto di Corrispondenza Archeologica (Rome), the Archaeo-logical Society (Athens) and the Society of Arts and Sciences (Batavia). The affiliated museums with collections of Egyptian art in Turin, Florence, London and Paris also received copies of this first publication.

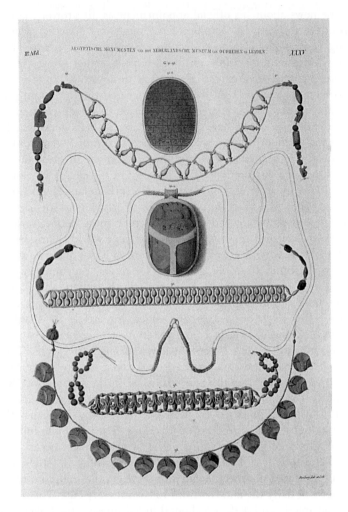

Figure 10.1 Lithograph from the first edition of the *Monuments Egyptiens* by
C. Leemans, 1839. It shows scarabs and jewellery from the d'Anastasy
collection.

With the opening of the museum to the public, the appointment of
Leemans as director and the start of publication of the catalogues, which
continued to be published throughout the nineteenth century, a new chapter
opened in the history of the National Museum of Antiquities: a period of
consolidation after the restless pioneer years, in which archaeology and the
Museum of Antiquities had had to struggle for their existence in the difficult
cultural climate of the early nineteenth century.

APPENDIX 1

LIFE OF C.J.C. REUVENS

1793: Born in The Hague, son of Jan Everard Reuvens (1763–1816) and Maria Susanna Garcin (1759–98)

1798: Death of his mother

1805: Pupil at the Latin School in The Hague

1808: Student of Greek and Latin at the Athenaeum Illustre in Amsterdam

1810: Student of law and classical languages at the University of Leiden

1811: Jan Everard Reuvens moved to Imperial Court of Cassation, Paris; Caspar follows his father and continues his studies of law and classical languages

1813: Doctoral thesis: *De rebus creditis: Du prêt, du depôt et du mandat.* Thèse Université Impériale, Paris, 2 juillet 1813

1815: Travels to Pyrmont for health reasons. Visits the brothers Grimm in Kassel

1815: Publication of *Collectanea Litteraria*

1816: Appointed as professor of Greek and Latin at the University of Harderwijk

1816: Death of Jan Everard Reuvens in Brussels

1818: Appointed as *professor extraordinarius* of Archaeology at the University of Leiden

1819: Travels to the provinces of Drenthe and Groningen. Meets Nicolaas Westendorp

1819: Travels to Oxford, Cambridge, London and Paris

1820: Travels to Antwerp: inspection of the first collection of B.E.A. Rottiers

1821: Acquisition of the first Rottiers collection; meeting with J.E. Humbert; acquisition of the first Humbert collection

1822: Travels to Antwerp: inspection of the second Rottiers collection; marriage in Leiden to Louise Sophie Blussé; membership of the Royal Academy of Sciences and Arts in Amsterdam; travels (with his bride) to Düsseldorf, Cologne, Bonn, Trier, Mainz, Frankfurt, Dresden and Berlin

1823: Birth of Reuvens' eldest daughter, Maria

1824: Birth of Reuvens' son Louis

1825: Travels to Antwerp, Brussels and Ghent

1826: Travels to Antwerp; appointment as *professor ordinarius* at the University of Leiden

1827: Birth of Reuvens' second daughter, Margaretha

1827: Start of the excavations at Voorburg (Arentsburg/Forum Hadriani)

1828: Travels to Antwerp

1829: Travels to Paris, together with C. Leemans; studies of the Egyptian collection in the Louvre

1830: Corrects the Borgia manuscripts with J.E. Humbert; revolution in Belgium

1831: Travels to Nijmegen; C. Leemans joins the Dutch troops during the 'Ten Days' War'

1833: Field survey in the province of Drenthe; travels to Trier, where he studies the Roman remains

1834: End of the excavations at Voorburg (Arentsburg/Forum Hadriani); travels to the province of Zeeland: description of local antiquities; excavations in Nijmegen with C. Leemans

1835: Travels to London with his wife; dies in hospital in Rotterdam, at the age of 42

APPENDIX 2

THE *DISCORSO PRELIMINARE*
OF RAFFAELE GARGIULO
Classifying Greek vases

The history of the study of vase-painting, like the history of all studies, offers entertainment to the curious or cynical mind and is sometimes useful for understanding older books and papers. But it is also instructive. Although there are rare students of genius, most are clever only in detail, normally uncritical of their methods or presumptions and blind to the further consequences of their arguments. So such fashionable theories as the Etruscan origin of painted vases, the representation of the ancient Mysteries and the artistic dominance of Ionia have in their time been accepted as fundamental truths. We may laugh at these past follies, but they are also a warning to look for equal follies of our own.

R.M. Cook, *Greek Painted Pottery*,
London, 1997, p. 311

In 1829 the archaeological agent J.E. Humbert travelled to Naples to start negotiations with the antiques firm Pacileo, Gargiulo and De Crescenzo. As described in Chapter 7, his aim was to acquire a collection of about 1,500 Greek vases for the museum in Leiden. A selection of the vases was illustrated in a catalogue, which Humbert took with him to the Netherlands.[1] The preface to the catalogue was written by Raffaele Gargiulo, who combined his academic work in the Museo Borbonico with the more lucrative trade in Greek vases. His introduction to the catalogue, the discorso preliminare, is interesting because it explains the specific composition of the vase collection on sale, and gives a chronological division of the vases, which is linked with the supposed places of production. The text is translated from the Italian and published here for the first time.

* * *

Magna Graecia, that is, Italy and Sicily, were regions where the fine arts flourished. The reasons for this advantage were the beautiful situation and the agreeable climate, which enticed the peoples banished after the Peloponnesian War to live there. They brought with them their rites, costumes and arts, which they had fostered in their own countries.

Everybody knows what heights of perfection the old Greeks reached in the arts of painting, sculpture, architecture, carving in hard stone, smelting and coinage. The enormous number of art objects that embellishes so many museums in Europe testifies to this.

Among the many art forms the ancient Greeks practised, one can also mention the fabrication of Italic-Greek vases. They brought this art to such perfection, that no other people after them has succeeded in making similar vases.

This collection of vases will be of great general interest, because of the subjects depicted on them, their forms and variety of fabric, their various ages, kinds of clay and glaze. As far as I can I will give an introduction to the study of these vases, which are interesting to scholars because of their lovely artistry, to craftsmen because of their peculiar and varied shapes, and to scientists because of the diverse types of clay and glaze. In this catalogue there will be a description of the various types, of the different periods in which the vases were made and of the places where they were found – a necessary element for such a big collection – which has never been done before.

These vases were not only made by the ancients for their sacred ceremonies and mysteries, but they were also offered as prizes in contests and used for domestic purposes. The fact that the vases are only found in tombs and not in other places could give rise to the idea that they were made exclusively for funerary rites, but we must be aware of the continuous wars and devastations which Magna Graecia suffered before the final destruction of so many important cities. The barbaric victors destroyed and pillaged everything. The graves, however, were regarded as sacred and inviolable, which is the reason why we find so many objects in these places. The ancient Greeks used to bury these vases with their deceased as a particular funerary rite but in some cities they had the singular custom of smashing the most precious vases and throwing the fragments on the funerary pyre. It is impossible to retrieve all those fragments.

Apart from these ceramics the ancients also buried everything that in life had been useful or dear to the departed, and so we find a suit of armour in the grave of a warrior, beautiful furniture or household objects in the tomb of a woman, and holy utensils in the grave of a priest, and so on.

The Kingdom of Naples, the former Magna Graecia, is the source of antiquities and it has supplied large quantities to museums abroad, but in these collections there is no good representation of the various types, periods and other interesting aspects of vase painting. In this collection the owners have accurately observed the above-mentioned diversity and it was with this aim that the collection has been assembled. This makes the collection very precious in view of the number of vases and of the representations, which show subjects that are interesting for the study of mythology, of the fine arts and of various other aspects of history.

The fabrication of this kind of Italic-Greek vases can be divided into six periods. The First Period comprises the kind of vases which until our days were called Egyptian, more specifically those of bright yellow clay with an overall pattern of animals and sometimes with human figures. These vases, however, have been proven to be not Egyptian, but the oldest kind of Greek manufacture, which was either introduced by the people who came to populate Magna Graecia, or was made with clay that was imported from their regions, because research has proved that this kind of clay is not found in our regions, whereas the clay of the other types is.

The vases that are decorated with black figures against an orange background are assigned to the Second Period. They were called 'Sicilian', because most of them were found on Sicily, but others have come to light in Locri, in Capua, in Nola and in Cuma. Nowadays they are described as *Greco antico*.

The Third Period was the best, during which they reversed the style of painting: they made the background black, and left the figures in the colour of the clay. The different places of manufacture were Locri, Nola, Nocera and Cuma. Pieces are found also in S. Agata de'Goti and Sorrento.

The vases on which the art of decoration begins to deteriorate are attributed to the Fourth Period. They were made in Bari, Ruvo, Canosa, Ceglio, Bitonto, Conversano and other small colonies of Campania like Avella, Altella, Cajazzo, Calvi, etc. Although the art of decoration might have deteriorated during this period, the craftmanship reached new heights, with bizarre forms and large sizes. In this period white paint is very often used and also additions of red colour.

In the Fifth Period not much changed, but the art of drawing deteriorated more and more, and the variety of shapes increased. The main centres of manufacture were Armento, Anzi, Pomarica, Calvello, San Arcangelo, Torre di Mare and Laurenzano.

The Sixth Period, the last, is called the period of decadence. To this period belong all the vases with a poor style of painting. There are also imitations of the preceding three original periods. This was caused by the yoke of submission and the continuous persecutions suffered by the Greeks, who lacked welfare and artists under Roman rule.

APPENDIX 3

EARLIEST MUSEUM
PUBLICATIONS, 1818–40

Hamaker, H.A., *Diatribe philologico-critica monumentorum aliquot Punicorum nuper in Africa repertorum interpretationem exhibens*, Leiden, 1822.

—— *Miscellanea Phoenicia sive commentarii de rebus Phoenicum, quibus inscriptiones multae lapidum ac nummorum, nominaque propria hominum et locorum, explicantur, item Punicae gentis lingua et religiones passim illustrantur*, Leiden, 1828.

Humbert, J.E., *Notice sur quatre cippes sépulcraux et deux fragments, découverts en 1817, sur le sol de l'ancienne Carthage*, The Hague, 1821.

Janssen, L.J.F., *Musei Lugduno-Batavi inscriptiones Etruscae*, Leiden, 1840.

Leemans, C., *Dissertatio antiquario-litteraria, exhibens Horapollinis Niloi Hieroglyphica, lectionis diversitate, versione Latina, hieroglyphicorum imaginibus et indicibus instructa*, Amsterdam, 1835.

—— 'Observations on three Roman sepulchral inscriptions found at Watermore near Cirencester in Gloucestershire, in 1835 and 1836', *Archaeologia*, 1837, vol. 27, pp. 211–28.

—— *Bibliotheca Reuvensiana*, Leiden, 1838.

—— *Lettre à M. François Salvolini, sur les monumens Egyptiens, portant des légendes royales, dans les Musées d'Antiquités de Leide, de Londres, et dans quelques collections particulières en Angleterre, avec des observations*, Leiden, 1838.

—— *Epistola ad Leonardum Joannem Fredericum Janssen de vita Caspari Jacobi Christiani Reuvensii*, Leiden, 1838.

—— *Aegyptische monumenten van het Nederlandsche Museum van Oudheden te Leyden*, Leiden, 1839.

—— *Description raisonnée des monumens Egyptiens du Musée d'Antiquités des Pays-Bas à Leide*, Leiden, 1839.

—— *Korte opgave der Aegyptische monumenten van het Nederlandsche Museum van Oudheden te Leyden*, Leiden, 1840.

Reuvens, C.J.C., *Oratio de laudibus archaeologiae*, Leiden, 1819.

—— 'Epimetrum de quibusdam monumentis cum Pollionis historia conjunctis', in J.R. Thorbecke, *De C. Asinio Pollione*, Leiden, 1820.

—— *Periculum animadversionum archaeologicarum ad cippos Punicos Humbertianos Musei Antiquarii Lugduno-Batavi*, Leiden, 1822.

—— 'Oudheden door den graaf van Elgin uit Griekenland medegebracht', *Antiquiteiten*, 1822, vol. II, 1, pp. 1–62.

—— 'Oudheden door den graaf van Elgin uit Griekenland medegebracht', *Antiquiteiten*, 1823, vol. II, 2, pp. 55–98.

—— 'Disputatio de simulacris quibusdam tympanorum Parthenonis, ad Taylorem Combium, Musei Britannici Antiquitatibus Praefectum', *The Classical Journal*, 1823, vol. 55, pp. 175–83; 1823, vol. 56, pp. 273–87.

—— 'Aus Holland: C.J.C. Reuvens Boettigero amico S.P.D.', *Amalthea*, 1825, vol. III, pp. 420–22.

—— *Verhandeling over drie groote steenen beelden, in den jare 1819 uit Java naar de Nederlanden overgezonden*, Amsterdam, 1826.

—— 'Nieuwste ontdekkingen omtrent den ouderdom der Aegyptische gedenkstukken, omtrent de dierenriemen, en den waarschijnlijken sleutel der hieroglyphen', *Antiquiteiten*, 1826, vol. III, 1, pp. 1–34.

—— 'Drentsche veenbrug: oudheden in derzelver nabijheid gevonden, en zoogenaamde legerplaatsen, en stad Hunso', *Antiquiteiten*, 1826, vol. III, 1, pp. 115–33.

—— *Oratio de archaeologiae cum artibus recentioribus conjunctione*, Leiden, 1827.

—— *Redevoering over het verband der archaeologie met de hedendaagsche kunsten*, Leiden, 1827 (translation from the Latin lecture by P.O. van der Chijs).

—— 'Incrementa Musei Antiquarii anno 1827–1828', *Annales Academiae Lugduno-Batavi*, Leiden, 1828.

—— *Korte beschrijving en plan der Romeinsche bouwvallen, gevonden bij de opdelvingen der jaren 1827–1829, ter waarschijnlijke plaatse van het Forum Hadriani, op de hofstede Arentsburg, onder Voorburg, bij 's-Gravenhage*, Leiden/The Hague/Amsterdam, 1829.

—— *Notice et plan des constructions romaines, trouvées dans les fouilles faites en 1827–1829, sur l'emplacement présumé du Forum Hadriani, à la campagne nommé Arentsburg, Commune de Voorburg, près de la Haye*, Leiden/The Hague/Amsterdam, 1829.

—— *Lettres à Mr Letronne (membre de l'Institut et de la Légion d'Honneur, inspecteur-général de l'Université de France, etc.), sur les papyrus bilingues et grecs, et sur quelques autres monumens gréco-égyptiens du Musée d'Antiquités de l'Université de Leide*, Leiden, 1830.

—— 'Incrementa Musei Antiquarii Lugduno-Batavi annis 1822–1832', *Annales Academiae Lugduno-Batavi*, Leiden, 1832.

Rottiers, B.E.A., *Itinéraire de Tiflis à Constantinople*, Brussels, 1829.

—— *Description des monumens de Rhodes*, Brussels, 1830.

APPENDIX 4

LE VOYAGEUR

A wanderer's song

In 1822, before departing for the first archaeological mission to Tunisia, J.E. Humbert composed a romantic song about his life as a wanderer. During the archaeological mission he often described himself as *Le solitaire des ruines*. The same melancholy is evident in these lines, which were printed in Leiden and distributed among Humbert's family and friends. The song was adorned with an engraving by T.C. Bruining, which shows an Egyptian temple, an Arab with a camel, a European traveller (Humbert) and a recently dug grave. The only remaining copy belonged to Reuvens and is now kept in the library of Leiden University. The initials J.E.H. are completed in pencil by Reuvens' wife with the letters 'umbert'. Between brackets she added 'Oom Turk' (Uncle Turk, the nickname of Humbert in the Reuvens family).

Le Voyageur

Romance

Sur l'air: Un castel d'antique structure

Chers amis, partagez ma peine,
Je pars, je quitte ces climats,
Bientôt vers la rive africaine
Le devoir va guider mes pas;
De vous revoir j'ai l'espérance,
Mais que cet espoir est trompeur!
Peut-on compter sur l'existence
Ou le retour du *Voyageur* (bis)

Bien souvent dans mes traversées,
Bravant la tempête en courroux,
Mes souvenirs et mes pensées
Me conduiront auprès de vous;
Et si quelquefois mon image

Venait vous attrister le coeur,
Dites: le monde est un passage
Où l'homme n'est que *Voyageur* (bis)

Lorsque dans vos heureux ménages,
Avec des parens, des amis,
Vous parlerez de longs voyages,
Pensez à moi dans vos récits:
Au sein d'une tendre famille
Formez des voeux pour mon bonheur;
A votre fils, à votre fille,
Nommez souvent le *Voyageur* (bis)

Si le destin jaloux m'envie,
Amis, de revoir vos foyers;
Si je dois terminer ma vie
Loin de ces lieux hospitaliers:
Qu'au moins, en travaillant la terre,
Le pauvre Arabe laboureur
Respecte l'endroit solitaire
Où repose le *Voyageur* (bis)

J.E.H.

NOTES

1 INTRODUCTION

1 Quotation from a letter of Reuvens to Falck, 6 February 1824, Museum Archive, 17.1.1/1.
2 Royal decree, 13 August 1821, National Archive-II, State Secretary, 1248.
3 Royal decree, 24 December 1826, National Archive-II, State Secretary, 2636.
4 Royal decree, 26 May 1828, National Archive-II, State Secretary, 2983.

2 EARLY COLLECTIONS OF CLASSICAL ART

1 Gerard Reijnst (1599–1658) and Jan Reijnst (1601–46) belonged to the city's elite. See for the history of this family and their collecting activities: A.M. Logan, *The 'Cabinet' of the Brothers Gerard and Jan Reynst*, Amsterdam–New York, 1979.
2 See for the Vendramin collection: T. Borenius, *The Picture Gallery of Andrea Vendramin*, London, 1923; E. Jacobs, 'Das Museum Vendramin und die Sammlung Reynst', *Repertorium für Kunstwissenschaft*, 1925, vol. 46, pp. 15–39; T. Borenius, 'More about the Vendramin collection', *Burlington Magazine*, 1932, LX, pp. 140–45; K. Pomian, 'Antiquari e collezionisti', in *Storie della cultura veneta*, 4/I, Vicenza, 1983, p. 497. M. Zorzi (ed.), *Collezioni di antichità a Venezia nei secoli della Repubblica*, Roma, 1988, pp. 78–9; Irene Favaretto, *Arte antica e cultura antiquaria nelle collezioni Venete al tempo della Serenissima*, Roma, 1990, pp. 143–51. Frequent mention of the collection is made in: *Venezia e l'archeologia*, RdA suppl. 7, Roma, 1990.
3 V. Scamozzi, *Idea dell'architettura universale*, Venezia, 1615, III, p. 305.
4 Logan, op. cit., p. 100.
5 J.W.C. van Campen (ed.), *Aernout van Buchell, Notae Quotidianae*, Utrecht, 1940, pp. 77–8.
6 Aernout van Buchell in: van Campen, op. cit., pp. 94–5.
7 Logan, op. cit., p. 57: 'antique statues displayed in cases in the courtyard.' The Dutch word *casse* is used in the seventeenth century also for the housing of saints' figures.
8 See for example: A. Schnapp, *The Discovery of the Past*, London, 1996, p. 125.
9 A complete list is to be found in: Logan, op. cit., pp. 55–66.
10 The statues were heavily restored, cf. Favaretto, op. cit. (1990), pp. 149–50: 'In effetti quello che colpisce nella collezione di Andrea Vendramin è la quasi assoluta mancanza di sculture lasciate allo stato frammentario, come si trovavano invece di frequente nelle collezioni cinquecentesche, dove pure era praticato il restauro, ma non condotto in modo così invadente. Tutte le statue o i busti che

furono di Andrea appaiono come fossero stati integri in ogni loro parte: teste, braccia, basi, panneggi e attributi. Sembra che l'ala del tempo non sia mai passata su queste figure, nelle quale solo raramente e quasi per vezzo si è lasciato il moncherino di un braccio.'

11 *Mercurius Publicus*, 8 November 1660, and *Parliamentary Intelligencer*, 12 November 1660.

12 Portrait of a woman, described in the *Icones* as 'Faustina', at present at Hampton Court. See: Logan, op. cit., pp. 85–6.

13 About the Smetius collection see: H. Brunsting, *Johannes Smetius als provinciaal-Romeins archeoloog*, Nijmegen, 1989; A.V.M. Hubrecht, 'Die Sammlung Johannes Smetius, Vater und Sohn, in Nijmegen, 1618–1704', in *Festoen, Festschrift A. Zadoks-Josephus Jitta*, Groningen/Bussum, pp. 335–42; S. Langereis *et al.*, *Johannes Smetius, Nijmegen: stad der Bataven* (introduction and Dutch translation), Nijmegen, 1999.

14 Tacitus, *Historiae*, IV, 14.

15 See for the most recent discussion of the piece and a review of earlier interpretations: S. Böhm, 'Zur Ehrenrettung des Leidener Asklepiosreliefs', *BABesch*, 2001, vol. 76, pp. 71–7.

16 C.J.C. Reuvens, *Lettres à Mr Letronne (membre de l'Institut et de la Légion d'Honneur, inspecteur-général de l'Université de France, etc.), sur les papyrus bilingues et grecs, et sur quelques autres monumens gréco-égyptiens du Musée d'Antiquités de l'Université de Leide*, Leiden, 1830.

17 Description by Matthaeus Brouerius van Nidek, quoted in: J.T.P. Bijhouwer, *Nederlandsche tuinen en buitenplaatsen*, Amsterdam, 1942, p. 58. The original work by Brouerius van Nidek was published in 1729 under the title *Zegepralend Kennemerland*.

18 See for the sarcophagus of Marcellus: F.L. Bastet and H. Brunsting, *Corpus signorum antiquorum*, Zutphen, 1982, pp. 141–3, no. 254 (with earlier literature); M. Immerzeel and P. Jongste, 'Technologie, style et iconographie: le sarcophage paléochrétien de Leyde en tant que produit industriel', *OudhMeded*, 1993, vol. 73, pp. 77–92.

19 David van Hoogstraten and Jan Lodewijk Schuer, *Groot Algemeen Historisch, Geographisch, Genealogisch en Oordeelkundig Woordenboek*, Amsterdam, 1725–33. Citations from: I.Q. van Regteren Altena and P.J.J. van Thiel, *De portretgalerij van de Universiteit van Amsterdam en haar stichter Gerard van Papenbroeck, 1673–1743*, Amsterdam, 1964, pp. 29–30.

20 Quote from the notary Isaac Beukelaar, cited in: Van Regteren Altena and Van Thiel, op. cit., p. 40.

21 Resolution of the trustees 22 April 1744, cited in: Bastet and Brunsting, op. cit., p. xxii.

22 Drawings by Jacob van Werven, City Archive, Leiden, Topographical Atlas, no. 16002.

23 MDCCXXXXIV AET.MEM.ET HONORI AMPL.VIRI GERARDI PAPENBROECKII AMSTEL.URBIS SCABINORVM OLIM PRAESIDIS OB GRAECA LATINAQVE ANTIQVITATIS MONVMENTA ACAD.LVGD.BAT. TESTAMENTO LEGATA POSVERVNT ACAD.CVRAT.ET VRBIS COSS. L.M.Q.

24 F. Oudendorp, *Oratio de veterum inscriptionum et monumentorum usu, legatoque Papenbroekiano*, Leiden, 1745, p. 36.

25 Oudendorp, op. cit., p. 37.

26 Oudendorp, op. cit., p. 39.

27 F. Oudendorp, *Brevis veterum monumentorum ab amplissimo viro Gerardo Papenbroekio Academiae Lugduno-Batavae legatorum descriptio*, Leiden, 1746.

28 Now in the Leiden University Library: Manuscript Papenbroek no. 17.

29 Donations were made by De Bosch, Van Hollebeeke, Allamand, Fremeaux, De Hochepied, Bollaert and De Mayne. The first director of the archaeological museum, C.J.C. Reuvens, commented: 'If the Trustees of this university had followed and aided the zeal and patriotism of these individual persons, then Leiden would have possessed a collection which could compete with many other cabinets in Europe.' (Reuvens to Minister Falck, 25 November 1820, Museum Archive, 17.1.1/1).

30 Reuvens to Minister Falck, 25 November 1820, Museum Archive, 17.1.1/1.

3 C.J.C. REUVENS AND THE ARCHAEOLOGICAL CABINET

1 Information about Reuvens' life is to be found in the *Vita Reuvensii* (1838), written after his death by his successor Conrad Leemans (Appendix 3). The correspondence between Reuvens father and son contains many biographical details. In the notes this correspondence (now in a private collection) is referred to as the 'Reuvens Archive'. For an extensive account of Reuvens' early years see: J.A. Brongers, *Een vroeg begin van de moderne archeologie: leven en werken van Cas Reuvens (1793–1835)*, Amersfoort, 2002, pp. 53–78. More literature concerning Reuvens is to be found in: J.A. Brongers, op. cit., pp. 150–54.

2 His doctoral thesis was titled: *De rebus creditis: Du prêt, du depôt et du mandat*, Thèse Université Impériale, Paris, 2 juillet 1813.

3 Roland to David, 17 October 1792, cited in: S.M. Pearce, *Museums, Objects and Collections*, Leicester, 1992, p. 100.

4 See for Vivant Denon: M.-A. Dupuy, I. Le Masne de Chermont and E. Williamson, *Vivant Denon, directeur des Musées sous le Consulat et l'Empire, Correspondence (1802–1815)*, Paris, 1999; M.-A. Dupuy, *Vivant Denon, l'oeil de Napoléon*, Catalogue Louvre, Paris, 1999.

5 In this aspect his endeavours can be compared with the ideals of Sir William Hamilton and the influence of his publications on the design of the Wedgwood factory. See: I. Jenkins and K. Sloan, *Vases and Volcanoes: Sir William Hamilton and his Collection*, London, 1996.

6 C.J.C. Reuvens, *Collectanea litteraria, sive conjecturae in Attium, Diomedem, Lucilium, Lydum, Nonium, Ovidium, Plautum, Schol. Aristoph., Varronem, et alios; passim manuscriptorum librorum ope factae, et maximam partem ad Romanorum rem scenicam pertinentes; quibus accedit disputatio de linguae Graecae pronunciatione*, Leiden, 1815.

7 C.J.C. Reuvens, *Oratio de litterarum disciplina animos ad studia severiora et ad vitam communem praeparante*, Harderwijk, 1816. Reuvens complained to his father that nobody in the audience had paid any attention to his words (he was the last to speak) and that such a lecture was a necessary evil, with the only benefit that the payment would start. His father reprehended him harshly, whereupon the young professor had 'cried like a child': letters in Reuvens Archive, 28 January 1816 and 4 February 1816.

8 An official enquiry proclaimed his death a case of murder, but, considering all documents, suicide is the most probable reason for his drowning. See: H.D. Ploeger, 'Het dossier Reuvens I–II', *Ius Civile*, 1996, vol. 4, pp. 11–20 and 33–54.

9 Documents in: State Archives-II, State Secretary, 632.

10 Falck to Willem I, 10 June 1818, State Archives-II, State Secretary, 632.

11 Royal decree, 13 June 1818, no. 100: State Archives-II, State Secretary, 632.

12 Museum projects in: Museum Archive, 15.1/1.

13 Ibid.

14 Ibid.

15 See: H. Dorsman, 'A visit to the Old Schools in 1819', *The Ashmolean*, 1999, vol. 37, p. 14.

16 For a good account of the nineteenth-century British Museum, see: I. Jenkins, *Archaeologists and Aesthetes in the Sculpture Galleries of the British Museum, 1800– 1939*, London, 1992.

17 Reuvens to trustees, 21 July 1818, Museum Archive, 17.1.1/1.

18 Trustees to Reuvens, 15 August 1818, Museum Archive, 17.1.2/1.

19 Reuvens to trustees, 8 April 1819, Museum Archive, 17.1.1/1.

20 The financial part of this transaction was taken care of by the Dutch Consul-General May, 28 September 1819, Museum Archive, 17.1.1/1.

21 'The undersigned asks respectfully that it might please Trustees to allow him to ask His Excellency the Minister for a extraordinary subsidy of Fl. 1,200.' Reuvens to trustees, 5 October 1819, Museum Archive, 17.1.1/1.

4 COLLECTIONS AND CONFLICTS

1 Reuvens to Van Ewijck, 25 November 1820, Museum Archive, 17.1.1/1.

2 The first English edition was published in 1687: *A Catalogue of All the Cheifest Rarities in the Publick Theater and Anatomie-hall of the University of Leyden.*

3 F.L. Bastet and H. Brunsting, *Corpus signorum antiquorum*, Zutphen, 1982, p. 206, no. 380, pl. 112. The probable provenance from Teos is put forward by: Wolf-R. Megow, 'Zwei Köpfe im Rijksmuseum van Oudheden in Leiden', *Antike Plastik*, 23, 1994, pp. 59–79.

4 Reuvens to Van Ewijck, 17 February 1828, Museum Archive, 17.1.1/3.

5 Reuvens to Falck, 25 November 1820, Museum Archive, 17.1.1/1.

6 Ibid.

7 C.J.C. Reuvens, *Verhandeling over drie groote steenen beelden, in den jare 1819 uit Java naar de Nederlanden overgezonden*, Amsterdam, 1826.

8 Reuvens to Baud (governor-general of the East Indies), 29 August 1832, Museum Archive, 17.1.1/4.

9 Ibid.

10 Ibid.

11 Ibid.

12 Reuvens to De Jonge, 8 November 1824, Museum Archive, 17.1.1/1.

13 De Jonge to Reuvens, 10 November 1824, Museum Archive, 17.1.2/1.

14 Reuvens to De Jonge, 24 November 1824, Museum Archive, 17.1.1/1.

15 Reuvens to Van Ewijck, 20 April 1825, Museum Archive, 17.1.1/1.

16 Ibid.

17 Reuvens to Van Ewijck, 27 April 1826, Museum Archive, 17.1.1/2.

18 See: J. Hoftijzer, 'Liste des pierres et moulages à textes Phéniciens/Puniques à Leyde', *OudhMeded*, 1963, vol. 44, pp. 89–98.

19 Reuvens to Van Ewijck, 12 May 1826, Museum Archives, 17.1.1/2.

20 Ibid.

21 H.A. Hamaker, *Miscellanea Phoenicia sive commentarii de rebus Phoenicum, quibus inscriptiones multae lapidum ac nummorum, nominaque propria hominum et locorum, explicantur, item Punicae gentis lingua et religiones passim illustrantur*, Leiden, 1828. His work was criticized for the inaccuracies of the illustrations and the transcriptions. In the catalogue of the Punic monuments of 1842, Reuvens' successor Conrad Leemans chose to follow the reading and translations of the German professor G. Gesenius from the University of Halle: *Scripturae linguaeque Phoeniciae monumenta quotquot supersunt, edita et inedita ad autographorum optimorumque exemplorum fidem edidit, additisque de scriptura et lingua Phoenicum commentariis illustravit G. Gesenius*, Leipzig, 1837.

22 C.J.C. Reuvens, *Lettres à Mr Letronne sur les papyrus bilingues et grecs, et sur quelques autres monumens gréco-egyptiens du Musée d'Antiquités de l'Université de Leide*, Leiden, 1830.
23 *Antiquiteiten* I, 1820, preface.
24 'Whoever lives in his country and scorns learning about his country, will be a stranger in my view, and not a compatriot.'
25 He published a Latin translation of his article in England: C.J.C. Reuvens, 'Disputatio de simulacris quibusdam tympanorum Parthenonis, ad Taylorem Combium, Musei Britannici Antiquitatibus Praefectum', *The Classical Journal*, 1823, vol. 55, pp. 175–83; 1823, vol. 56, pp. 273–87.
26 *Antiquiteiten* III/1, 1826, preface.

5 THE GREEK COLLECTIONS OF B.E.A. ROTTIERS

1 Falck to Reuvens, 2 November 1820, Museum Archive, 17.1.2/1.
2 A biography and a detailed description of his archaeological activities are in: F.L. Bastet, *De drie collecties Rottiers te Leiden*, Leiden, 1987.
3 J.T. Reinaud, *Lettre à M. le Baron Silvestre de Sacy sur la collection de monuments orientaux de S. Exc. M. le Comte de Blacas*, Paris, 1820. On p. 14 mention is made of Rottiers' collection.
4 B.E.A. Rottiers, *Itinéraire de Tiflis à Constantinople*, Brussels, 1829.
5 See for this diplomatic climate for example: W. St. Clair, *Lord Elgin and the Marbles: The Controversial History of the Parthenon Sculptures*, Oxford, 1998.
6 A diplomat with a somewhat tarnished reputation because of his double-dealing at the auction of the Aegina marbles. See: C.P. Bracken, *Antiquities Acquired: The Spoliation of Greece*, Newton Abbot, 1975.
7 Painter, collector, dealer and diplomat. See: *Dictionaire de biographie française*, XIII, pp. 805–6.
8 B.E.A. Rottiers, *Les Monumens de Rhodes*, Brussels, 1830, p. 273, no. 1.
9 Giuracich to Testa (Dutch ambassador in Constantinople), 18 May 1819, State Archives, Consulate Athens 1816–1830, 97.
10 See C.W.J. Eliot, 'Coastal demes of Attica: a study of the policy of Kleisthenes', *Phoenix*, 1962, supplementary vol. 5, 6–24.
11 Reuvens to Falck, 25 November 1820, Museum Archive, 17.1.1/1.
12 Ibid.
13 Reuvens to Falck, 8 February 1821, Museum Archive, 17.1.1/1.
14 Ibid.
15 '. . . he sold his vases to Mr Jean Rotier jr [sic], and also some medals'. Origone to ambassador Testa, 14 September 1821, State Archives-II, Legation Turkey and the Levant, 97.
16 Rottiers to Reuvens, 6 March 1822, Museum Archive, 17.1.2/1.
17 Reuvens to Falck, 5 June 1822, Museum Archive, 17.1.1/1.
18 Rottiers to Reuvens, 6 May 1823, Museum Archive, 17.1.2/1.
19 Delescluze to Reuvens, 29 July 1826, Museum Archive, 17.1.2/2.
20 Reuvens to Van Ewijck, 15 August 1826, Museum Archive, 17.1.1/2.
21 Ibid.
22 Falck to Willem I, 23 June 1824, State Archives-II, Ministry of the Interior, 57.
23 Van Ewijck to Reuvens, 16 July 1824, Museum Archive, 17.1.2/1.
24 Reuvens to Van Ewijck, 3 August 1824, Museum Archive, 17.1.1/1.
25 Reuvens to Van Ewijck, 5 October 1824, Museum Archive, 17.1.1/1.
26 The documents are now in the State Archives-II, Legation Turkey and the Levant, 12. It is not clear if Rottiers acted on impulse or was asked to do so.

27 Rottiers to Reuvens, 27 April 1825, Museum Archive, 17.1.2/1.
28 Unofficial note of Van Ewijck to Reuvens, undated, Museum Archive, 17.1.2/1.
29 State Archives-II, Legation Turkey and the Levant, 815 (10–5–1825).
30 Bastet, op. cit., p. 98.
31 B.E.A. Rottiers, *Description des monumens de Rhodes*, Brussels, 1830, p. 10. In fact the arrival of the Dutch ambassador on Melos put an end to the availability of the crew of HM *Diana*, which had to escort the diplomat to Smyrna.
32 *Courier des Pays-Bas, Journal de Bruxelles*, 28 December 1825.
33 Reuvens to Van Ewijck, 3 April 1826, Museum Archive, 17.1.1/2.
34 Ibid. The most recent publication of the Melian mosaic dates it in the beginning of the third century AD: E.M. Moormann, 'Imperial Roman mosaics at Leiden', *OudhMeded*, 1991, vol. 71, p. 103.
35 'Rottiers Painter and workshop'. See: J.N. Coldstream, *Greek Geometric Pottery*, London, 1968, pp. 181–5.
36 R.A. De Vertot d'Aubeuf, *Histoire des Chevaliers Hospitaliers de Saint Jean de Jérusalem appellés depuis Chevaliers de Rhodes, et aujourd'hui Chevaliers de Malte*, Paris, 1726.
37 'A very important mummy, which was found long ago in a cavity cut in the rock near Famagusta on Cyprus', Rottiers to Reuvens, 22 November 1826, Museum Archive, 17.1.2/2.
38 Reuvens to Van Ewijck, 3 April 1826, Museum Archive, 17.1.1/2.
39 Ibid.
40 Reuvens to Van Ewijck, 19 December 1826, Museum Archive, 17.1.1/2. The most important finds were in his view the mummy with its three cases, the altar, the priest's head and the mosaics from Melos, the kouros head from Santorini and a sundial from Athens.
41 Ibid.
42 Ibid.
43 Reuvens to Van Ewijck, 5 October 1824, Museum Archive, 17.1.1/1.
44 Rottiers to Van Ewijck, 10 June 1826, Museum Archive, 17.1.2/2.
45 Reuvens to Rottiers, 10 February 1827, Museum Archive, 17.1.1/2.

6 JEAN EMILE HUMBERT: THE QUEST FOR CARTHAGE

1 The archaeological activities of Humbert are described in: R.B. Halbertsma, 'Benefit and honour: the archaeological travels of Jean Emile Humbert (1771–1839) in North Africa and Italy in service of the Kingdom of the Netherlands', *MededRom*, 1991, vol. 50, pp. 301–16; R.B. Halbertsma, *Le solitaire des ruines: de archeologische reizen van Jean Emile Humbert (1771–1839) in dienst van het Koninkrijk der Nederlanden*, Leiden, 1995.
2 D.P.G. Humbert de Superville, *Essai sur les signes inconditionnels dans l'art*, Leiden, 1827–39.
3 A British friend in Tunis wrote: 'You must sometimes regret that Nature has been so bountiful to you: for you, "beaux esprits", are like pretty women, always with a cortège, & consequently are obliged to hear in such a sejour as this terrestrial purgatory insipid observations of the "soi disant" literati or the profound diplomatick remarks of Tunesian politicians . . .' J.D. Hodge to J.E. Humbert, undated, Museum Archive, 19.3.1/46.
4 Project designed by Louis-Alexandre d'Herculais. See: *Dictionnaire de biographie française*, XVII, p. 1049.
5 *OMNES NATVRA IVDICES FECIT SED NON ARTIFICES*: 'Nature has given everyone the ability to criticize, but not to construct something.' Documents

about the project in the Museum Archive, 19.3.3/11.

6 Report written about the increasing tensions in 1802 by Vice-Admiral J.W. de Winter, State Archives-II, State Secretary, 518.

7 For example Th. Shaw, *Voyages de Monsieur Shaw dans plusieurs provinces de la Barbarie et du Levant*, I–II, The Hague, 1743.

8 Quotes by M.M. Noah, *Travels in England, France, Spain and the Barbary States in the years 1813–14 and 1815*, New York/London, 1819.

9 E. Malakis (ed.), *F.R. de Chateaubriand, Itinéraire de Paris à Jérusalem (1812)*, Baltimore, 1946, II, p. 287.

10 See for a detailed description of Borgia's activities: V. Ciccotti, *Camillo Borgia (1773–1817), soldato ed archeologo*, Velletri, 1999; V. Ciccotti (ed.), *Atti del convegno internazionale di studi Camillo Borgia (1773–1817)*, Velletri, 2000.

11 See for a description of his activities in Tunisia: J. Debergh, 'Camillo Borgia, ricerche archeologiche di un esule in Tunisia (1815–1816)', *Levante*, XLVIII, 3, pp. 7–26.

12 J.E. Humbert, *Notice sur quatre cippes sépulcraux et deux fragments, découverts en 1817, sur le sol de l'ancienne Carthage*, The Hague, 1821. Humbert published the inscriptions before they became the property of the Dutch Government.

13 G.B. Niebuhr, *Römische Geschichte*, 1844, p. 371, note 3: 'Dem Oberst Hömberg [sic], einem rechtlichen, offenen, redlichen, geraden Soldaten.'

14 Humbert wrote: 'l'Homme est entouré de destruction: il ne touche que ce qui est détruit, ou va l'être. Il forme des liens qui doivent se rompre, des liaisons qui doivent finir: bientôt il n'a plus que des souvenirs que le tems vient effacer encore, avant de l'entrainer lui-même dans le néant . . .' Letter dated 27 November 1819, Museum Archive, 19.3.1/46.

15 Reuvens to Falck, 9 March 1821, Museum Archive, 17.1.1/1.

16 Reuvens to Falck, 3 June 1821, Museum Archive, 17.1.1/1.

17 Ibid.

18 Ibid.

19 Humbert to Reuvens, undated (June 1821), Museum Archive, 17.1.1/2.

20 Reuvens to Falck, 27 November 1821, Museum Archive, 17.1.1/1.

21 'J'ai fait quelques infidelités au bon sens. Je ne conviendrai pas cependant que je suis devenu infidèle à mon pays pour n'avoir pas suivi sur les bords de l'Arno les usages des bords de l'Amstel.' Letter 10 January 1823, Museum Archive, 19.3.1/ 21. His meeting during the carnival with a certain Margherita Terreni would have serious consequences for the second expedition of 1826–30, as shall be described later.

22 Inventory book 1818–24, Museum Archive, 1.1/1. The statue used to be identified with the *Flora* found in Utica by Borgia, and donated to Gierlew, but in reality has nothing to do with Borgia's find, see: J. Lund, 'Il console Gierlew e il Conte Borgia in terra d'Africa', in *Atti del convegno internazionale di studi Camillo Borgia (1773–1817)*, Velletri, 2000, pp. 80–81. The whereabouts of the *Flora* still remain unknown.

23 Now in Copenhagen, Nationalmuseet, inv. ABb 1. The history of this statue is described in: J. Lund, 'En draperet kvindestatue fra Utica i Nationalmuseets Antiksamling', *Klassisk Arkaeologiske Studier*, 1995, vol. 2, pp. 195–214. About Falbe's activities as an antiquarian: J. Lund, 'The archaeological activities of Christian Tuxen Falbe in Carthage in 1838', *Cahiers des études anciennes*, 1986, vol. 18, pp. 8–24; J. Lund, 'Royal connoisseur and consular collector: the part played by C.T. Falbe in collecting antiquities from Tunisia, Greece and Paris for Christian VIII', in Bodil Bundgaard Rasmussen *et al.* (eds), *Christian VIII and the National Museum*, Copenhagen, 2000, pp. 119–49.

24 Reuvens to Falck, 12 March 1823, Museum Archive, 17.1.1/1.
25 Humbert to Falck, 16 August 1822, Museum Archive, 17.1.1/2.
26 See for a recent discussion of these stones: U. Wurnig, *Reliefstele der Dea Caelestis: Studie zu Religion und Kunst im römischen Nordafrika*, Würzburg, 1999.
27 Humbert to Reuvens, 3 June 1822, Museum Archive, 17.1.1/2.
28 Sections for archaeological drawings were not new, see for example the 'section through an excavation near Nola', published in M. Dubois-Maisonneuve, *Introduction à l'étude des vases antiques*, Paris, 1817, p. 101 (also reproduced in: I. Jenkins and K. Sloan, *Vases and Volcanoes: Sir William Hamilton and his Collection*, Catalogue British Museum, London, 1996, p. 55, fig. 24).
29 C.T. Falbe, *Recherches sur l'emplacement de Carthage*, Paris, 1833, p. 43.
30 'Oui, la mémoire fait jouir / c'est un des nos plus doux partages. / Plaisirs, vous seriez trop volages / sans le bienfait du Souvenir.' The original poem has not been found *in situ*, but it is cited in a letter of Humbert dated 26 July 1822, Museum Archive, 19.3.1/21.
31 Humbert to his friend Falchi, 22 October 1823, Museum Archive, 19.3.1/21.
32 Humbert to his friend Luzac, 10 January 1823, Museum Archive, 19.3.1/47.
33 Reuvens to Van Ewijck, 4 January 1826, Museum Archive, 17.1.1/2.
34 Humbert grew tired of the ever increasing list with questions of Reuvens and Hamaker: 'The erudite scholar, who travels around the world sitting in his comfortable library chair asks from a traveller too often knowledge which is beyond his reach, and research which is impossible to do.' Humbert to Van Ewijck, 31 October 1827, Museum Archive, 17.1.2/3.
35 Reuvens to Van Ewijck, 25 February 1825, Museum Archive, 17.1.1/1.
36 His description of Spain was famous at the time: A.L.J. De la Borde, *Voyage pittoresque et historique de l'Espagne*, I–II, Paris, 1806–20.
37 See for a full account of these transactions: R.B. Halbertsma, 'Il fondo Borgiano di Leida' in V. Ciccotti (ed.), *Atti del convegno internazionale di studi Camillo Borgia*, Velletri, 2000, pp. 37–44.
38 As title she suggested *Voyage dans la Régence de Tunis par le comte Camille Borgia*.
39 All documents regarding this purchase in: Museum Archive, 19.2.2/19.

7 STATION LIVORNO:
THE ETRUSCAN AND EGYPTIAN COLLECTIONS

1 See about Hamilton and his vase collection: I. Jenkins and K. Sloan, *Vases and Volcanoes: Sir William Hamilton and his Collection*, Catalogue British Museum, London, 1996.
2 See for the fate of the immense Campana collection: S. Sarti, *Giovanni Pietro Campana 1808–1880: The man and his collection*, Oxford, 2001.
3 For example: E.C. Hamilton-Grey, *A Tour to the Sepulchres of Etruria*, London, 1841; G. Dennis, *The Cities and Cemeteries of Etruria*, London, 1848.
4 See F.L. Bastet and H. Brunsting, *Corpus signorum antiquorum*, Zutphen, 1982, nos. 267–9, 271–2 and 278 (with earlier literature).
5 'Mr Champollion knew the urns I bought. He wanted to buy them also and wrote about them to France. I had the good luck to outstrip him in fastness.' Humbert to Reuvens, 30 January 1827, Museum Archive, 17.1.2/3. Champollion's mistress Angelica Palli lived in Livorno. Humbert and Champollion met each other regularly at her salon.
6 Museum Archive, 19.3.5/1.
7 Ibid.
8 Ibid.

9 Reuvens to Humbert, 30 November 1826, Museum Archive, 17.1.1/2.

10 Museum Archive, 19.3.5/1.

11 Humbert to Reuvens, 30 January 1827, Museum Archive, 17.1.2/3.

12 See about Cortona and the Museo Corazzi: A. Neppi Modona, *Cortona Etrusca e Romana nella storia e nell'arte*, Florence, 1977; P. Barocchi and D. Gallo (eds), *L'Accademia Etrusca*, Milan, 1985; *Bibliotheca Etrusca: fonti letterarie e figurative tra XVIII e XIX secolo nella Biblioteca dell'Istituto Nazionale di Archeologia e Storia dell'Arte*, Rome, 1986; P. Zamarchi Grassi and M. Scarpellini, *Tesori ritrovati: reperti archeologici etruschi rinvenuti nel territorio di Castiglion Fiorentino dal sec. XVIII ad oggi*, Montepulciano, 2002.

13 Reuvens to Van Ewijck, 9 August 1826, Museum Archive, 17.1.1/2.

14 Humbert to Van Ewijck, 2 October 1826, State Archives-II, Ministry of the Interior, 4314.

15 Reuvens to Van Ewijck, 23 October 1826, Museum Archive, 17.1.1/2.

16 Van Gobbelschroy to Willem I, 15 November 1826, State Archive-II, State Secretary, 2636.

17 King Willem I to the minister of the interior, 24 December 1826, State Archives-II, Ministry of the Interior, 4314.

18 Humbert to Van Ewijck, 12 March 1827, Museum Archive, 17.1.2/3.

19 The first publications were: L.J.F. Janssen, *Musei Lugduno-Batavi inscriptiones Etruscae*, Leiden, 1840. L.J.F. Janssen, *De Etrurische grafreliëfs uit het Museum van Oudheden te Leyden*, Leiden, 1854. L.J.F. Janssen, *Les inscriptions grecques et etrusques des pierres gravées du Cabinet de S.M. le Roi des Pays-Bas*, The Hague, 1866.

20 L.J.F. Janssen, *Musei Lugduno-Batavi inscriptiones Etruscae*, Leiden, 1840, p. 2.

21 Inv.nr. H III S 1. See: R.B. Halbertsma, *Le solitaire des ruines – de archeologische reizen van Jean Emile Humbert (1771–1839) in dienst van het Koninkrijk der Nederlanden*, Leiden, 1995, pl. 25.

22 See: A.M. Donadoni Roveri, 'Il Museo Egizio di Torino', in *L'Egitto fuori l'Egitto*, Bologna, 1991, pp. 191–9.

23 See: M.L. Bierbrier, W.R. Dawson and E.P. Uphill, *Who Was Who in Egyptology*, London, 1995, pp. 99–100.

24 Bierbrier, Dawson and Uphill, op. cit., p. 15.

25 Reuvens to Van Ewijck, 17 July 1827, Museum Archive, 17.1.1/2.

26 Rosellini was preparing an expedition to Egypt together with Champollion, which took place in 1828–9. See Bierbrier, Dawson and Uphill, op. cit., pp. 362–3.

27 Reuvens to Van Ewijck, 19 October 1827, Museum Archive, 17.1.1/2.

28 A Dutch businessman with many contacts in the Mediterranean and an informant of Reuvens.

29 Reuvens to Van Ewijck, 19 October 1827, Museum Archive, 17.1.1/2.

30 Humbert to Reuvens, 7 December 1827, Museum Archive, 17.1.2/3. Reuvens was furious about such remarks. On a piece of scrap paper he jotted down: 'Humbert mustn't say the ultimate price is 400,000 francs [. . .]. He knows that he has bought two collections for less than half of the asking price. With this expression he seems to be our opponent, and not our agent. He must give his opinion calmly, with knowledge about people and trade.' Draft of Reuvens, Museum Archive, 17.1.1/2.

31 Reinhold to Humbert, 15 December 1827, Museum Archive, 19.3.1/28.

32 Humbert to Van Ewijck, 24 December 1827, Museum Archive, 17.1.2/4.

33 Reinhold to Humbert, 29 December 1827, Museum Archive, 19.3.1/28.

34 Reinhold to Humbert, 24 January 1828, Museum Archive, 19.3.1/28. The Minister alludes to the Medway Raid of June 1667 when Admiral De Ruyter sailed into the Thames estuary and captured the British flagship H.M. *Royal Charles*.

35 Reuvens to Van Ewijck, 29 February 1828, Museum Archive, 17.1.1/3.
36 Ibid.
37 State secretary to the minister of the interior, 24 March 1828, Museum Archive, 17.1.2/4.
38 Reinhold to Humbert, 26 April 1828, Museum Archive, 19.3.1/28.
39 Reuvens to Van Ewijck, 29 March 1830, Museum Archive, 17.1.1/4.
40 In 1821 both famous collections were merged and placed in the palazzo of Giovanni Tiepolo. A year later this Nani-Tiepolo collection, which was renowned for its Greek artefacts, was put on sale. When Humbert saw the collection parts of it were already dispersed. See: I. Favaretto, *Arte antica e cultura antiquaria nelle collezioni Venete al tempo della Serenissima*, Roma, 1990, pp. 206–20.
41 To Leiden he sent an interesting *apperçu historique* of the Museum Nanianum, made by Costantino Cavaco, vice-consul of the Netherlands in Venice, 18 August 1829, Museum Archive, 17.1.2/5.
42 Now in the Leiden Museum Archive, III/2 (HIt 10 a-b).
43 Gargiulo's system, which is correct in view of the relative chronology (except for the last category), is not mentioned in Cook's history of the study of vase-painting. See: R.M. Cook, *Greek Painted Pottery*, London, 1997, pp. 275–311, with the splendid remark: 'We may laugh at these past follies, but they are also a warning to look for equal follies of our own' (Cook, op. cit., p. 311).
44 Catalogue and drawings in the Museum Archive, 3.2/10–11.
45 Humbert to Reuvens, 7 February 1830, Museum Archive, 17.1.2/6.
46 See: G.T. Martin, *The Memphite Tomb of Horemheb, Commander-in-chief of Tutankhamun*, London, 1989.
47 Reuvens was angry that Humbert had missed this piece with a royal cartouche. It can be identified with the Viennese Horemheb fragment inv. 214. See: H.D. Schneider, *De Laudibus Aegyptologiae*, Leiden, 1985, p. 23. The receipt of the Castiglione purchase in: Museum Archive, 19.3.1/39.
48 C.T. Falbe, *Recherches sur l'emplacement de Carthage*, Paris, 1833.
49 The gravestone did not survive. A year after Humbert's death the *cimitero* was moved to the Via Mastacchi in Livorno, and the skeletal remains were put in an ossuary in the form of a round temple with the names of the 339 deceased engraved on a marble plaque (communication by Vincenzo Ciccotti).

8 FORUM HADRIANI: DIGGING BEHIND THE DUNES

1 See for Reuvens' ideas about archaeological fieldwork and also a description of his activities at Forum Hadriani: J.A. Brongers, *Een vroeg begin van de moderne archeologie: leven en werken van Cas Reuvens (1793–1835)*, Amersfoort, 2002, pp. 93–108.
2 De Jonge to Reuvens, 18 January 1826, Museum Archive, 17.1.2/2.
3 Reuvens to Van Ewijck, 10 February 1826, Museum Archive, 19.2.1/57.
4 Reuvens to Van Ewijck, 1 January 1827, Museum Archive, 19.2.1/57.
5 Van Ewijck to Reuvens, 4 January 1827, Museum Archive, 19.2.1/57.
6 Reuvens to Van Ewijck, 11 January 1827, Museum Archive, 19.2.1/57.
7 A short description of the excavation is in: J.A. Brongers, 'An early nineteenth-century excavation in the Netherlands', *Berichten van de Rijksdienst voor het Oudheidkundig Bodemonderzoek*, 1974, vol. 24, pp. 191–4.
8 Olden to Reuvens, 8 June 1827, Museum Archive, 19.2.1/57.
9 All the finds were listed in the Arentsburg Diaries, Museum Archive, 19.2.1/53.
10 Official gazette (*Nederlandsche Staatscourant*), 12 October 1827, Museum Archive, 19.2.1/57.
11 Ibid.

12 Ibid.
13 Ibid.
14 Official gazette (*Nederlandsche Staatscourant*), 5 September 1828, Museum Archive, 19.2.1/57.
15 Reuvens to Van Ewijck, 1 March 1829, Museum Archive, 19.2.1/57.
16 Collection Muséum d'Histoire Naturelle, inv.nr. 24913 (kept in the depots of the Musée de l'Homme): 'Modèle en plâtre d'un squelette, que l'on croit être celui d'une femme romaine, trouvé en 1828 à Arentsburg, près de la Haye, sur l'emplacement du forum Hadriani. Don Reuvens, Directeur du Musée des Antiquités à Leyde.' With thanks to Dr J.-C. Moreno, Muséum d'Histoire Naturelle and Dr Philippe Mennecier, Musée de l'Homme.
17 Diary excavations Arentsburg, Museum Archive, 19.1.2/53.
18 'It has done me much grief that since my days on Arentsburg an alienation between us has taken place. The principal reason lies not with you, nor with me: of this I am assured.' Van der Chijs to Reuvens, 11 June 1829, Museum Archive, 17.1.2/5.
19 Diary excavations Arentsburg, Museum Archive, 19.1.2/53.
20 Sir Mortimer Wheeler, *Archaeology from the Earth*, Oxford, 1954, p. 8.
21 Aloys Senefelder (1771–1834) published his *Vollständiges Lehrbuch der Steindruckerei* in 1818 in Munich and Vienna. It was translated immediately into English and French.
22 Reuvens to Van Ewijck, 23 May 1829, Museum Archive, 19.2.1/57.
23 Reuvens to Minister Van Doorn, 11 October 1832, Museum Archive, 19.2.1/58.
24 Reuvens to Minister Van Doorn, 19 February 1833, Museum Archive, 19.2.1/58. In his diary he noted: 'In any case, Holland isn't the only country where sciences and arts have to yield pride of place to nobility and richness.'
25 Caan to Reuvens, 3 October 1833, Museum Archive, 19.2.1/58.
26 See: J.A. Brongers, *Air Photography and Celtic Field Research in the Netherlands*, Amersfoort, 1976. The same author has described Reuvens' observations in Drenthe: J.A. Brongers, *1833: Reuvens in Drenthe*, Bussum, 1973 (text in Dutch and English).
27 Later interpreted as the foundation of a Gallo-Roman temple: H. Brunsting, 'Opgraving bij het Fort Krayenhoff te Nijmegen in 1834', *OudhMeded*, 1949, vol. 30, pp. 49–65.

9 THE IDEAL MUSEUM: DREAMS AND REALITY

1 Projects and sketches in: Museum Archive, 15.1/1.
2 About the new arrangement of the antiquities in Leiden see: R.B. Halbertsma, 'Treasures around the temple: the new installation at the National Museum of Antiquities in Leiden', *Minerva*, 2001, vol. 12, no. 4, pp. 8–13.
3 See for Reuvens' visit to Cambridge and Oxford: H. Dorsman, 'A visit to the Old Schools in 1819', *The Ashmolean*, 1999, vol. 37, pp. 14–15.
4 Reuvens to King Willem I, 29 March 1826, Museum Archive, 17.1.1/2.
5 Trustees to Reuvens, 6 May 1826, Museum Archive, 17.1.2/2.
6 Ibid.
7 Reuvens to trustees, 7 February 1824, Museum Archive, 15.1/1.
8 Zeger Reijers (1790–1857) was a successful architect in The Hague. He received his training in France, Germany and Italy, where he developed a palladian style of architecture.
9 Informal notes by Reuvens, 3 December 1826, Museum Archive, 15.1/1.
10 Reijers to Reuvens, 1 December 1826, Museum Archive, 15.1/1.

NOTES

11 C.J.C. Reuvens, *Oratio de archaeologiae cum artibus recentioribus conjunctione*, Leiden, 1827.
12 Reuvens to King Willem I, 2 June 1827, Museum Archive, 17.1.1/2.
13 Ibid.
14 From: C. Sol, 'Mummies op de schopstoel – Thorbecke over het nut van universitaire musea en verzamelingen', *Leidsch Jaarboekje*, 1998, vol. 90, p. 109.
15 Reuvens to Van Ewijck, undated (May 1830), Museum Archive, 17.1.1/4.
16 Ibid.
17 Ibid.
18 Ibid.
19 Ibid. In a later note Reuvens added that this corrosion only occurred when a surface was coloured with paint containing lead.
20 Ibid.
21 Ibid.
22 Reuvens to trustees, 18 June 1832, Museum Archive, 17.1.1/4.
23 Reuvens to trustees, 16 August 1832, Museum Archive, 17.1.1/4.
24 M. Siegenbeek, *Geschiedenis der Leidsche Hoogeschool: van hare oprichting in den jare 1575, tot het jaar 1825*, Leiden, 1829–35.
25 Ibid., p. 132.
26 Thorbecke (a former pupil of Reuvens!) to Van Rappard, 4 October 1834, in: Sol, op. cit., p. 109.
27 Ibid.

10 END OF THE PIONEER YEARS, 1835–40

1 Conrad Leemans, *Epistola ad Leonardum Joannem Fredericum Janssen de vita Caspari Jacobi Christiani Reuvensii*, Leiden, 1838.
2 National Museum of Antiquities, inventory number SR.
3 'The learned Englishmen, who were present at the auction, admired Reuvens' singular cleverness and zeal', Leemans, op. cit., p. 52.
4 'With very few and incoherent words.' Leemans, op. cit., p. 55.
5 Conrad Leemans, *Dissertatio antiquario-litteraria, exhibens Horapollonis Niloi Hieroglyphica, lectionis diversitate, versione Latina, hieroglyphicorum imaginibus et indicibus instructa*, Amsterdam, 1835.
6 Leemans to trustees, 15 August 1835, Museum Archive, 17.1.1/5.
7 Ibid. (Salvolini cited by Leemans).
8 Leemans to trustees, 16 August 1835, Museum Archive, 17.1.1/5.
9 A year later Leemans was even more pessimistic about this publication. To publish the excavation of Arentsburg alone was 'generally not important enough', but Reuvens' idea of a complete description of all Roman remains in the Netherlands was of an 'immeasurable scale and almost impracticable'. Leemans to trustees, 26 October 1836, Museum Archive, 17.1.1/5.
10 His lecture was published a year later in *Archaeologia*: C. Leemans, 'Observations on three Roman sepulchral inscriptions found at Watermore near Cirencester in Gloucestershire, in 1835 and 1836', *Archaeologia*, 1837, vol. 27, pp. 211–28.
11 See for a summary of his correspondence: W.F. Leemans, *L'egyptologue Conrade Leemans et sa correspondance: contribution à l'histoire d'une science*, Leiden, 1973.
12 Humbert to Luzac, 9 January 1837, Museum Archive, 19.3.1/47.
13 Leemans to the Ministry of the Interior, 20 January 1837, Museum Archive, 17.1.1/5.
14 The visitors' books were in use during the nineteenth and early twentieth century. Also the names of Heinrich Schliemann, Hans Christian Andersen and Sigmund Freud can be found in the visitors' lists.

15 Official gazette, 9 April 1839.

16 Leemans to trustees, 12 February 1839, Museum Archive, 17.1.1/6.

17 Official gazette, 11 January 1840. See for the Danish interest in the archaeology of America: Klavs Randsborg, 'Archaeological globalization: the first practitioners', *Acta Archaeologica*, 2001, vol. 72, no. 2, pp. 1–53.

18 C.T. Falbe, *Recherches sur l'emplacement de Carthage*, Paris, 1833.

19 Grenville T. Temple, *Excursions in the Mediterranean, Algiers and Tunis*, London, 1835.

20 A.J.C.A. Dureau de la Malle, *Recherches sur la topographie de Carthage*, Paris, 1835.

21 L.H.H. Prince von Pückler-Muskau, *Semilasso in Afrika. Aus den Papieren des Verstorbenen*, Stuttgart, 1836.

22 Leemans to trustees, 26 October 1836, Museum Archive, 17.1.1/5.

23 Leemans to trustees, 3 May 1837, Museum Archive, 17.1.1/5.

24 Recent interest in the activities of Camillo Borgia led to extensive use of the Borgia manuscripts *cum annexis*. The results were published in: V. Ciccotti, *Camillo Borgia (1773–1817), soldato ed archeologo*, Velletri, 1999; V. Ciccotti (ed.), *Atti del convegno internazionale di studi Camillo Borgia (1773–1817)*, Velletri, 2000.

25 Correspondence about this exchange (for which Leemans forgot to ask the king's permission) in: Museum Archive, 17.1.1/6 and 17.1.2/8.

26 'In the past Etruria had yielded little painted pottery, but during the spring of 1828 the necropolis of Vulci was found and by the end of 1829 over 3,000 painted vases had been unearthed. The lucky proprietors (of whom the luckiest was Napoleon's slippery brother Lucien, the Prince of Canino) were soon selling off their booty to European collectors [. . .]' R.M. Cook, *Greek Painted Pottery*, London, 1997, p. 281.

27 Lucien Bonaparte, *Museum Etrusque de Lucien Bonaparte, Prince de Canino, Fouilles de 1828 à 1829*, Viterbo, 1829.

28 Humbert to Van Ewijck, 15 December 1839, Museum Archive, 17.1.2/5.

29 It is clear that he followed the classification of Eduard Gerhard, see Cook, op. cit., pp. 281–2.

30 Only years later Leemans wrote about the king's role in this purchase: 'This purchase was one of the manifold proofs of the benevolence of our late King towards the arts and sciences [. . .] and it is very gratifying to be able to mention now that the collection has been bought with the King's own finances and placed in the museum as a gift.' C. Leemans, *De zangles: eene Grieksche beschilderde schaal van het Nederlandsche Museum van Oudheden*, Leiden, 1844, pp. 18–19.

31 L.J.F. Janssen, *Musei Lugduno-Batavi inscriptiones Etruscae*, Leiden, 1840.

APPENDIX 2

1 Catalogue in the Museum Archive, 3.2/10–11.

BIBLIOGRAPHY

The abbreviations of periodicals follow those of the *Archäologischer Anzeiger*, 1997, pp. 612–24.

Barocchi, P. and D. Gallo (eds), *L'Accademia Etrusca*, Milan, 1985.

Bastet, F.L., *De drie collecties Rottiers te Leiden*, Leiden, 1987.

Bastet, F.L. and Brunsting, H., *Corpus signorum classicorum musei antiquarii Lugduno-Batavi*, Zutphen, 1982.

Bibliotheca Etrusca: fonti letterarie e figurative tra XVIII e XIX secolo nella Biblioteca dell'Istituto Nazionale di Archeologia e Storia dell'Arte, Rome, 1986.

Bogaers, J.E., 'Voorburg-Arentsburg: Forum Hadriani, *OudhMeded*, 1971, vol. 52, pp. 128–38.

Borenius, T., *The Picture Gallery of Andrea Vendramin*, London, 1923.

Brongers, J.A., *Reuvens in Drenthe*, Bussum, 1973.

—— 'An early nineteenth-century excavation in the Netherlands', *BROB*, 1974, vol. 24, pp. 191–4.

—— *Air Photography and Celtic Field Research in the Netherlands*, Amersfoort, 1976.

—— *Een vroeg begin van de moderne archeologie: leven en werken van Cas Reuvens (1793–1835)*, Nederlandse Archeologische Rapporten 23, Amersfoort, 2002.

Brunsting, H., 'Een opgraving van Reuvens en Leemans bij het Fort Krayenhoff te Nijmegen in 1834', *OudhMeded*, 1949, vol. 30, pp. 47–65.

—— 'Geschiedenis van het verzamelen in Nederland', in *Klassieke kunst uit particulier bezit. Nederlandse verzamelingen 1575–1975*, Leiden, 1975.

Ciccotti, V., *Camillo Borgia (1773–1817), soldato ed archeologo*, Velletri, 1999.

—— (ed.), *Atti del convegno internazionale di studi Camillo Borgia (1773–1817)*, Velletri, 2000.

Debergh, J., 'Carthage, archéologie et histoire, les ports, Byrsa', *Studia Phoenicia*, 1983, vol. II, pp. 151–7.

—— 'Ombres et lumières sur la topographie de Carthage punique: les errances de Byrsa', *Studia Phoenicia*, 1988, vol. VI, pp. 91–9.

—— 'Autour du port de commerce de Carthage', *Studia Phoenicia*, 1992, vol. IX, pp. 283–97.

—— 'L'aurore de l'archéologie à Carthage au temps d'Hamouda bey et de Mahmoud bey (1782–1824): Frank, Humbert, Caronni, Gierlew, Borgia', in *Geografi, viaggiatori, militari nel Maghreb: alle origini dell'archeologia del Nord Africa* (L'Africa romana. XIII convegno internazionale di studi, Djerba, 10–13 dicembre 1998), Roma, 2000, pp. 457–74.

—— 'L'esilio in Tunisia. Il fascino dell'antichità', in *Atti del convegno internazionale di studi Camillo Borgia*, Velletri, 2000, pp. 45–71.

—— 'Camillo Borgia, ricerche archeologiche di un esule in Tunisia (1815–1816)', *Levante*, 2001, vol. XLVIII, 3, pp. 7–26.

Dorsman, H., 'A visit to the Old Schools in 1819', *The Ashmolean*, 1999, vol. 37, pp. 14–15.

Elen-Clifford Kocq van Breugel, E., *Opgravingen in Tripolitanië: de collecties Griekse oudheden van Jhr. J.F.H. Clifford Kocq van Breugel in het Rijksmuseum van Oudheden 1838–1988*, Den Haag, 1988.

Favaretto, I., *Arte antica e cultura antiquaria nelle collezioni Venete al tempo della Serenissima*, Roma, 1990.

Halbertsma, R.B., 'Benefit and honour: the archaeological travels of Jean Emile Humbert (1771–1839) in North Africa and Italy in service of the Kingdom of the Netherlands', *MededRom*, 1991, vol. 50, pp. 301–16.

—— *Le solitaire des ruines: de archeologische reizen van Jean Emile Humbert (1771–1839) in dienst van het Koninkrijk der Nederlanden*, Leiden, 1995.

—— 'Il fondo Borgiano di Leida', in *Atti del convegno internazionale di studi Camillo Borgia*, Velletri, 2000, pp. 37–44.

Holwerda, J.H., *Arentsburg, een Romeinsch militair vlootstation bij Voorburg*, Leiden, 1923.

Hooiberg, T., *De geschiedenis van een ruim tachtig jarig leven uit herinneringen samengesteld*, Epe, 1893.

Hubrecht, A.V.M., 'Die Sammlung Johannes Smetius, Vater und Sohn, in Nijmegen, 1618–1704', in *Festoen, Festschrift A. Zadoks-Josephus Jitta*, Groningen/Bussum, 1976, pp. 335–42.

Jenkins, I., *Archaeologists and Aesthetes in the Sculpture Galleries of the British Museum, 1800–1939*, London, 1992.

Lancel, S., *Carthage: A History*, Oxford, 1997.

Leemans, W.F., *L'egyptologue Conrade Leemans et sa correspondance: contribution à l'histoire d'une science*, Leiden, 1973.

Lelièvre, P., *Vivant Denon, homme des lumières, 'Ministre des Arts' de Napoléon*, Paris, 1993.

Logan, A.M., *The 'Cabinet' of the Brothers Gerard and Jan Reynst*, Amsterdam–New York, 1979.

Lund, J., 'The archaeological activities of Christian Tuxen Falbe in Carthage in 1838', *Cahiers des études anciennes*, 1986, vol. 18, pp. 8–24.

—— 'Il console Gierlew e il conte Borgia in terra d'Africa', in *Atti del convegno internazionale di studi Camillo Borgia*, Velletri, 2000, pp. 75–84.

Neppi Modona, A., *Cortona Etrusca e Romana nella storia e nell'arte*, Florence, 1977.

Neppi Modona, L. (ed.), 'Humbert, Jean Emile/Giampietro Vieusseux: les Barbaresques et les Chrétiens', in *Atti del gabinetto scientifico letterario G.P. Vieusseux*, Florence, 1983.

Otterspeer, W., *De vesting van de macht: de Leidse universiteit*, 1673–1775, Leiden, 2002.

Regt, W.M.C., 'De familie Humbert en Humbert de Superville', *Algemeen Nederlandsch Familieblad*, 1901, vol. 14, pp. 131–40.

Sandys, J.E., *A History of Classical Scholarship*, New York, 1958.

Schneider, H.D., 'Van Archaeologisch Kabinet tot Rijksmuseum van Oudheden', *Nederlandse Musea/Dutch Museums VI*, Leiden, 1981, pp. 7–42.

—— *De Laudibus Aegyptologiae: C.J.C. Reuvens als verzamelaar van aegyptiaca*, Leiden, 1985.

—— 'Egypt outside Egypt: the Leiden Chapter', in *L'Egitto fuori dell'Egitto, dalla riscoperta all'egittologia, atti del convegno internazionale*, Bologna, 1990, pp. 391–402.

Van der Meer, L.B., 'The Etruscan urns from Volterra in the Rijksmuseum van Oudheden at Leiden', *OudhMeded*, 1975, vol. 56, pp. 75–126.

Van Regteren Altena, I.Q. and Van Thiel, P.J.J., *De portretgalerij van de Universiteit van Amsterdam en haar stichter Gerard van Papenbroeck, 1673–1743*, Amsterdam, 1964.

Watson, V., *The British Museum*, London, 1973.

Zamarchi Grassi, P. and Scarpellini, M., *Tesori ritrovati: reperti archeologici etruschi rinvenuti nel territorio di Castiglion Fiorentino dal sec. XVIII ad oggi*, Montepulciano, 2002.

Zorzi, M. (ed.), *Collezioni di antichità a Venezia nei secoli della Repubblica*, Rome, 1988.

INDEX

For Product Safety Concerns and Information please contact our EU
representative GPSR@taylorandfrancis.com Taylor & Francis Verlag GmbH,
Kaufingerstraße 24, 80331 München, Germany

Printed and bound by CPI Group (UK) Ltd, Croydon, CR0 4YY
08/05/2025
01864458-0001